ethics. It is meant to provoke a recognitio of the issues of life and death in today's worl and the awareness of the possibility of man resurrection through the Cross.

JAMES W. DOUGLASS is assistant professor of religion at the University of Hawaii. Born in British Columbia, he is both an American and Canadian citizen. He received his master's degree from the University of Notre Dame in 1962 and studied theology at the Gregorian University in Rome from 1962 to 1964. During Vatican Council I, he served as theological adviser to several British and American bishops on questions of peace and war. He has contributed to several books and has published in *Cross Currents, Commonweal, New Blackfriars, Continuum,* and many other periodicals.

THE NON-VIOLENT CROSS

THE
NON-VIOLENT CROSS

A Theology of Revolution and Peace

BY

JAMES W. DOUGLASS

THE MACMILLAN COMPANY, NEW YORK
COLLIER-MACMILLAN LTD., LONDON

Library of Congress Catalog Card Number: 68-31276

First Printing

The Macmillan Company, New York
Collier-Macmillan Canada Ltd., Toronto, Ontario

Printed in the United States of America

The author wishes to thank the following for permission to
reproduce copyrighted material: Rider and Company, Lon-
don, for *Gandhi to Vinoba* by Lanza Del Vasto; Simon and
Schuster, Inc., for *I Found No Peace* by Webb Miller, Copy-
right 1936, © 1963 by Webb Miller; Young Friends Movement,
Philadelphia Yearly Meeting of the Religious Society of Friends,
for *A Saint at Work, A View of Gandhi's Work and Message,*
William Penn Lecture, 1950, by Amiya Chakravarty; National
Catholic Welfare Conference, for *Pastoral Constitution on the
Church in the Modern World;* St. Louis Review, for "Cardinal
Ritter's Intervention," published as a copyrighted article by
the *St. Louis Review;* Duke University Press, for *War and the
Christian Conscience* by Paul Ramsey, used also with the per-
mission of Paul Ramsey; Los Angeles *Free Press,* for "Police
Riot Mars Peace March" by James Shafikh, June 26, 1967;

Charles Scribner's Sons, for *For Whom the Bell Tolls* by Ernest Hemingway; Alfred A. Knopf, Inc., and Faber & Faber, Ltd., for *Markings* by Dag Hammarskjold, translated by Leif Sjoberg and W. H. Auden, Copyright © 1964 by Alfred A. Knopf, Inc., and Faber & Faber, Ltd.; National Council of the Churches of Christ, for several short passages of Scripture from the Revised Standard Version of the Bible, copyrighted 1946 and 1952; Uchida Rokakuho Publishing House, for *Children of the A Bomb,* compiled by Dr. Arata Osada, translated by Ruth Sieben-Morgan and Jean Dan, original English-language edition published by Uchida Rokakuho Publishing House, Tokyo, Japan (Japanese original edition: *Genbaku No Ko* by Iwanami Shoten, Tokyo, Japan); Atheneum Publishers and Martin Secker & Warburg Limited, London, for *The Last of the Just* by André Schwarz-Bart, Copyright © 1960 by Atheneum House, Inc., translated from the French by Stephen Becker, originally published in French under the title *Le dernier des Justes,* © 1956 by Editions du Seuil, Paris.

The author also wishes to make acknowledgment to the following periodicals, which published condensed versions of some of his chapters: *Gandhi Marg* (India), January 1968, for "From Gandhi to Christ: God as Suffering Love," and *Commonweal,* November 24, 1967, under the title "A Non-Violent Christology"; *New Blackfriars* (England), September 1967, for "From Bonhoeffer to Gandhi: God as Truth"; *Fellowship,* July 1966, for "The Non-Violent Power of *Pacem in Terris*" under the title "Pope John and Gandhi: Proof That Non-Violence Is Power"; *Continuum,* Autumn 1966, for "André Schwarz-Bart and Vatican II."

To the Two Hermenes

Acknowledgments

THE SCATTERED COMMUNITY which was the sustaining power for every word of this book includes more people than I can name here. Those belonging to it who are not mentioned below have been no less present to us during our two years living and writing in Hedley. I hope they find something of themselves in the book, even if their names are lacking.

I wish to thank the Fellowship of Reconciliation and the Franz Jägerstätter Foundation for grants which made possible the period of study and writing. It is an honor to have been associated with both the FOR and Jägerstätter, two names which represent so much of the meaning of peace today. I am especially grateful to Gordon Zahn, President of the Jägerstätter Foundation, for the help he has given me in many ways.

Few writers have had the benefit of more discerning and demanding critics. Each of the following has contributed significantly to a dialogue on particular chapters: Richard Brilliot, Father John Dunne, C.S.C., Father M. Eusebius, O.C.S.O., M. A. Fitzsimons, William Hamilton, Thomas Merton, Kristin Morrison, Paul Ramsey, and John Howard Yoder.

I would not have been exposed to much of the background of this book had it not been for the Church Peace Mission's Committee on Issues and Direction. I shall always be grateful to the CPM, and particularly its Executive Secretary, Paul Peachey, for a community of theological discourse which helped to shape these issues into their present form.

For introducing me to the issues ten years ago at the University of Santa Clara and for continuing encouragement along the way I am grateful to my friends Herbert C. Burke and Gerhardt Steinke. To have had such professors is to know the possibilities of teaching and the responsibilities of learning. One of my deepest hopes for my book is that I have not let these men down.

In much the same way I am indebted to Dorothy Day and Thomas Merton. With many American Catholics I have come to know and love the Church through Dorothy Day and the Catholic Worker Movement. It is impossible to say where I would be personally without the Catholic Worker but it is certain that this book would never have been written. The Catholic Worker opened the way, as did my reading of Thomas Merton and my correspondence and visits with him. The power of contemplation in the world is what one learns from Merton, almost unwillingly.

There have been a number of crucial moments when the writing would have ceased were it not for the various kinds of help given by some beautiful people: Fathers Daniel and Philip Berrigan, Mr. and Mrs. Graham Carey, Rabbi and Mrs. Everett Gendler, Father John Loftus, Father Bill Marrin, Bishop John J. Wright.

Chapters 4, 5, and 6 were originally given as talks at a *Pacem in Terris* Convocation in Los Angeles, at the University of Santa Clara, at Temple Isaiah (Los Angeles), and at the Hebrew Union College-Jewish Institute of Religion (Los Angeles). Chapter 1 was written at the invitation of Ned O'Gorman for his book *Essays on Revolution*. I am grateful for each of these invitations not only for the encounters they led to but for giving the book an initial substance.

Bishop Christopher Butler has been gracious in permitting me to quote freely from our correspondence during the fourth session of the Vatican Council. My continuing gratitude to him and to the other Fathers of Vatican II whom I knew during our years in Rome comes from the grace of having seen a living Spirit in the Church.

Finally I wish to thank Maureen Graham and Margaret Pitkethly for making our move to Hedley possible and beautiful;

Our pastor, Father Richard Peedle, whose life and sermons have helped to deepen the themes treated here;

The Macmillan Company and my editor, Elizabeth Bartelme, for their help and patience.

The book is dedicated to Mrs. Hermene J. Eisenman and Mrs. Hermene Evans, without whom everything would have been inconceivable. Their faith passed beyond measure long ago, but I hope not beyond the "Shalom" this book is meant to say to them.

My mother and father have never ceased believing and helping in every way possible.

My wife, Sally, has shown me all the way with her life and beauty that the meaning of existence is love.

JAMES W. DOUGLASS

Hedley, British Columbia
January 10, 1968

Contents

INTRODUCTION by Everett Gendler   xiii

PART ONE: Cross and World
1   The Revolution of Peace   3
2   From Bonhoeffer to Gandhi: God as Truth   26
3   From Gandhi to Christ: God as Suffering Love   48

PART TWO: Cross and Church
4   The Non-Violent Power of *Pacem in Terris*   81
5   Toward a New Perspective on War:
     The Vision of Vatican II   100
6   André Schwarz-Bart and Vatican II   137
7   Anatomy of the Just War   155
8   Christians and the State   182

PART THREE: Cross and History
9   Cain and the Cross   217
10   Is There a Politics Without Violence?   257
11   The Crux of History   284

INDEX   293

Introduction

"Victory cannot tolerate truth, and if that which is true
is spread before your very eyes, you will reject it,
because you are a victor.
Whoever would have truth itself, must drive hence
the spirit of victory; only then may he prepare
to behold the truth."

—RABBI NAHMAN OF BRATZLAV
(*18th–19th centuries*)

GUERNICA, DRESDEN, HIROSHIMA, AUSCHWITZ, etc., etc., etc.—has
there ever been an age that, in so short a period of time, has
provided so many massive monuments to man's defeats? Yet has
there ever been an age that has heard, from so many public
platforms, such incessant talk of man's victories? Small wonder,
then, with mostly "victors" audible, that truth has seemed in short
supply.

But beneath the clashing sounds of "victorious" voices, others,
less voluble but also less vacuous, may be heard: still, small
voices; voices of those meek who shall yet inherit the earth
(Psalm 37:11)—if earth there remain to inherit; voices of those
who, having driven forth the blinding spirit of victory, behold,
then speak the truth they see.

Such a person is James Douglass, and such a voice is his. It is
critical, penetrating, precise, and truthful. It is also loving. In it

"love and truth are met, justice and peace have kissed" (Psalm
85:11).

He is severely critical of the Church, but loving—and always
appreciative of the redemptive potential that inheres, even now,
in the non-violent cross. He is centrally concerned with this central Christian symbol, but treats it not primarily in self-contained
Christian categories but rather by relevant and deeply felt references to exploitation, the nuclear situation today, Gandhi, the
Lamed Vav, Ernie Levy, Malcolm X, Martin King, Dag Hammarskjöld, the *ebed Yahweh* of Isaiah, Martin Buber, and John
XXIII.

The dangers of such exegesis are obvious: caricatures in place
of persons, distortions in place of descriptions, apologetics in
place of appreciations. Yet somehow these dangers are largely
avoided, the spirit of truth keeps at bay the victory-seeking spirit
of particularist pleading, and the result is twofold: on the one
hand, the liberation of a symbol from the too-narrow confines of
particular dogma so that it may serve, in some measure and
however qualifiedly, for all men as a dynamic symbol of human
hope and process; on the other hand, a deeper appreciation of
the meaning of these men and symbols for adherents of their
"own" traditions (if one may speak so parochially of such men
and symbols!).

Is there anywhere so moving or so profound an appreciation
of *The Last of the Just*? When I first read this essay on Schwarz-
Bart and Vatican II, I was so stirred that I was moved to include
nearly all of it in our Yom Kippur service at the Jewish Center of
Princeton, and I still find it one of the most affecting essays I
have ever read.

Again with the *ebed Yahweh* (Servant of the Lord), Mr. Douglass speaks with such sympathy, such reverence, such identification, and in so broad and non-partisan a spirit, that one feels
keenly those respects in which this religiously contested figure, so
tragically divisive through the centuries, might yet serve to relate
and draw closer those now estranged by the painful history of
this suffering symbol.

Similarly, would not a Gandhian find his appreciation of Gandhi's meaning increased by Mr. Douglass' treatment of him? Or the Hammarskjöld–United Nations admirer find new understanding of their full significance in the sweep of redemptive history? Even those whose favorites come in for rather severe criticism—just-war buffs and Vatican Council enthusiasts—will find, I am sure, deeper understanding possible because of the sympathetic and non-hostile manner of Mr. Douglass' analysis.

In a remarkable way, Mr. Douglass' manner of approach contributes to those very ends he seeks. Deeper personal understanding, mutual critical appreciation, a recognition of "the other's" humanity—in fact, some measure of "convergence"—are both the spirit of this volume and its felt effects.

This is not to suggest, of course, that everything each of us might have desired is to be found fully developed in this single volume. Personally, I wish there had been a more specific treatment of "the way of truth" that "in a world of injustice is revolution," especially as it relates to the wretched of the earth, the state, and the real responsibility for the political arrangements in/under which we live. I also wish that not only the redemptive power of suffering but something more of the natural joy of Creation had been articulated, for I know how sensitive Mr. Douglass is to this dimension of our existence.

Yet I confess that this is a dark age indeed, darker than the artificial glare and glitter permit us to discern, and so the prevailing sobriety of tone is finally appropriate.

But darkness itself, as Mr. Douglass suggests, may, penetrated, reveal both beauty and hope. In the words of Isaiah: "I will give you treasures of darkness, and hidden riches of secret places, that you may know that I am the LORD . . ." (Isaiah 45:3). Mr. Douglass' book, deeply affirmative without avoiding the overwhelming tragedy of our times, is, it seems to me, precisely such a "treasure of darkness."

Everett Gendler

What counts today, the question which is looming on the horizon, is the need for a re-distribution of wealth. Humanity must reply to this question, or be shaken to pieces by it.

FRANTZ FANON, *The Wretched of the Earth*

We must undertake an evaluation of war with an entirely new attitude.

SECOND VATICAN COUNCIL,
Constitution on the Church in the Modern World

The Christians say they love Christ, but I think they hate him without knowing it. So they take the cross by the other end and make a sword out of it and strike us with it.

ERNIE LEVY IN *The Last of the Just*

ONE

Cross and World

1

The Revolution of Peace

To SEE REALITY in our time is to see the world as crucifixion. Our age is defined by the kind of events, from Auschwitz to Vietnam, whose depth of evil imposes night on the eyes of countless victims at the same time that the executioners, removed yet responsible, comfort themselves with blindness or the self-righteousness of an ideology. To see reality is to cut through the blindness of self, whether that self be one of the individual alone or, more commonly, the extended self of family, race, or nation. To see reality is to cut through every self of our time so as to go out from the blindness of a few into the beauty and darkness of the world of man, given over to agony and despair by absent executioners. To see reality is to be wholly present at the crucifixion of the world; to live reality is to enter into that crucifixion, but to do so, in the phrase of Albert Camus, as neither victim nor executioner. The life of the living is a suffering with the world, yet not as a passive victim but suffering in resistance and in love, experiencing the darkness of crucifixion without surrendering the hope and strength and revolution of resurrection.

The event which revealed the essence of our age of global crucifixion took place in a city. It has been described more accurately by Shintaro Fukuhara, a boy then in the fourth grade, than by the distant objectivity of the movie camera recording the scene from within the B-29 bomber flying overhead. Shintaro was the B-29's target:

The all-clear had just sounded after an alert and I was idly watching the increasing numbers of my friends who were arriving at school. A red dragon-fly came swooping by and alighted on the top of the wall right before my eyes. I saw it clearly. When I think back on it I realize that even then I was hearing the characteristic sound of a B-29 engine, but lulled by the security and relief of the all-clear, I let the sound go in one ear and out the other. My little brother had just put out his hand to catch the red dragon-fly on the wall when in that instant there was a flash and with my whole body I received a shock as if I had been thrown into a furnace. I was blasted into the angle of the wall. Even now when I think about it I wonder when and how it was that I, after being slammed around as one in a delirium from inside a swirl of light rays into instantaneous blackness, ever got hold of my little brother's hand and began to run. Only fragmentary glimpses of those scenes are left printed on my retina as on a photographic film.

When I opened my eyes after being blown at least eight yards, it was as dark as though I had come up against a black-painted fence. After that, as if thin paper was being peeled off one piece at a time, it gradually began to grow brighter. The first thing that my eyes lighted upon then was the flat stretch of land with only dust clouds rising from it. Everything had crumbled away in that one moment, and changed into streets of rubble, street after street of ruins. I, who had unconsciously taken my little brother's hand and started to run, when I saw the cruelly burned passengers come rolling out one after another from a trolley-car, only ran the more wholeheartedly toward home, with fear for the safety of my family tightening itself around my chest.

The countless miserable things that happened at that time are quite beyond my pen and my tongue. Because of that calamity I lost my most beloved father and older sister. I will never be able to see my father and sister again forever. I know there are others who have lost equally—or rather, there are hundreds of thousands whose misery is many times greater than this, who have been deprived of everything that gave them happiness, and my feeling of indignation is only stirred up the more by the immensity of the disaster.[1]

Between the moment Shintaro's little brother reached out to

catch the red dragonfly on the wall and the moment the two children began to run hand-in-hand through rubble and agony, man entered the age of his most critical self-revelation. He did not enter it accidentally or without warning. In terms of the sheer enormity of murder involved, even Hiroshima and Nagasaki were exceeded by the prior events of Auschwitz, Buchenwald, Dresden, and Tokyo. From a moral standpoint, the coming of Hiroshima was foreseeable in the triumph and weary indifference with which Allied populations had responded to the reports of mounting atrocities by their own forces, thereby signifying their blind approval of the next step. Hiroshima was no moral break from the pattern of obliteration bombing of German and Japanese cities. But it was a significant power break in the history of mankind, inasmuch as it revealed on a global scale the power equivalent of man's moral capacity for self-destruction and did so in such a way, in the agony of Shintaro and his city, that the new power instantly became one with the old drive to kill. Hiroshima became the wedding place of eschatological weapons —those weapons through which mankind can commit its final act —with the death instinct that prompted Cain to destroy his brother in the field. That new period which in technological terms is the Nuclear Age has therefore become, in temporal and moral terms, the Eschatological Age, in which man's power of global self-destruction has forced him into a confrontation with the depths of his spiritual self. Hiroshima, where Bomb and Cain-instinct joined forces above Shintaro in the playground, has pressed on the human conscience the absolute identity of that being who killed millions in gas chambers and burning cities with the being who today possesses a power capable of ending history. There can be no escape from our age and its primary threat: that man will commit his final act of murder.

The Nuclear Age has therefore brought man's quest for security through ever-greater destructive power to an absolute end. The historical pursuit of security through superior weapons has arrived instead at the insecurity of threatened extinction. For the first time in history, any further increase in man's destructive power is irrelevant to his situation in time. Whether the existing arms are capable of ending the human race once or a thousand times is irrelevant to the conscience of man, to whom a new revelation of the nature of power has been given. Military power has put mankind on the cross. The new threat of global suicide has redefined military power at its height as ultimately powerless, because its ultimate use would terminate the life of man. The possession of such power renders man impotent because he cannot survive its use, yet remains committed to it in principle through a mythology of power relations. The only genuine power which eschatological weapons have for man is the power to provoke in him a complete re-examination of the nature of power itself. For to have pursued a form of it to the edge of self-destruction is indication enough that his pursuit has been after a disastrous illusion. The powerlessness of man in possession of eschatological weapons is a sign, after centuries of pursuing power, that any real power for peace and security is virtually unknown to him at that near-terminal point in history when he most needs it. Man has developed what he thought was power to the point where its emergent reality as self-destruction has rendered him impotent, and where only a repudiation of the illusion of power and a committed search for its true existence elsewhere can deliver him from himself.

But short of the actual use of eschatological weapons, mass murder has already become the mark of our age. Nor is it confined to the atrocities of Algeria, Hungary, and Vietnam. Its global presence and nature can be defined factually and statistically: "the amount of money spent on armaments today (by a few major powers) is equal to the total national income, not of any one country, but of the combined continents of Asia, Africa, and South and Central America." [2] While half of the world's population, according to the director general of the UN Food and Agriculture Organization, is "underfed or badly fed or both," the greatest industrial power in the world spends $30 billion a year to wage war in Vietnam.[3] The reverse side of the arms race and Vietnam is the sustenance gap and places like

Palma di Montechiaro, a town typical of Sicily which when submitted to an inquiry into health and sanitary conditions

brought to light, among other facts, that tests for worms showed that
"out of 267 children examined 74.9 per cent had threadworms, and
out of 235 persons of all ages, mostly children, 34.5 per cent had
dwarf tapeworms and 11.1 per cent had common round worms." That,
naturally, "90.2 per cent of the houses are without running water and
86.4 per cent without lavatories. Only three of the eighty-two lavatories have a proper bowl and seat and only one of these is placed in
a separate room." That, naturally, "the drains are practically non-
existent and their place is taken by rivulets of black water which cut
stinking furrows in the surface of the street." That out of 20,429 inhabitants, 4,964 are on assistance, most of these being under-em-
ployed. That "only one house, out of 600, was entirely free from mice
and rats." And so on and so on . . .[4]

The world of Vietnam and the world of Palma di Montechiaro
are identical: they are the two arms of a single global cross. What
is done by enormous resources of technology turned to destruction in the one is left undone by the lack of knowledge and technology in the other. The Vietnamese from war and the desperate
in Sicily, India, and Latin America from indifference are victims
of the same murderous process. As one economist has put it,
"Now all scarcity—and this is really the most important thing—
all scarcity, all need felt in the world, is henceforth due to human interference, human stupidity and human greed. The means
are there, the knowledge is there; what is needed is the will to
apply them." [5]

The growing reality of mass hunger alongside the growing
affluence of military states emphasizes the impotence of destructive power to effect any truly human change in the world, and
the guilt of those who choose impotence. The power of the
affluent not only threatens global destruction but actually carries
it out in widening circles of famine and destitution. The jealous
possession of such power renders man powerless to make peace
both because it commits him to the end of all peace on earth
and because it already wages global war against the hungry.

To the man of conscience, as defined by his sense of humanity, the growing fact of such a world raises the moral imperatives of resistance and revolution. Any political or economic system which can preach an ideological crusade against the poor, punctuating it with napalm and TNT, or can tolerate worms in the stomachs of children, deserves not allegiance but uprooting. To the human family's threatened murder by nuclear weapons and to its on-going murder by privilege and indifference, the response of human conscience is "No!" In such a world, revolution is not a question and a possibility. It is an obligation and a necessity. One must either revolt against the disorder of the present system, for the sake of each man's right to the means of a human life, or cease being human oneself. The process of inhumanity and slow murder has already gone too far to allow an intermediate choice.

The revolutionary is the man of conscience in today's world. There is and can be no other man of conscience today, for the world as man has thus organized it, socially and economically— as distinct from its created forms and life—is intolerable. To tolerate the morally intolerable is gradually to lose life, as a man who lets the water close above him; to fail to see the intolerable, as most do, is to live in less than the world, and for less than man. The revolutionary both sees and acts with all his power. Given his recognition of the global size of injustice, nothing less will do for him, and not even that will begin to do for man. Revolution begins in the revolutionary himself by his response to the present world, creating through the crisis of vision and shared agony the kind of power which rises anew to meet a torn world with the word of love and the act of transformation. The revolutionary has no other choice in love than to seek with his whole being a new heaven and a new earth. Anything less is an infidelity to the suffering family of man and to his own vision born of crisis. His commitment is to man made whole again and to a community restored to visible love. What begins as a recognition of massive injustice must grow into a commitment to global love. Thus the man of conscience faces the world today as a revolutionary seized by the crisis of injustice, and thus he prepares to act in it.

But the revolutionary of the Nuclear Age, as the man most sensitive to the moral realities of his time, must recognize that he especially lives under the cloud of man's ultimate powerlessness through military power. It is the revolutionary who above all must lead the search for a new power that can free man from the fatal illusion of power which eschatological weapons represent. The facts of power in the Nuclear Age have emphasized a truth of revolution as such, that to seek revolution through destruction is to commit the crime of denying the end by the means.

For to revolt against injustice is at the same time to revolt for life, life in the world and life in oneself. As revolution passes from conscience to act, to remain true to its genesis it must express itself in living forms, in means as well as in ends. The death of the Russian Revolution, and a danger sign of all mass movements, lay in its subordination of actual life to a theory of life, of living men to a principle and technique concerning their eventual happiness. When the revolutionary divorces ends and means and oppresses for the sake of liberation, he loses life and the source of his power. The new order takes on the bitterness of the old, and the revolutionary-become-tyrant transfers his struggle against injustice to a struggle with the world as such, in all its forms and beauty.

But given its inspiration in a cry of the living for the life they were created for, revolution cannot then bridge the living and the life they seek by a sword. It cannot fulfill life through death. It cannot create a new order of justice by murdering all those who supported injustice, for injustice will have merely changed hands.

Pasternak's description of the revolutionary, Strelnikov, lays bare the temptation, and if accepted, the end of revolution:

In order to do good to others he would have needed, besides the principles which filled his mind, an unprincipled heart—the kind of heart that knows of no general cases, but only of particular ones, and has the greatness of small actions.

Filled with the loftiest aspirations from his childhood, he had looked upon the world as a vast arena where everyone competed for perfection, keeping scrupulously to the rules. When he found that it was not like that, it did not occur to him that he was wrong in over-simplifying the world order. Shutting up his grievance deep inside himself for years, he conceived the thought that he would some day be the judge between life and the dark forces which distort it, be life's champion and avenger.[6]

Strelnikov's fixation on Marxist principle, at the expense of an openness to life and humanity, sapped his revolution of power and drove it in the direction of nihilism.

Only the revolutionary of the unprincipled heart, with the greatness of small actions, can carry revolution through to the end. Resistance to injustice grants to no man the power, born of frustrated idealism, to draw a line between life and the oppressor. Such a power can be seized only from beyond revolution, and works ultimately against it. Revolution is instead the uprooting of death by the power of life. Life itself resists the doctrinaire's program of judgment and fire; it will not surrender the justice of revolution to an injustice of means. The original power of the revolution is maintained not in the ruthless idealism of Strelnikov, but in Zhivago, who says, "Man is born to live, not to prepare for life. Life itself—the gift of life—is such a breathtakingly serious thing!"[7] What was true for Zhivago is even more true today: The powerlessness of destruction to attain life stands in contrast to the profound power of life itself, and the revolutionary therefore chooses life.

For the same reason revolution cannot become an instrument of ideology. Hungary and Vietnam have proven that each of the opposing ideologies of the world is murderous at its core. For any oppressed people to rely on the assistance of a major state today for their freedom is for them to risk involvement in corruption, deceit, and finally their renewed suppression in the name of some exalted value that will be visible only to the ideological leader, for whom philosophy is the servant of special interests. Revolution must occur today against the oppressor without at the same time taking on the murderous form of a counter ideology. Neither the East nor the West can any longer be

trusted to deliver global man from his agony. The future, if it is
to be saved for anyone, must be recognized as belonging to a
different kind of power than ideology or weapons technology,
and to a different kind of man than the leader defined by the
interests of a party.

Where, then, is genuine revolution, a revolution of resistance
and of life, a revolution which seeks peace by making peace?
Where does one find the currents of deep change and ultimate
transformation whose existence in a world of growing agony
conscience is compelled to believe in?

One finds real revolution, first of all, not by scanning the
world from the summits of the power that has been revealed
as impotence, as most commentators do, thus seeking and finding
merely rebellious forms of that impotence, but rather by im-
mersing oneself in the dark beauty of space and time where the
crucifixion of man is felt most deeply and where need is given
its deepest human response. One finds the signs of a revolutionary power in man not in mass movements and uprisings but in
persons, and even there in persons whose status in society is
usually that of outcast and criminal. The first revolution demanded of a man for his involvement in the revolution of peace
is his recognition of a truth fundamental to the works of
Dostoevsky:

Is the meaning of life buried so deep then that the wise man who
perceives it can appear among us only as one misunderstood, only
as a fool, the strong man who holds it in his hands, only as weak, the
healthy man who draws his nourishment from it, only as sick? Is then
the true interpretation, the meaning of all that happens on earth, so
fully crowded out into the margin that only those who themselves
are in some way out there—harlots, murderers, and the insane—can
follow its trail and understand it? And that, wherever this meaning,
this interpretation, is brought again into the center, it immediately
seems to be a disruption of all that is customary—ridiculous naiveté,
idiocy, something totally foreign, unprecedentedly different from
everything that has previously happened and been thought? [8]

The revolution of peace proceeds from a recognition of first
the need, then the power of those "crowded out into the margin

of the earth." Wisdom and power come not from the privileged, but from those who know life from having found it in death, and light from having perceived it in darkness. For those on the margin of the earth, who today comprise most of the human race, need has given birth to power, but a power virtually unrealized and unexplored. One finds both the need and the power implicit in the recital of the life of a Sicilian laborer:

Now I've got five sons. To earn enough to feed them, I worked both on the land and at sea, fishing at night and digging by day. For nearly all the summer, I'd never have more than three hours sleep out of the twenty-four, and I led this sort of life for ten or twelve years, so that my hair was white by the time I was 35. I used to throw down the hoe in the street outside the house at five o'clock in the evening and be off to the fishing. We'd fish all night, although we were worn out by the work in the fields, and then in the morning we were off again ploughing. When we were at sea, we used to lie down on the seats of the boat and sleep while the nets were down, while the fish, the anchovies, were getting caught in them.[9]

The primary resource for the revolution to transform a world of increasing suffering into a world of human respect is to be found in the depths of suffering itself. The weak have strength in their weakness and will learn to fight not with the guns of the powerful, but with the resource of their own strength forged in the poverty and suffering imposed on them by others and by life. What will change to make the native strength of the poor a primary and not an incidental factor in their struggle for life and justice is an emerging understanding of suffering not as weakness but as power. What will, on the other hand, deliver the powerful from the impotence of their weapons will be the emerging power of those without any weapon except the one weapon available to those on the margin, suffering for truth and justice, which to those at the center appears as no weapon at all. This is not to say that suffering imposed by others is either desirable or justified. It is to say that suffering especially is redemptive and that it teaches the powerless something about life and about their very being which is capable of providing an enormous power against the oppressor responsible for that suffering. The seed of revolution is suffering: the endurance of suffering is both the impulse and the potential strength of those who must and will rise up for a just and human order. But while suffering is for the powerless the matter of power, it must be informed by something beyond itself in order to fulfill itself and make the revolution real.

In a confused way short of this fulfillment, the native power of the weak over the apparently strong is evident in Vietnam, where the greatest military force in the world, operating with ruthless efficiency, has been unable to subdue a force of peasants in black pajamas. In this case the strength of the weak can be understood as radically distinct from military weapons, which have confused rather than expressed the Vietnamese people's strength. The further truth about war today is that not only is it murderous in the hands of the rich but it is irrelevant in the hands of the poor, whose enormous power *to endure* war is frustrated from achieving any beneficial ends by *their waging* of war.

It has been said accurately that the object of war is to change the enemy's mind by making him suffer. Commander Stephen King-Hall formulated the normal logic of war as that of "bringing physical pressure to bear on the body so that its brain says: 'To avoid further misery I will give in and concede to the victor what he demands.'" [10] The waging of war presumes that a rise in the enemy's suffering will provoke a rising fear of further punishment and finally the surrender which would avoid it. This general logic of war is particularly true in modern war, in which the strategy of massive land armies forcing surrender by occupation has given way to immediate annihilation from the air. Today especially, in the age of napalm, massive bombing, and nuclear weapons, the enemy is expected to be reasonable enough to surrender before his suffering has become literally inconceivable, or to use Herman Kahn's criterion, before the living envy the dead. The logic of war, especially modern war, is that the suffering created by our weapons will eventually impose defeat on the enemy's mind and make him obedient to our will.

This logic of military power has been powerless against the kind of people the United States is fighting in Vietnam and will likely fight elsewhere. For in addition to the powerful's own moral corruption, the problem which they face in fighting the poor and the weak is that such an enemy expects deep suffering as the very essence of life.[11] To assume that the enemy wishes to avoid death, pain, and material destruction enough to surrender is to assume that he knows well what the alternatives would be. But the poor and the weak know life itself as suffering. What is done in war by bombs has been done in peace by exploitation, by the indifference of the privileged, and by the natural resistance to life of an undeveloped area. What the rich only fear the poor suffer daily and in Southeast Asia have endured for centuries. William Pfaff has cited a Korean officer in South Vietnam as observing that Americans expect of life that they can be happy; Koreans and Vietnamese, he claimed, do not expect this.[12] And because the poor expect suffering instead as their normal lot, the great suffering a rich enemy adds to their lives through war is borne with an endurance beyond the rich's comprehension and their calculations of victory. The weak have the power to endure a suffering they expect of life, and even as their suffering increases under enemy guns, their power of endurance is upheld and strengthened by the justice of their cause and by the injustice and inhumanity of the powerful.

But if the weak have the power to endure suffering, and to that extent the power to revolt against the powerful, the waging of war confuses and compromises this power. When both sides commit atrocities, as happens in any war, each is provoked to the justification of further violence by the injustice of its enemy. When the weak wage their revolution with the weapons of the powerful, they only justify the powerful's more extensive and more efficient use of such weapons, and on the other hand, compromise the great strength of their own suffering for justice's sake. While the weak can endure the powerful's more intensive warmaking, the conflict of war remains by its nature the special battlefield of military power per se, and there the weak cannot draw sufficiently on their greatest natural strength, their capacity to endure suffering, to transform their endurance into victory. To prevail and not simply endure, to match the power of the power-less directly against the weakness of the strong, the revolution of the poor must be informed and transformed by a Power identi-fied with suffering without being limited by war, and thus deeply present in pain while transcendent to retaliation. Suffering is the matter of a crucified world and the flesh of its unrealized power; Love is its spirit and its life, the world's Power made real and the world's oppressed set free. Love is suffering divinized. Love is the world both crucified and overcoming.

The reality of a revolution of peace, obscure and compromised in the jungles of Vietnam, is found clear and radiant on certain roads of India. It is a reality present in the work of Vinoba Bhave, a follower of Gandhi who remains almost unknown in the West despite his impact on the social structure of India.

Vinoba is the originator of the *Bhoodan-Gramdan* movement, which works to persuade the landowners of India, large and small, to surrender the bulk of their land to the poor and dispos-sessed. A seventy-three-year-old ascetic, Vinoba has for seventeen years been walking from village to village in India, accompanied by a growing number of followers and preaching the message of non-violence and *Bhoodan*. "Bhoodan" means "land gifts," and "gramdan" "village gifts." Yet it is not the pleasure of an arbitrary generosity but a sense of the urgent demands of justice that Vinoba arouses in his listeners. "I am not begging for alms," he says, "I am demanding what is owed to the poor." By 1962 Vinoba's campaign for the landless poor, which has spread from a one-man revolution to about 20,000 co-workers, had been given seven million acres for redistribution—still considerably short of his goal then of fifty million acres, one-sixth of the peninsula's cultivable land and an area about the size of the whole of France. Vinoba's movement has since graduated to the concept of "gramdan," the village in which enough land has been given to communize ownership in the village as a whole, and strong appeals have now begun to go out for *district-dan* and even *state-dan*. By August 1966 almost 25,000 villages had been secured and transferred from individual to communal ownership. This has all been accomplished without force or fear by a man who has never ridden in an automobile, yet who understands profoundly the meaning of power in the Nuclear Age.

The impossible nature of his task, from its conception to whatever end it reaches, is acknowledged by Vinoba in his interpretation of the movement's beginning.

On April 18, 1951, at Pochampalli, when Vinoba had finished speaking to the people on peace, there was silence among them. Then some pariahs came forward and said:

"We, too, love peace, but we are workers and have no land to work. What do you want us to do? Instead of talking to us about peace, give us land and we'll always live in peace."

Vinoba looked down, as though abashed, and was plunged in thought. Then, turning toward his audience, he cried:

"There are some rich men among you and it is to them I am speaking now. You have been listening to my words of peace and you have all approved of them, it seems.

"Is it possible that none of you is willing to show that he has understood them, by relieving, say, the land famine from which these poor laborers are suffering?"

A man immediately stood up and offered one hundred acres. Those who had put forward their request only as a challenge were overwhelmed in the midst of the general astonishment.

"On that day," Vinoba says, "God gave me a sign. I meditated on it the whole of the following night and ended up by finding out what I had to do. . . .

"Without this hint on His part I should never have made up my mind to preach *Bhoodan*, so impossible did it seem to clever people to heal by this means one of the greatest sores of India and of the world. I should never have had the audacity for it, even if I'd had the idea.

"But I put my trust in Him. And even if my reason showed me that the task was an immense one, I felt that if I did not undertake it, my non-violence would be shown up as only cowardice and good for nothing.

"That is why I received the Sign with gratitude and went forward with the adventure." [13]

Vinoba's adventure in non-violence represents today a more living hope to the Indian poor than either the programs of their government or the promises of Marxism. Vinoba has had the inspiration to attack directly, with his marching feet and a guiding spirit of truth and love, a problem which the Marxists claim can be solved only by violence. The Marxists have watched him with sympathy and jealousy, incredulity at his success and skepticism of its continuation. One of them once said to him:

"Your end is good, but your means are ridiculous. How can you hope to obtain great changes without using violence?"

"Tell me, my friend, did not a great change take place in you the day you became a Communist?"

"Yes, everything changed that day for me."

"But did you become a Communist of your own free will, or did someone force you with a gun to join the party?"

"What an idea! I read Marx, I found what he said true, and that is all there was to it."

"Then why do you think it impossible to obtain from others what Marx obtained from you?" [14]

Vinoba's question and the challenge of his revolution are as pertinent to Christianity as they are to Marxism. The fact is that neither of these great apocalyptic theologies, Marxism or Christianity, has shown much faith in its ability to change men by the power of truth. In the most crucial issues and conflicts, neither Marx nor Christ has been thought sufficient by his followers to obtain from their opponents the same victory won over them and predicted by them for mankind, the victory of an overcoming truth. In both Marxism and Christianity, an apocalyptic faith in one's own truth as the future form of man's being has not been strong enough to include the immediate opponent, considered instead unredeemable by truth and thus subject to violence. In the one case, the contradiction between faith in the ultimate truth of Marxism and the use of violence against the unconvinced is found in Marx himself, who believed in violence as a necessary means for the victory of his truth, thus denying the adequacy of that truth on the level of truth itself. But in the case of Christianity, the contradiction raised by Vinoba—between a belief in the transforming power of truth and a resort to violence in the name of an apparently powerless truth—seems a perversion of the life and teaching of Christ. For it was the man of violence, Pilate, who asked despairingly, "What is truth?"; and the victim, Christ, who answered with the faith of the cross. A faith in truth's power to overcome the world by love and accepted suffering is as essential to an understanding of the Gospel as it is lacking in a Christianity which continues to endorse warfare. The renewed presence of such faith, in the non-violence of Gandhi and Vinoba, has begun once again to reveal crucifixion as power.

The crucifixion of the world taking place from Vietnam to Palma di Montechiaro can be seen with relation to both executioners and victims: as related to the executioners, the act is violence and murder. Violence is the willed destruction of another, or to use Simone Weil's phrase, the transformation of a man into a thing. The avoidance of the destitute by turned consciences is as much an act of violence as their repression by guns and bombs. To refuse a response to one afflicted is to deny his humanity. It is to turn him into a corpse, first in terms of one's own attitude toward him and finally in terms of his actual condition.

Nevertheless, however deep the guilt of the privileged, the executioners of the world cannot be identified simply by wealth, position, or power, so that one could confine responsibility or guilt to particular peoples. The truth is that no man alive is free in conscience from the guilt of the executioner any more than he is free in feeling from the suffering of the victim. Every man is both executioner and victim, executioner to the extent that he has worked the destruction of his fellow man and victim to the extent that he has experienced that destruction from others.

The reverse side of the world's crucifixion, then, is the reverse side of man: man not as executioner but as victim, not violent but suffering. The reverse side of violence is suffering, and in the interaction of these two forces in the world, the force of violence and the force of suffering, the nature of true power is gradually revealed in man's history. Power is revealed not as violence, which destroys, nor even simply as suffering, which endures, but as Truth, which resists injustice through voluntary suffering, and as Love, which in that suffering resistance opens victim to executioner and thus raises their relationship from the level of objects, passive and active, to that of persons, confronting and confronted. Men are neither victims nor executioners when mediated by Love but persons transcending their guilt toward each other. In the confrontation by violence by Truth and Love, the activity of violence is revealed as passive and futile and the passivity of suffering as active and overcoming. From this confrontation Power emerges as the ability to redeem from inhumanity both victim and executioner in the overcoming reality of Truth and Love.

A faith in the power of Truth is not abstract or idealistic but deeply incarnational, a faith lived in human suffering and death but turned toward life and an open tomb. The incarnation of Truth is found in the dust raised by the sandaled feet of Vinoba and his followers, whose humble way is necessary to serve the poor and truly represent their need. Truth can exert its enormous power only by being incarnated in the humility and apparent weakness of suffering Love, a Love which therefore raises no obstacles to Truth by violence but, on the contrary, affirms the other's existence at its very base by service and sacrifice and opens him to dialogue with the one confronting him. Truth is powerless without suffering Love as its medium. Given that medium, however, Truth takes hold in men as the power to raise them from the death of injustice and war to the life of community.

The revolution of peace has taken hold also in the land of Palma di Montechiaro, northwest Sicily, home of the Mafia and site of the most violent and corrupt social milieu in Western Europe. In the "triangle of hunger," which bred the famous bandit Giuliano, the non-violent revolution of Danilo Dolci has begun to work changes in a society with virtually a Stone Age ethos.

Dolci is a forty-four-year-old former student of architecture whose campaigns for justice on behalf of the hungry of Sicily have combined the functions of sociologist, publicist, relief worker, and follower of Gandhi. Since 1952, when he moved from northern Italy to live with the Sicilian poor, Dolci has kept up a sustained protest against the inhuman conditions prevailing under a corrupt power alliance of the Mafia and the Christian Democratic government, supported by the Church in Sicily. What began as a personal crusade has expanded through Dolci's books, broadcasts, demonstrations, and fasts into a community of volunteer workers. The community has been organized by Dolci into cells, each built around an agro-technician and a welfare group, which have been sent out to establish centers in the most desperately deprived areas and under the constant threat of violence. Their purpose is to stimulate local employment and encourage a consciousness toward self-help. Each worker was to be, in Dolci's words, "a moral reference point," in an area of 430,000 inhabitants, containing only four people with degrees in agriculture, no competent authority on education or sociology, and with an average of one murder every five days.[15] It is this work and the conditions that prompted it, as described in Dolci's book *To Feed the Hungry,* which became a direct source of inspiration for President Kennedy's founding of the Peace Corps.

In September 1962 Dolci underwent a sustained fast as an appeal to the Italian government for the building of a dam essential to the area's development. He fasted until the ninth day when, as his health took a dangerous turning point, the government agreed to begin work on the dam within five months. Dolci warned officials that he would fast again if there were delays, and the work on the dam began as promised.

A year later Dolci fasted for another large dam. On the tenth day of the fast the government pledged it would build the second dam. As a result of these two fasts, but above all, of the Truth and Love expressed through the man who suffered them, the people of Sicily will soon be served by an irrigation network that will be the envy of larger states.

Dolci has often been called ingenuous and a dreamer. He replies: "I'd say that he who hasn't yet understood that the discovery of truth is the strongest force of all, he's the ingenuous one, he's the dreamer." [16]

Dolci's revolution is rooted in the people, whose life he shares and whose hopes he has concentrated into a non-violent attack against the very structure of injustice. "There is God in these people," he has written, "like the fire that smolders under the ashes." "This land is like one of the many beautiful little girls you see in the alleys of its townships. The beauty is often there beneath the scabs, the raving hair, the wild and tattered rags: and already you can picture what an appearance of graphic and noble intelligence a good upbringing would give to those features. . . ." [17]

It is this deeply lived vision and faith which prompted a friend to say of Dolci: "Danilo transforms others. It's a kind of moral strength which can transform even politics." [18]

Revolution is synonymous with transformation. The radical change which is revolution means change affecting the very nature of man in the world, inasmuch as man's nature has become conformed through the ages to structures and institutions radically incapable of meeting the needs of the human family today. The structure of the nation-state, in an age dependent for its existence on a global community, is obsolescent and deserves no more allegiance by the global citizen who is man today than to those programs which widen and deepen his sense of community. In the Nuclear Age the institutions of war and private wealth are not only murderous of persons, but murderous of man's future. To grant them existence by means of one's life, whether that life be spent in military service, in the payment of heavy taxes to a war machine, or in the accumulation of private security, is to sow death across man's destiny. Revolution means transformation because man deformed by such structures and institutions must pass into a fire of truth consuming his very nature as he has built it up—a nature fragmented in body and committed in spirit to a power which is impotent—and thus in the heat of suffering love take on the new and more deeply human forms of non-violent power and total community.

Whether such a transformation of man is an historical possibility is a way of asking whether man himself is a continuing historical possibility. For it is clear that man as he has thus far shaped and understood himself, and as he is confronted by nuclear power and global misery, has remaining only the future symbolized in the Book of Revelation. The transformation of politics, in and through the transformation of political man, is not a subject for meditation or a theory to be debated by theologians, but a mandate of conscience, of principled action, for every man who lies awake in an age of suffering. Transformation is possible, and thereby political, wherever injustice exists and Truth and Love lie dormant. Transformation is the mode of politics in the Nuclear Age because it is the mode of continuing life, and thus hope and the art of the possible become one: to be politic is to believe in and practice the art of transforming man. A future opens only to those who live and spread the belief that man can become what he has not been, and that the widening of community is a constant possibility.

It is just such a politics of the spirit which has been embodied successfully by Dag Hammarskjöld and U Thant in the United Nations, and toward which John Kennedy was struggling at the end and gave expression to in his American University Address. The greatest politician of our time, however, in the sense of having been the deepest practitioner of global community, was Pope

John XXIII. In his quest for the universality of a Universal Church, Pope John inevitably became the prophet of political transformation as well, for a truly worldwide Church must seek the harmony of man divided. To see Truth is to begin to bring it into being, and Pope John's vision of *Pacem in Terris* has impelled man toward his goal of global convergence. Yet it is the suffering love of Pope John and Hammarskjöld, as of Vinoba and Dolci, which incarnated their vision of peace on earth.

In the crucifixion of the world, suffering is transformed into power by Truth and Love, and thus redeemed, it strikes at the roots of injustice in man. Suffering Love has the power to transform the oppressor, as it has already transformed the oppressed; it has the power to widen the community of strength. Gandhi's greatest victory was the liberation not of the Indians, but of the British, who came into power only as they relinquished it. Suffering love joins the oppressed, and finally the oppressor, in a growing reality of global community. It confirms humanity by community.

But when resistance to suffering Love rises in a backlash of fear and strikes down the prophet of non-violence, as America struck down Martin Luther King, the power of transformation becomes a power of judgment, if not judgment by fire then by the inward curl of a society unable to confront power in the service of a world community and thus committed by fear to the sterility of self. Yet transformation continues in the midst of fear and pushes back the effects threatened by the blind. If in the end the sword is still taken, only he who takes it has been said to perish. Love and its community remain.

For it is true of the suffering poor who fill the earth that there is God in these people, like the fire that smolders under the ashes. There is no God other than the Fire under these ashes. If God appears dead in the Nuclear Age, it is because he has not been sufficiently liberated from his bondage in suffering man. The presence of God in mankind is, above all, the presence of man crucified. It is a presence dimly seen and scarcely felt when the crucified of mankind are crowded out into the margin of the earth. God lives where men are beaten and die, but He lives to bring them and their murderers to life, and His life comes to life only when He emerges from them as Truth and as Love. The life of God is the life of the crucified, but while He is deeply present in crucifixion the unveiling of His presence is in resurrection, a resurrection which can be seen and felt only by those in whom Love and Truth have taken hold. God is dead where men lie dying and unseen. He lives where crucifixion is seen and felt and entered into, as neither victim nor executioner but as Love suffering and as Truth overcoming. Crucifixion becomes redemptive precisely when the victim recognizes his divinity. Man takes that step when he responds to injustice with Love: suffering, resistant, and overpowering. Man becomes God when Love and Truth enter into man, not by man's power but by raising him to Power, so that revolution in Love is revealed finally as the Power of resurrection.

To join the revolution of peace is to enter the Fire smoldering under the ashes of men suffering and to feel the intensity of its promise. It is to discover that Fire rising already into flame at the beginning of the greatest revolution in history. The Fire of Truth and Love rising from the ashes and restoring the ashes to flame is the only power remaining in the Nuclear Age. To enter that Fire is to become one with God in man, as God has revealed himself in such servants of man as Gandhi, Vinoba, and Dolci, and as Pope John, Dag Hammarskjöld, and U Thant. The revolution of peace is the rising flame of man daring to become truly human, the flame of man beginning to live with himself without fear by uniting himself with the Power of Truth. It is a Fire which has only begun in man and which will end only when it has burned his image from earth into the heavens, transfiguring man into the God who is his Power.

NOTES

1. *Children of the A-Bomb*, compiled by Dr. Arata Osada (G. P. Putnam's Sons: 1963), pp. 151–52.

2. J. D. Bernal, "The Human Family: A Map of Need," in *Peace on Earth: The Way Ahead,* ed. Walter Stein (Sheed and Ward, London: 1966), p. 62.
3. Dr. B. R. Sen of FAO made the first half of this statement during the week of October 16, 1966, as quoted by Louis B. Fleming in the *Vancouver Sun,* October 27, 1966. As the number of U.S. forces in Vietnam rises above 500,000, the estimate of $30 billion a year as the American cost of the war may even be low. The significance of this figure is evident in the fact that one year of the Peace Corps is equal to the cost of thirty-two hours of the Vietnam War.
4. Danilo Dolci, *Waste* (Macgibbon & Kee, London: 1963), p. 15.
5. Bernal, p. 66.
6. Boris Pasternak, *Doctor Zhivago* (Fontana Books: 1965), p. 248.
7. *Ibid.,* p. 292.
8. Eduard Thurneysen, *Dostoevsky* (John Knox Press: 1964), p. 27.
9. Danilo Dolci, *The Outlaws of Partinico* (London, Macgibbon & Kee: 1960), pp. 168–69.
10. Stephen King-Hall, *Defense in the Nuclear Age* (Fellowship Publications: 1959), p. 31. King-Hall also believed, however, that an enemy's mind could be changed by an appeal to reason and that non-violent methods are the only effective defense in the Nuclear Age.
11. For this point I am indebted to a short but penetrating article by William Pfaff, "The Strategy of the Weak," *Commonweal* (July 22, 1966), pp. 456–57. Felix Greene developed the same point in a series of articles for *The Vancouver Sun* after he returned from three months in North Vietnam. See especially his "Paradox of 'Bombed-Out' North Viet Nam: People Strong Because They're Poor," *The Vancouver Sun,* July 6, 1967.
12. Pfaff, p. 457.
13. This account and Vinoba's comments are drawn from *Gandhi to Vinoba: The New Pilgrimage* by Lanza del Vasto (London, Rider and Company: 1956), p. 85.
14. *Ibid.,* pp. 171–72.
15. The details about Dolci's workers are given in an excellent biography: *Fire Under the Ashes: The Life of Danilo Dolci* by James McNeish (London, Hodder and Stoughton: 1965), p. 163.
16. *Ibid.,* p. 156.
17. *Ibid.,* pp. 68, 169.
18. *Ibid.,* p. 217.

2

From Bonhoeffer to Gandhi: God as Truth

THE WORLD AS suffering and as entering transformation is crucifixion. At the heart of the world is the continuation and working out of Golgotha. The revolution of peace is the world in the critical process of overcoming its self-resistance to unity through the upward convergence of love, a process animated by the union of God and man.

But the world is creation as well as crucifixion, natural growth as well as divine revolution. Man is born in the cathedral of earth and sky, reaches out to the infinite silence of the universe, and begins to form himself in a rhythm of creation and self-recognition. Man is growing and maturing through time, provoking and provoked by a progressive self-understanding. Today the world as creation is man's cumulative discovery of himself in time, not at his deepest self-identity—for his deepest manhood is found through his suffering union with God, through crucifixion not creation, or through that *unique creation* which is crucifixion. But the world as evolving creation is man's growing discovery of himself as distinct and fully responsible, as that one called from childhood to recognize and affirm the possibilities of a world come of age.

In *The Secular City* Harvey Cox has effectively described the present point of the world as creation in terms of secularization, of "man turning his attention away from worlds beyond and toward this world and this time." [1] The age of the secular city is a liberation of man from religious world views whose orientation distracted him from the task of building the earth. It is therefore an affirmation of human responsibility and maturity. The secular metropolis today stands as both the pattern of men's life together and the symbol of their view of the world, because secularization "occurred only when the cosmopolitan confrontations of city living exposed the relativity of the myths and traditions men once thought were unquestionable." [2] Cox suggests that the secular city even supplies us with the most promising image for understanding the Kingdom of God. Since the Kingdom is the partnership of God and man in history, our responsible shaping of the secular city is the Kingdom in the process of realizing itself. Cox later expresses his awareness, however, that "secularization is not the Messiah." In itself secularization is simply "a dangerous liberation; it raises the stakes, making it possible for man to increase the range of his freedom and responsibility and thus to deepen his maturation. At the same time it poses risks of a larger order than those it displaces. But the promise exceeds the peril, or at least makes it worth taking the risk." [3] On this level of his analysis, Cox's positive response to the secular city is a necessary reawakening of Christian concern for the world as continuing creation, and for man as he actually confronts this stage of his evolving history.

Yet granted the need to celebrate creation, which today means an increasingly secular creation, it is impossible to understand the height to which the stakes have been raised by our age unless one recognizes the enormous tension between what is and what must become, and unless one anchors that recognition in a radical distinction between the secular city and the Kingdom of God.

The distance from the secular city to the Kingdom of God is infinite, not because the Kingdom is nowhere present in the city but because it is present as transcendence and therefore active

as revolution. In the technological society that is rapidly covering
the earth the city must be a locus for the revolution of peace but
it is not its reality. The city as such is pragmatic and profane,
beautiful and ugly, calling for both celebration and transformation. The city is all things to those gathered within it, joy and
terror on the same block. But the city as city is unredeemed.
It remains the city of man, where God's work of love within man
is unsettling and explosive. For in terms of justice, the city is
more static than mobile and often meets the challenge of non-
violent love with violent hatred, revolution with repression. Man's
coming of age in the secular city is not identical with the coming
of love. Where the two intersect, as they do in the man of truth,
a crucifixion takes place, for the city is not prepared to accept
the fulfillment of its promise and will exact the penalty of suffering from the prophet. The presence of transcendence in time is
loving and abrasive, non-violent and aggressive. The name of
transcendence is Truth. In its revolution of peace Truth cannot
make peace with the city until the city has taken the form of that
new heaven which is a new earth.

It is not so much secularity as technology, the source and sustaining power of the city, which represents the peril and risk of
our time. Secularity has brought man a sense of absolute autonomy; technology has given him the power to press his autonomous self into experiments with inconceivable effects on his life
and psyche. Yet technology is not simply a huge power complex
of machines and apparatus. It is a state of mind, and as such it
has formed the frame of reference in which we all live.   .

The effect of technology on the entire world has been to impel
mankind toward a single, all-embracing civilization, a civilization
characterized largely by the domination of machines over men,
but even more by the domination of standardization over spon-
taneity and of means over ends. Technique means the pursuit
by quantitative calculations of the one best means in every
area of human life. It is a question of the specialist determining
everywhere not the best relative means, in which a subjective
choice would be made among several possibilities, but the best

means in the absolute sense, on the basis of objective numerical calculation. Thus the expansion of technique into the whole of life has meant the creation of a science of means, a science touching very different areas with the same methodology of absolute technical calculation. "It ranges from the act of shaving to the act of organizing the landing in Normandy, or to cremating thousands of deportees. Today no human activity escapes this technical imperative." [4] It is the aggregate of all these means and the machines embodying them, each the best by calculation in a specific field, which produces technical civilization. We have become, in the words of Jacques Ellul, the foremost analyst of this phenomenon, "a civilization of means." [5]

It is within this context of technique, of the technological society, that the question of truth must be consciously reraised by man today. As men of technique we are actually incapable of seeking truth in any other context—we can only conceptualize within our "civilization of means"—but we are both able and likely to seek truth without conscious recognition of the extent to which our efforts have been managed by our age, and our end predetermined by our beginning. The question of truth must be raised critically, with direct reference to our world and its particular kind of dominance over us, or we shall be as much the victims of a passing mythology, in this case imposed by the thought patterns of the secular city, as was any noble savage. On the other hand, there can be no question of aspiring to a timeless, disembodied truth unaffected by the relativities of history. To grow in truth, which is both present and transcendent, relative to life and infinite in reach, man today must do so in terms of, and in response to, the technological society which is forming his world.

Considerations such as these moved Dietrich Bonhoeffer to pose, in his prison cell in 1944, his now-famous questions about God and man in the contemporary world: "The thing that keeps coming back to me is, what *is* Christianity, and indeed what *is* Christ, for us today? . . . We are proceeding toward a time of no religion at all: men as they are now simply cannot be religious any more. . . . How do we speak of God without religion, i.e. without the temporally influenced presuppositions of metaphysics, inwardness, and so on? How do we speak in a secular fashion of God?" [6]

To judge from two of the current efforts "to speak in a secular fashion of God," those of Harvey Cox and Leslie Dewart, discourse on God in the contemporary world may have to become increasingly wrapped in silence. Cox feels that due to the fatal equivocality of the word "God" and its equivalents in our secular civilization, we may have to take a moratorium on speech until a new name for the reality of God arrives. This new name will come through a continuing revelation in history, "through the clash of historical forces and the faithful efforts of a people to discern His presence and respond to his call." [7] Dewart suggests in his valuable book *The Future of Belief* that in the meantime we should be engaged in a progressive dehellenization of the Christian doctrine of God, especially with regard to such concepts as being, omnipotence, eternity, and the supernatural. What will begin to emerge is a new restraint in applying any name to the Christian God, motivated by the desire to render His presence more immediate to us.[8]

It would be difficult to deny the value of any proposal which would reduce radically the invocations to God in a civilization which holds God Himself as a means ready to sell its every crime and product. Nor is there anything intrinsically sacred in the name "God." For that Reality whose presence evokes awe and a self-crucifying love, the name of "God," with both its pagan and modern connotations, may be a conceptual reduction verging on blasphemy. On the other hand, it is not blasphemy but belief to signify by our withdrawal of his name that the God who can justify total victory in Vietnam should be declared totally dead.

Yet granting the problem of "God" and the Christian precedents besides, from Dionysius the Areopagite through St. John of the Cross, for a position which would at certain heights deny him every name and attribute, it can still be questioned whether an historicized version of negative theology is the fulfillment of

Dietrich Bonhoeffer. If to speak meaningfully of God in the technological society is to speak of Him less or not at all, then we must still either take on the task of forging a new and living credo for our more restrained speech, or, in the case of total negation and silence, suppose in modern man a ready response to that burning awareness of the divine presence which moved the mystics, and would presumably move ourselves, beyond thought and language. If it is more possible to witness to the divine presence without "God," and even then sparingly, it remains impossible, except in rare instances, to speak of Him by denying Him speech. If God lives to give birth to others, then His presence must be granted the witness of living words. What Bonhoeffer has proven equally by his life and his writings, and what Harvey Cox has restated so well, is that the peculiar idiom in which this presence can be conveyed to modern man, if it can be conveyed at all, is political rather than metaphysical:

A church which eschews politics, or worse still, uses politics to shore up its own position in the world, will never speak to secular man. Ministers and nuns on picket lines for racial justice today are not just signs of the church's "social concern." They are evangelists, telling modern man what the Gospel says. The church which remains securely within the "spiritual realm" will annoy no one and convince no one, for secular man is a political animal *par excellence*. . . .[9]

To speak in a secular fashion of God means, first of all, to speak of Him in direct response to the suffering and injustice in the world today, and moreover, to speak in so specific and pointed a fashion that there can be no question of one's meaning and position. To speak meaningfully of God to secular man is therefore to act decisively on the faith that conscience can and must seek out and discern the will of God where secular man lives, in concrete events, and that conscience can do so regardless of how much "the people with watch-chains," as Pasternak referred to the enemies of life,[10] have obscured by doubt and profaned by presumption the fulfilling of such a mandate. There can be no living speech about God, under any name, except where injustice is resisted by love in witness to His presence in the suffering.

Discourse on God can only take on meaning with specific reference to suffering man, which is not to deny the truth of transcendence but to affirm the reality of its incarnation and continuing presence.

Because secular man is "a political animal *par excellence*" he will confront God primarily in a political idiom. If the God of Love seems absent there, as was the case when Karl Marx took up the cause of the workers, then secular man will give Him up as dead. A God who is not present in political life today is dead to man's conscience because the decisions, or lack of them, which bring life and death to the majority of mankind now take place in the realm of politics. To speak of God in a secular fashion is to testify to His presence where life and death matter most to man, yet precisely where God has in fact usually been claimed by the forces of injustice and oppression. To cut through the Christian mythologies of class and nation to the core of concern, however, it is clear that the man, Jesus, who was crucified by Rome as a dangerous insurgent can neither be divorced from the political realm nor enlisted as a counter-revolutionary.[11] The judgment of the Romans, who at least discerned in Jesus the fact of revolution, however wrong their interpretation of it, was more accurate than that of modern Christians, whose conception of Christ makes him unworthy of crucifixion if it does not in fact place him among the executioners.

It is not necessary to search through Bonhoeffer's early commentaries as Cox does,[12] for a clue to a specific starting point for "a worldly interpretation of Christianity." Bonhoeffer was quite specific on the point in the same prison cell, three months after he posed his initial questions:

God allows himself to be edged out of the world and on to the cross. God is weak and powerless in the world, and that is exactly the way, the only way, in which he can be with us and help us. Matthew 8:17 makes it crystal clear that it is not by his omnipotence that Christ helps us, but by his weakness and suffering.
This is the decisive difference between Christianity and all religions. Man's religiosity makes him look in his distress to the power of God in the world; he uses God as a *Deus ex machina*. The Bible

however directs him to the powerlessness and suffering of God; only a suffering God can help. To this extent we may say that the process we have described by which the world came of age was an abandonment of a false conception of God, and a clearing of the decks for the God of the Bible, who conquers power and space in the world by his weakness. This must be the starting point for our "worldly" interpretation.[13]

Only a suffering God can help, the God of the Bible, who conquers power and space in the world by his weakness. To speak in a secular fashion of God is to speak of this God of the Bible, crucified and resurrected, and to draw forth the implications of his revolutionary crucifixion for the believer in the technological society. If we are to take Bonhoeffer seriously, it would seem that a fundamental reason for secular man's indifference to God is that Christianity has failed to introduce him to Jesus crucified. Yet it is not apparent that this introduction will be accomplished by celebrating the secular city and making God its appendix. A closed secularity is overcome not so much by speaking less of God as it is by speaking more of man, at that precise point where man meets God in suffering and in revolution. But to speak today of God in the fashion of His man it is imperative that the man of the cross be seen outlined against the totalitarian power of our civilization of means.

In the modern world the meeting of man and God has most closely approximated the revolution of the cross in the person of Mohandas Gandhi. While it cannot be said that to preach Gandhism is to preach Christ, it is always necessary to preach Christ in terms of his continuing presence in man and of the upward revolution of cross and open tomb; their primary exponent in our time is Gandhi. The significance of Gandhi is that more than any other man of our century, except Pope John XXIII on a different level of politics, he has testified to the active presence of God in the world of political man and has done so after the pattern of Jesus. In Gandhi belief met secularity in suffering love and an empire changed. The questions which Bonhoeffer asked, and to which he gave the cross as the beginning of an answer, have their further response in Gandhi.[14] Moreover, this response was such that it offers perhaps the only way to resist effectively and finally transcend the technological determinants of our civilization.

Gandhi's faith and politics were inseparable. He wrote in the introduction to his autobiography:

What I want to achieve,—what I have been striving and pining to achieve these thirty years,—is self-realization, to see God face to face. I live and move and have my being in pursuit of this goal. All that I do by way of speaking and writing, and all my ventures in the political field, are directed to this same end.[15]

Gandhi rejected the popular description of himself as a saint trying to be a politician; he said that the truth was the other way around. Yet the extent to which Gandhi as a politician made his goal, that of seeing God face to face, determine and form each of his concrete actions and policies sets him far apart from any other believing politician. He made God his end not as a terminal point and his particular salvation but as the Reality to be progressively found through his daily politics, the ground and measure of every decision, and as an end already visible in the faces of a people resisting oppression with love. Gandhi was both saint and politician because his deepening vision of God was realized in and through his political vision for man. "If I could persuade myself that I should find Him in a Himalayan cave, I would proceed there immediately. But I know that I cannot find Him apart from humanity." [16] His faith became incarnate in his suffering people. He was once moved to write: "It is no exaggeration, but the literal truth, to say that in this meeting with the peasants I was face to face with God, Ahimsa and Truth." [17] Because Gandhi saw God already present in man he was able to move man to a revolution toward God.

Gandhi's God was Truth, a name he arrived at after much searching but one which so deepened in his consciousness that his final formulation of it passed from "God is Truth" to "Truth is God":

I came to that conclusion [that Truth is God] after a continuous and relentless search after Truth, which began nearly fifty years ago. I then found that the nearest approach to Truth was through love. But I also found that love has many meanings in the English language at least, and that human love, in the sense of passion, could become a degrading thing also. I found, too, that love, in the sense of *Ahimsa* [avoiding injury to anything on earth], had only a limited number of votaries in the world. But I never found a double meaning in connection with Truth, and not even atheists had demurred to the necessity or power of Truth. But, in their passion for discovering Truth, the atheists have not hesitated to deny the very existence of God—from their own point of view rightly. And it was because of this reasoning that I saw that rather than say that "God is Truth," I should say that "Truth is God." [18]

Gandhi titled his autobiography *The Story of My Experiments with Truth*. Truth is limitless. It is gained gradually on an infinite ascent through a painful methodology of search and self-sacrifice. Truth, or God, is so intimate to life that it is the subject of deep personal experimentation and the essence of political action; Truth so transcends life that its way is without end and its power without limit. Yet man can grow into Truth's infinite power only by first recognizing his own powerlessness and in humility reducing himself to zero. "Satyagraha," or truth-force, is that Power which in itself can overcome any injustice on earth but whose fullness is blocked by the individual's lack of faith and his continuing self-assertion. The extent of each person's commitment to Truth goes beyond all religious and secular loyalties to define his real allegiance to God. A man knows Truth as relative, but if he worships that relative truth and deepens in it, he is certain to attain the Absolute Truth.

Gandhi's answer to the question: How do we speak in a secular fashion of God? was to speak of Truth. The one name God possesses for every man of good will, believer or not, is Truth; or to put the emphasis where Gandhi wanted it, Truth is God. The Truth Gandhi spoke of and witnessed to was a living Truth. It could shape his life and politics because it exists at the very center of life:

Truth gives perennial joy. . . . Truth is Knowledge also. It is Life. You feel vitality in you when you have got Truth in you. Again, it gives Bliss. It is a permanent thing of which you cannot be robbed. You may be sent to the gallows, or put to torture, but if you have Truth in you, you will experience an inner joy.[19]

In his friendships with professed atheists who shared his social concern, Gandhi found the identity of God and Truth the necessary bridge for mutual understanding. For a marriage between two atheists in his Ashram he substituted the words "in the name of Truth" for "in the name of God" without compromising either his or their beliefs. On the existential plane the key to belief was love, for as he told one friend: "You may call yourself an atheist, but so long as you feel akin with mankind you accept God in practice." [20] Truth incarnated in suffering love was belief. Another atheist, by expounding his belief in man's dignity as unhindered by a repressive God, forced Gandhi to admit:

Yes, I see an ideal in your talk. I can neither say my theism is right nor your atheism wrong. We are seekers after truth. We change whenever we find ourselves in the wrong. I changed like that many times in my life. I see you are a worker. You are not a fanatic. You will change whenever you find yourself in the wrong. There is no harm as long as you are not fanatical. Whether you are in the right or I am in the right, results will prove. Then I may go your way or you may come my way; or both of us may go a third way.[21]

The man who received this response was overwhelmed by Gandhi's openness and understanding. He became a member of Gandhi's "family" and later wrote a book on their continuing dialogue and friendship, *An Atheist with Gandhi.*[22]

The correspondence between Gandhi's understanding of truth and the thought of the Catholic philosopher Leslie Dewart in *The Future of Belief* is remarkable enough to quote Dewart at length:

Belief in the *true God* means not simply belief in a god which, (logically enough), we must *presuppose* to be true, under pain of otherwise not being able to believe at all. It means belief in God precisely *as true.* It would not be inexact, therefore, to say that belief in God really means to have an ultimate commitment to the truth; I mean, to all truth, totally and universally—not particularly to a transcendent, subsistent Truth, that is, not to the presumed Truth of

God's self-identity, which is a hellenization of the Christian experience, but to the transcendent truth which is immanent and manifested in every truth. I am talking about the truth which evokes the attitudes of honesty and truthfulness—I mean, that precise sort of openness which is apt to earn self-respect. I refer to that truth which calls for fidelity to the truth wherever and whatever it might be.[23] (Italics in original.)

Dewart cites as the hallmark of the commitment to God *as true* "a certain conditioning of one's belief by the willingness to admit the real possibility of disbelief—both by another and by oneself."[24] Or as the man of our time whose intensity of belief was second to none put it to an atheist: "I may go your way or you may come my way; or both of us may go a third way." Unlike Christianity, which has allowed its belief to become fixed on a narrowing conception of God at the expense of its openness to truth, especially as found in its own Gospel, Gandhi felt in no way threatened by an absolute commitment to truth as it opened out to him. For Gandhi God was "up ahead" in the deeply living sense that his experiments in Truth were drawing him farther and farther into the mystery of a loving goal of life and history. God as Truth opened him to every aspect of man's search for dignity and meaning. Truth is therefore not the adequacy of our representative operations but, in Dewart's words, "the adequacy of our conscious existence," "the fidelity of consciousness to being."[25] There was no hesitation in Gandhi's pursuit of all truth, on a rigorously disciplined way, because God's very presence could be separated from no truth.

It is perhaps in this direction as indicated by Gandhi, the identification of God's presence with a loving, existential growth in truth, that the proper approach lies to what Dewart has suggested is the basic problem for Christian philosophy: to demonstrate whether, in what sense, in what way, and with what consequences, God is *present*.[26] If God is present as truth, grounded in suffering love, then the previous deadlock between theism and atheism takes on a new dimension, one in which there is a response to Bonhoeffer when he writes: "I often ask myself why a Christian instinct frequently draws me more to the religionless than to the religious, by which I mean not with any intention of evangelizing them, but rather, I might almost say, in brotherhood.'" [27]

In Gandhi's framework, insofar as the religious have sacrificed the search for truth, which is God's very presence, for a particular notion of God, which in becoming merely abstract and static proclaims the absence of God, they have in effect lost God Himself. The religionless, on the other hand, lacking any allegiance to a deity jealous of its own truth, have been free to press forward into God's actual presence as Truth and Love. Bonhoeffer's brotherhood with the religionless was that of a still freely seeking believer with those whose non-belief was an affirmation of God's presence. To recognize God's presence as truth, loving and liberating, is to shatter dogmatic barriers and reveal the existential ground of genuine faith. It is not surprising therefore that Christianity in the modern world, where it has so often sheltered tradition and institution from an openness to truth itself, is experiencing the death of God. The demise of living truth is the death of God. To speak in a secular fashion of God is to speak meaningfully to men to whom God is already existentially present as vital truth, but for whom religious belief has come to mean the end of truth: a profession of faith which seems to claim that final truth has been found, when in fact it is evident to any man of conscience that the fullness of truth is not given in time and that the way to it has not been luminous enough in the life of the Church. To speak meaningfully of God to secular man is to recognize God's presence in him as truth and to confess God's absence in oneself as untruth, evasion, and hypocrisy. It is, in the last analysis, less a question of language than of living: living in and through a naked commitment to truth as it opens man to history and frees him to feel the presence of the living God.

That vital truth which was the subject of Gandhi's experiments can be understood in terms of the human spirit's own transcendence opening more and more to the mystery that is the ground of all being, as experienced in and through every relative truth of life. By freely accepting the relative process of ever-widening truth, by surrendering himself without reservation to truth as the loving center and focus of his life, Gandhi simultaneously opened himself to the boundless mystery of Truth, which is God's self-communication. God is present as truth insofar as man is serious in his pursuit of it. Man is called to revere and grow in truth, not simply to control and use it, which is only technique and brings man efficiency, not life. Truth lies over the city like mist over rainy streets. Men are enveloped by it and pass through it. Some pause and are transformed. There is in every vital truth an element of contemplation.

We come then to the heart of our question, the question of truth raised critically in an age overcome by technique: How does Gandhi's approach to truth provide an effective response to the technique dominating our civilization of means? To put the question in this way, in terms of "how" and "effective," is already to concede one bias of our time, the view that truth is to be understood pragmatically. To ask it thus with critical reference to the technology behind pragmatism, however, is to adopt provisionally the criterion of effectiveness without committing oneself to the framework normally identified with it.

While it is true that "technopolitan man's understanding of truth is pragmatic," [28] it is the fatal weakness of technique that it is not itself pragmatic. In appearance technique functions effectively for man in the modern world; it is said to work for him. In reality it grants him a tightly contained control over a mechanized mode of life whose ultimate effect has been an operational totalitarianism doubling back on him. Technique has meant the convergence on man of a plurality, not of techniques, but of systems or complexes of techniques, each of them asserting in good faith that it leaves intact the integrity of its subject but whose cumulative effect on him has been totalitarian.[29] It is to be feared that in its over-all effect technique has functioned not so much for man as it has over and against him. The astounding efficiency of modern technology, from nuclear missiles to electric toothbrushes, has on the whole been efficient only when measured by its own particular technical aims. When measured by its subject, man, and his aspirations for world peace and justice, the overwhelming power generated by technique has coincided with moral impotence. By fostering the illusion of omnipotence over the deepening reality of impotence, technique has been fundamentally ineffective for man: it has freed him from much of his subjection to nature only to enslave him to technical processes.

A primary reason for technique's mastery of its master, man, is that technique has grown out of its machinery into a pervasive state of mind which continues daily to absorb more and more of mankind. Technique as a state of mind has overcome not only the man of the street but most of the potentially liberating intellects of our time. To each man it has dictated an approach to life, that of intense specialization directed toward a series of technical solutions, which has seemed to provide an effective response to every immediate problem of life while distracting him comfortably from most of its overarching questions. The unacknowledged premise is that man, by concentrating his technical skill industriously on each problem as it confronts him, will arrive finally at an effective end of some kind. In effect, this means adopting the technical answer of the specialist to a multitude of problems, with the consequent loss of any higher perspective. Technique is thought to possess all the answers. Thus President Kennedy was led by advisers through a series of technical problems and solutions into the Bay of Pigs, and was judged most severely afterward not for a failure of over-all wisdom but for refusing to employ the further technique of intensive bombing. Thus, on a different level, the American husband's most typical response to death is made through the technique of life insurance and the special advice of his agent. At least the financial aspect of death will have been put under control, which is all of death that deserves immediate attention since it alone admits of a technical solution (unless one takes the attitude that eternal life can be technicized through church donations and spiritual exercises).

The domination of technique over human intelligence and feeling has been nowhere more evident than in modern warfare and the military industry. The techniques of modern war, automatic and usually controlled at some point remote from their human victims, have made it possible for men to execute massive slaughters without feeling any of the normal pain or anguish implied in a single act of killing. Divorced from the living consequences of their actions, the technicians of military power have had no difficulty in justifying human carnage on their charts and boards, although few would wish to pour napalm personally over a child. In Vietnam the crushing victory of military techniques over any human feeling and reason has been so visible as to require no documentation. It was again a dedicated and brilliantly synchronized army of technicians that built the atomic bomb, and another skilled team of technicians that performed the task of dropping it on Hiroshima and Nagasaki. The connecting link between them, where wisdom is usually presumed by the weapons technician and seldom found, was the chief of state and his advisers. But they, too, were ruled by technique, the thought of "the one best way" to end the war. More recently, the thought of nuclear strategists such as Herman Kahn has offered further evidence of technique's victory over intelligence, by turning man from the morally imaginative task of building peace to devising the most surgical ways to wage a thermonuclear war (the justification of which has been the technical function of some moralists on the scene). The unthinkable for Kahn is the problem of peace on earth, because it has no technical solution.[30] Like Kahn, we have all been trained to think technically, yet technique in itself is ineffective in changing man, except on the most primitive level of fear, and can only divert us from the search for true power into further and ultimate destruction.

The common factor between Gandhi and the technical mind is experimentation: Whereas technique has experimented on man to the roots of his functioning being, Gandhi has experimented beyond the acknowledged limits of man's spirit. Both Gandhi and the technical mind have based themselves on experience: The technical mind has abstracted from laboratory experience the infinite variety of techniques which make up our civilization of means, with its claim to have a technical solution for every problem and the power to control life even as it threatens global death. In a very different laboratory, that of his own spirit understood in community, Gandhi sought the way to an enduring power for the powerless. As opposed to the magnitude and resources of technique, Gandhi's experiments were all but invisible. But measured by their pragmatic value for transforming man, Gandhi's tentative experiments in truth were the most effective events of our age. They staked out ground for real hope for political man where only skepticism had thrived in the past, in the correction of massive injustices through the power of truth. It is quite true that Gandhi himself employed techniques—no man is without them—but erroneous to suggest that he relied on or was dominated by them in a way paralleling that of the technical mind. He relied only on Truth and through it developed those non-violent techniques which could convey Truth most effectively. For that reason Gandhi's techniques, not autonomous but under the power of Truth, were effective for man. Because his experiments in truth were given precedence, and not the established techniques of conflict, which were already violent and becoming more so, Truth was at last mediated by a new choice and range of methods through which it could find genuine expression in conflict. Truth was shown for the first time on a modern political scale to have living power between opponents when it is not denied from the beginning by violence. Gandhi's experiments were a constant critical search for the means corresponding perfectly to the end of Truth. They can help us transcend our civilization of means if we can see in our own context Gandhi's painfully rediscovered truth that means are end-creating.

Even today with our concentration on technique, we are still accustomed to explain our actions in terms of their ends. The process is a natural one but overlooks the unnatural autonomy of our techniques. Whereas we now act, or rather submit—in terms of the pressures of our time—as if our techniques were autonomous, we continue to speak as if they were directed to some noble end, obscuring the fact that in reality technique has under its own power outdistanced any ideal we might formulate for it and has set its own ends. Every country in the world has been told conscientiously by the United States Government that the only reason for our increasing destruction of Vietnam is that we wish to bring a just peace to it. Yet few have seen any correspondence between our means and stated end, any more than they have recognized in themselves numerous cases, on a less murderous level, of the same practice of self-deception. One need not accuse government officials, or any of the dignitaries of our respectable crimes, of deliberate genocide: the truth is more complex. Our chosen means in Vietnam and across the world are themselves end-creating, but the ends brought into being by autonomous techniques, destructive of life and repressive of human dignity, are such that we can grant them no formal recognition. We can only hold righteously to our higher formulation of intent, peace and justice (through the repression and destruction of suspected Communists), as if the actually disastrous end already visible through our means were a somewhat unexpected step on the way. In our civilization of means, intended ends seem suddenly to disappear from sight, whereas in reality they have gradually been displaced by the unrecognizable (because unjustifiable) ends implicit in our means. The natural consequence of our studied fixation on apparently noble ends, sought through massive means creating their own, opposite ends, would be a forced recognition of the real character of our actions so that we would have to do ruthlessly the same crimes which for some time we have been in the process of doing righteously. Eventually our ideal end could scarcely justify criminal means even to ourselves because an actually criminal end arising from these means would have become more and more obviously dominant over the ideal. But even a barbarian honesty is not certain in such a process: self-righteousness is tenacious enough, and modern technology effective enough on its own terms, to admit the possibility of our doing today almost any evil in the name of good.

Every means tends to create its own end, unless it truly expresses and is continually formed by a seriously intended end.

"It is necessary to incarnate the end in the means themselves." [31] As Gandhi put it: "There is just the same inviolable connection between the means and the end as there is between the seed and the tree." [32] Or in Maritain's words, the means are "in a sense the end in the process of becoming." [33] The great danger central to our civilization of means is that we shall allow our technology to destroy the earth while we continue to hold self-righteously to an absurdly contradicted ideal. We are no longer even at the criminal stage of justifying our murderous means by a compromised end, but at the pathological stage of refusing to acknowledge, much less resist, the real and overwhelming end emerging from our civilization of means like the beast from the sea. Illusion and hypocrisy have never been so fatal as when wedded to modern technique. The alternative to deepening slaughter and guilt, and one seldom chosen in international politics, is repentance: the admission that the existential end implicit in the execution of our policies was criminal from the beginning.

An experiment in truth is an effort to realize God's presence as truth *both in and through* a particular action. It is concentrated on neither means nor end but seeks to affirm the integrity of life by an action already embodying as much as possible, and thereby creating, a worthy end. Rabbi Steven Schwarzschild has defined the criterion for a good action as the question of "whether it will be appropriate both for the hastening of the coming of the Kingdom in time and within the Kingdom itself once it is established." [34] An experiment in truth is, in terms of its end-means integrity, what the Jews call a *Mitzvah,* a divinely commanded deed. A *Mitzvah* transforms the world into the Kingdom of God in two ways:

In the first place, it establishes the Kingdom in this world for the split moment and in the very narrow space in which it is being performed, and, in the second place, it conquers that moment and that space as one out of billions in the forward-moving front on which the Kingdom conquers the world in history.[35]

If there is a difference between a *Mitzvah* and an experiment in truth, it would be in the latter's emphasis on a more tentative and probing search toward that deed which *is* divinely commanded. An experiment in truth takes place primarily in those murky regions of life and experience where the divine command has not yet been found for an action which could have a place in the actually established Kingdom, and where it has been given up by most as incapable of definition or realization: in day-to-day politics and in situations of intense conflict.

With respect to the technical process we have described, an experiment in truth can be viewed as the rejection of an autonomy of means for the integrity of means and end in truth, an understanding of which must eventually involve a radical critique and redefinition of all our proximate actions in the light of the truth capable of being present in them. Such an experiment is a sensitive probing of the possibilities of truth to which a particular moment and situation are open. It draws no pre-established lines concerning the ability of man to grow in truth, but tries instead to open him progressively and self-critically to the Power latent in and transcendent to each second of existence. Its ground and hoped-for justification lie in direct and usually painful experience. It is contemplation in action, a search for and expression of truth in the most spiritually resistant areas of life. In political life an experiment in truth is therefore a way of action which challenges traditional political theory at its perennially unresolved dichotomy of means and ends.[36] It meets conflict and its invitation to resolution through violence with the affirmation that life is whole and that the power of Truth is capable of being incarnated in each successive moment of it.

What Gandhi sought in his experiments was not simply his own salvation through a series of spiritual discoveries but an ever-widening, communal growth in truth, the convergence finally of whole races and peoples in an upward ascent of mutual recognition. Whereas the effect of autonomous technique on man is fragmentization, the effect of a growth in truth is unity, unity in the man of truth and unity in the community drawn upward by truth. A wholeness of life and a community of love are the fulfillment of truth in man. The purpose of experimenting in truth is not merely to free oneself from a murderous social context, but to realize the truth in unity within that very context and on continually higher levels: from city block to race, nation, and world. When God is sought as truth, he draws the seekers into a growing community of love. The concrete way in which Gandhi suffered toward this community of seeking men is the point at which his experiments coincide most perfectly with the life and death of Christ.

NOTES

1. Harvey Cox, *The Secular City* (Macmillan: 1965), p. 2.
2. *Ibid.,* p. 1.
3. *Ibid.,* p. 167.
4. Jacques Ellul, *The Technological Society* (Alfred A. Knopf: 1965), p. 21.
5. *Ibid.,* p. 19.
6. Dietrich Bonhoeffer, *Letters and Papers from Prison* (Macmillan paperback: 1962), pp. 162–64.
7. Cox, *The Secular City,* p. 266.
8. Leslie Dewart, *The Future of Belief* (Herder and Herder: 1966), "The Development of Christian Theism," pp. 171–215.
9. Harvey Cox, "Beyond Bonhoeffer?," *Commonweal* (September 17, 1965), p. 657.
10. In an early poem, *My Sister Life.* See Thomas Merton's essay, "The Pasternak Affair," in *Disputed Questions* (Farrar, Straus and Cudahy: 1960), p. 7.
11. New Testament historians have shown an increasing awareness of the charge of insurgency laid against Jesus. See, for example, Paul Winter, "The Trial of Jesus," *Commentary* (September, 1964), pp. 35–41, esp. pp. 38–39. I am indebted to Dr. George Edwards of Louisville Presbyterian Seminary for bringing this point to my attention.
12. Cox, *The Secular City,* p. 241, where the author reverts to Bonhoeffer's commentary on the Second Commandment, written many years before his imprisonment, in order to find "a much-needed clue" on how to speak in a secular fashion of God.
13. Bonhoeffer, *Letters and Papers from Prison,* pp. 219–20.
14. Bonhoeffer himself recognized his spiritual kinship with Gandhi and for several years considered going to India to live and work

with him. He was discouraged from doing so by the immediate need for a Christian witness in Germany. A friend who writes of his attraction to Gandhi says: "It was Bonhoeffer's high regard for suffering, I think, which drove him to Gandhi." Gerhard Jacobi, "Drawn Toward Suffering," in *I Knew Dietrich Bonhoeffer*, edited by Wolf-Dieter Zimmerman and Ronald Gregor Smith (Harper & Row: 1966), p. 73.

15. M. K. Gandhi, *An Autobiography or The Story of My Experiments with Truth* (Navajivan Publishing House: 1927), p. xiv.
16. M. K. Gandhi, *God Is Truth* (Bharatiya Vidya Bhavan: 1962), pp. 54–55.
17. Gandhi, *The Story of My Experiments with Truth*, p. 304.
18. Gandhi, *God Is Truth*, pp. 29–30. The editor of this book of extracts from Gandhi's writings does not explain why he chose a title that reverses Gandhi's own formulation.
19. *Ibid.*, p. 25.
20. Gora (G. Ramachandra Rao), *An Atheist with Gandhi* (Navajivan Publishing House: 1951), p. 31.
21. *Ibid.*, p. 44.
22. See above, fn. 20.
23. Dewart, *The Future of Belief*, p. 74.
24. *Ibid.*
25. *Ibid.*, p. 92.
26. *Ibid.*, pp. 184–85.
27. Bonhoeffer, *Letters and Papers from Prison*, p. 165.
28. Cox, *The Secular City*, p. 63.
29. Ellul, *The Technological Society*, p. 391.
30. See my review-article of Kahn's *On Thermonuclear War* and several other books in the "overkill genre," "Peace and the Overkill Strategists," *Cross Currents* (Winter, 1964), pp. 87–103. In justice to Kahn, however, it should be pointed out that in recent years his Hudson Institute has also sponsored the work of some scholars doing peace research.
31. P. Régamey, *Non-Violence and the Christian Conscience* (Herder and Herder: 1966), p. 202.
32. M. K. Gandhi, *Satyagraha (Non-Violent Resistance)* (Navajivan Publishing House: 1951), p. 10.
33. Jacques Maritain, *L'Homme et l'Etat*, p. 49. Quoted by Régamey, p. 200.
34. Steven Schwarzschild, "The Necessity of the Lone Man," *Fellowship* (May, 1965), p. 16.
35. *Ibid.*
36. See Joan V. Bondurant, *Conquest of Violence: The Gandhian Philosophy of Conflict* (University of California Press: 1965), "The Gandhian Dialectic and Political Theory," pp. 189–233.

3

From Gandhi to Christ: God as Suffering Love

BEFORE INQUIRING INTO Gandhi's relationship to Christ and from there into a non-violent Christology, it is necessary to consider first a phenomenon which provides a significant contrast to Gandhi's experiments in truth and which will suggest why Gandhi is so important today for an understanding of the Christian Gospel: the scandal of Western Christianity's denial of its own truth.

From the standpoint of both modern theology and the traditional teaching of the Catholic Church, there is no question that the truth of the Gospel is itself the living person of Jesus Christ; born, suffering, dying and redeeming, raised to lordship by the Father. The truth proclaimed by Christianity is the truth of a living person. The claim of the Gospel is that God's truth has become incarnate and redemptive, has been revealed in the person and life of Jesus. The further claim of the Church is that this living truth of Jesus is present today in the community of faithfully witnessing believers. Christian truth is Jesus Christ; the incarnate truth of Jesus remains present in the mystical identity between Christ and the faithful, whoever and wherever these may be. At the center of any definition of Christian truth is therefore its nature as incarnation, a truth whose fullness is the life of

Jesus and whose continuing presence is that same life as given in the Holy Spirit (but resisted by sin) in his followers. This is not to deny the truth of the dogmatic formulations of Jesus' self-revelation made by the Church, but rather to assert that these are true in a way guardian to the scripturally given incarnation of truth in Jesus himself. In terms of truth, the function of dogma is largely negative; in Karl Rahner's words, "to prevent the self-utterance of Jesus being distorted or truncated." [1] So profoundly vital and personal is the Incarnation that an objective observer should be able to discern this, the full truth of Christianity, simply in the normal life of Christians, without reference to dogma or even to scripture. Thus it was that Paul, for example, gave over his entire existence to the living truth of Christ; to encounter Paul at that stage was to encounter in him the incarnate truth of the Gospel. Such are the implications of Christian truth as defined fully in the person of Jesus of Nazareth. As Karl Barth has put it: "If Jesus Christ is the Word of Truth, then the truth of God is exactly this and nothing else." [2]

Yet it must be admitted that such a living truth has not always been reflected in the life of Christians. In a comment that cuts too deeply for nice ecumenism at the same time as it carries judgment for those who would dismiss it, a sensitive critic of Christianity has written: "The doctrine of the Incarnation, which says that redemption already exists in this world, has always tempted Christians to make their peace with whatever this world has been at any given time." [3] The form of the Incarnation Christians worship, that of humility, service, suffering love, and a sacrificial death, has seldom been matched by the cultural forms they have identified with "incarnationally." To judge from contemporary Christianity in particular, a belief in the Incarnation as true would seem to involve a built-in political and social conservatism, if not a fear-ridden reaction against all that lives and moves in the world under the banner of revolution. In terms of Christian truth, Christianity today is its own denial. What it has incarnated is not the living truth of Jesus. On the contrary, to take two specific examples from the Catholic Christianity professed by the writer: "The Word was made flesh, and dwelt respectably among us white citizens" describes a significant aspect of the incarnationalism of American Catholicism, just as "dwelt among us fascists" reflects the lived faith of another national Catholicism. An examination of these particular incarnations of Catholic Christianity, as they are analyzed in two current studies, will clarify the nature of the Christian contradiction, or "incarnational heresy," which is now evident everywhere. On the other hand, it may also indicate the promise of a truly Catholic faith.

"The Capitulation," an essay by the German Catholic writer Carl Amery,[4] presents us with both the profound failure of German Catholicism and the kind of framework needed to analyze in depth our own incarnational heresies. Amery compares the present state of West German Catholicism to that of the Church under those sovereigns following Constantine who assigned special tasks to her: tasks which guided the Church away from dangerous criticisms of the system while reinforcing the ruler's control over it. The effect on the Church was to leave her in a paradoxical state of power and powerlessness, established and muted; so, too, the Church in West Germany. Amery's thesis is that the new sovereign in Germany, whose power is unprecedented in any single monarch, is the milieu. German Catholicism is dominated by a lower-middle-class milieu which has stifled the primary Christian virtues under layers of honesty, punctuality, cleanliness, dependability, diligence—the kind of secondary virtues which, like Adolf Eichmann's obedience, can be pressed into any cause.

To such a system of values, framing the "decent" life and summed up in the slogan of the cultural mail-order business, "Decorate your house," German Catholicism has capitulated. An analysis of that capitulation, from 1933 onward, raises the critical questions that must become prominent among German Catholics today if belief is to be raised finally from a dying "Milieu-Catholicism." It was Milieu-Catholicism, with its ideals of solidarity and civic virtue, which provided the background and rationale for the individual capitulations to the Nazis, and it is Milieu-Catholicism which must be uprooted today to prevent an equally established and unconscious Church from arriving at its "1933."

Essentially, then, "The Capitulation" is an essay on power as understood in two dimensions, political or cultural power, and Christic power. Due to German Catholicism's almost complete domination by cultural power, Amery is able to suggest only faintly in his own context the kind of power which a genuinely Christocentric ecclesiology might attain. At first glance it may seem scarcely impressive: against the Nazis a Church drastically reduced in numbers and destined for perhaps total martyrdom. But a contrast to the powerless power of the compromised Church raises the necessary questions: In what, after all, does true power consist? Does not the Christian commitment to deep change in the world demand a total witness at every step, as opposed to the impotence of Milieu-Catholicism to achieve anything in or out of crisis beyond its own sterile survival? Would Pius XII's power to change men, for example, have been greater had his unquestionably sensitive conscience been less dominated by another Milieu-Catholicism? How can a faith defined as "catholic" ever be consistent in identifying itself with the alternately protective and oppressive institutions of a particular milieu? Questions such as these bring one to the threatening question: How long before the next capitulation?

The Segregated Covenant by William Osborne raises, at least by implication, the same kind of question in an American context. Osborne's book is a careful study of race relations and American Catholics. Predictably enough, the results of his survey do not add up to a very convincing imitation of Christ by American Catholics faced by "the nation's number one moral problem," as their bishops described the race question in 1958. The dismal pattern of segregated schools, hospitals, and churches, of a few courageous voices raised against massive apathy and hostility, is repeated in each successive region and city with a few outstanding exceptions: particularly the archdioceses of St.

Louis and Detroit where Cardinal Ritter and Archbishop Dearden have committed the Church to a strong attack on racism. But the over-all picture of a white church holding itself aloof from black agony for more than a century leaves little doubt in one's mind that Carl Amery's characterization of Milieu-Catholicism is applicable here. The dictation from culture to Church on race noted by Osborne in southwestern Louisiana holds true for the nation as a whole:

The basic relationship between the Church and its cultural setting remains precisely what it was before the Civil War. It can ameliorate slavery and segregation, it temporizes with them and even cooperates in their maintenance. Then as change becomes inevitable, again its best effort seems to be acceptance and cooperation with the new order. This remarkable ability to adapt to environment has been made possible, unwittingly of course, by an introverted theology narrowly focused on personal salvation via the sacramental system.

If American middle-class virtues have not been drafted for the building of crematoria, neither have they encouraged any resistance among Catholics to murderous techniques of white respectability. To put it sociologically, Catholics have been too preoccupied establishing themselves in a predominantly Protestant milieu to concern themselves dangerously over the plight of a much more beleaguered minority. But better, theologically, American Catholicism has by indifference and enmity pounded at least its share of milieu-given nails into the Black Christ. That it continues to do so with little hesitation, despite the publicized condemnations of racism by bishops and the long-overdue presence of clergy in demonstrations, shows that a catholic Church has hardly begun to be born beneath the mantle of a Milieu-Catholicism.

To return to the issue defined incarnationally, what do these portraits of Milieu-Catholicisms,[5] which comprise two of the supposedly most dynamic national Catholicisms of our time analyzed in terms of their major moral challenges, have to say about the presence of Christ in the modern Church? It is obvious that the most significant statements would have to be negative:

Christ was not visible here in the Church, nor his love and justice there; or more to the point, Christ was beaten here by the faithful, and crucified there over their curious stares. Milieu-Catholicisms, whether of Germany or America, or for that matter, of Spain, England, Italy, or whatever, have not only failed to reveal the presence of Christ in response to pressing moral issues, but have played a significant role in denying it even as a possibility. It has too seldom been thought prudent for the Church, in clergy or laity, to act immediately and instinctively with the reconciling power of an *agape* transcendent to a national ethos. Not a living Christ, present as transcendent love, but a dying milieu, incarnate in all its cultural controls, has been the apparent motif of national Catholicisms in the modern world.

But if Catholic Christianity is measured by the essence of its claim, by a faith in the universal truth of Jesus Christ, scripturally given and dogmatically protected, rather than by the conduct of its formal mebership, then the presence of Christ becomes in the last analysis independent of the corruption of a sinful Church. What this means in theological terms is the precedence of grace over nature in the unveiling of God's presence in man, thus eclipsing any natural claims to moral pre-eminence —including the religious pride and moral postures of self-proclaimed believers—by the dual mystery of God's frequent absence in belief and of his often striking presence in unbelief. What a genuinely "universal Catholicism" means further in regard to the presence of Christ in the world is that such a presence must be defined in a living way, as Christ himself defined it passively in terms of those in suffering need (Matt. 25:34-40) and as his own life and death unfolded his presence actively in terms of suffering love. In seeking out the presence of Christ in his world, Christians must therefore become less and less interested in themselves as Christians and focus instead on the living reality of Christ, whether in belief or unbelief, as the invitation of suffering need and as the graceful response of suffering love. What is then seen to be common to Christ's passive and active presence in the world is man in the state of suffering, as he first cries out in suffering for the aid of his brother and as he secondly as the brother lays down his goods and his life in suffering response to that cry. If it is then recognized that suffering is the one earthly reality with which God identifies himself universally in the person of Jesus Christ, who becomes present to suffering through the love of the Holy Spirit, it will be seen that the Catholic faith —by re-emphasizing the active presence of Christ as suffering love over those dogmatic formulations which, however true, have been frozen rather than fulfilled—can be true to its self-definition as a witness to the living and universal Christ.

It can be suggested therefore that a living and scripturally founded doctrine of the Incarnation, as opposed to the theory and practice of a Milieu-Catholicism, will center on suffering love as the redemptive reality and active presence of Christ in the world. From this standpoint, German Catholicism, and American Catholicism on race, can be understood and evaluated best as incarnational heresies, which is to say, as choices made for a theoretical faith to the exclusion of the living Christic reality of suffering love. The truth of Jesus, while remaining dogmatically protected, has not become flesh in a living, suffering belief. Modern Christianity has been incarnate instead only in the wrong flesh, that of self and of the extended culture-self.

The significance of Gandhi, for a Christianity which has capitulated to its various milieux and thus become an incarnational heresy, is that Gandhi concentrated his entire life and being on the Christic reality of suffering love. Moreover, through his experiments in truth he committed himself to suffering love in such a way that the power of Christ was demonstrated in terms of a social and political revolution.

It has become customary for contemporary theologians, in a genuine effort to respond to the needs of our time, to describe the Gospel as revolutionary. At this point in history, however, the revolution of the Gospel is hardly recognizable to a revolutionary dedicated to the transformation of a corrupt society. For it is too well known and accepted that revolution or "rebellion" (the conservative equivalent for revolution) is identified in Christianity with the root sin of Satan. Since rebellion is presumably satanic, and obedience is held to be holiness, a Milieu-Christianity will labor righteously to crush any revolution against its cultural deities. The object of damnation in a Milieu-Christianity is not the obedience of an Eichmann but the rebellion of a draft-card burner. It is not surprising therefore that in our vanishing Christendom there have been many Christian men of peace whose peace was held in honor so long as it was not pitted directly against the institutions of war, but few Christian revolutionaries, especially in this age of revolution. Yet peace divorced from that revolution which would right injustice is just as futile today as revolution divorced from that peace which would keep it radically just. The peacemakers and those who hunger and thirst for justice are blessed together because they are the same.

Gandhi recognized peace and revolution as integral. He experimented with the Christic power of peace, suffering love, to realize the social revolution demanded equally by conscience. By not involving himself in any Milieu-Christianities, Gandhi kept himself independent of incarnational heresies and worshiped none of the gods of established disorder. He was therefore free to reopen the way for a return to the Gospel of Peace and to the revolutionary power of the cross, which stands at its summit.

In view of the heresy characteristic of the West, the relationship of the Hindu Gandhi to the person of Christ can be described as the most living belief in the Incarnation given in our time, and that in full recognition of the fact that Gandhi did not confess Jesus as the only Son of God. For Gandhi had a profound sense of the suffering, loving Christ:

Though I cannot claim to be a Christian in the sectarian sense, the example of Jesus' suffering is a factor in the composition of my undying faith in non-violence which rules all my actions, worldly and temporal. And I know that there are hundreds of Christians who believe likewise. Jesus lived and died in vain if he did not teach us to regulate the whole of life by the eternal Law of Love.[6]

Gandhi rejected Christianity for the sake of Jesus:

Today I rebel against orthodox Christianity, as I am convinced that it has distorted the message of Jesus. He was an Asiatic whose message was delivered through many media, and when it had the backing of a Roman Emperor it became an imperialist faith as it remains to this day.[7]

Gandhi understood and revered Christ as catholic and could not reconcile the universal meaning he saw in him with the imperialist faith he met in Christianity. In rejecting the Milieu-Christianity of the West, he rejected as well the Church and doctrines he associated with it. Gandhi did not accept Jesus as the only Son of God because that doctrine as presented to him by friends anxious to claim him for Christianity always struck him as too exclusive: "It was more than I could believe that Jesus was the only incarnate son of God, and that only he who believed in him would have everlasting life. If God could have sons, all of us were his sons."[8]

At the same time Gandhi could give this testimony to the person of Jesus:

I refuse to believe that there now exists or has ever existed a person that has not made use of his [Jesus'] example to lessen his sins, even though he may have done so without realizing it. The lives of all have, in some greater or lesser degree, been changed by his presence, his actions, and the words spoken by his divine voice. . . . And because the life of Jesus has the significance and the transcendency to which I have alluded, I believe that he belongs not solely to Christianity, but to the entire world.[9]

For Gandhi, as for Bonhoeffer after him, "Jesus preached not a new religion, but a new life. He called men to repentance."[10]

To define the catholic Christ of Gandhi more precisely, one can say that Gandhi committed himself to Christ morally in the Sermon on the Mount and existentially in the cross. Concerning the Sermon on the Mount, which he felt "was delivered not merely to the peaceful disciples but to a groaning world,"[11] he wrote: "The teaching of the Sermon on the Mount echoed something I had learnt in childhood and something which seemed to be part of my being and which I felt was being acted up to in the daily life around me. . . . This teaching was non-retaliation, or non-resistance to evil."[12]

The cross was, again, a reality meant for all men: "The Cross, undoubtedly, makes a universal appeal the moment you give it a universal meaning in place of the narrow one that is often heard at ordinary meetings." [13] Gandhi followed Christ in identifying genuine faith and discipleship with the taking up of one's personal cross. In a talk given to a group of Christians on Christmas Day, he said: "We dare not think of birth without death on the cross. Living Christ means a living Cross, without it life is a living death." [14]

Gandhi's faith in the power of non-violence was therefore profoundly Christocentric with reference to:

1) The Sermon on the Mount:

If, then, I had to face only the Sermon on the Mount and my own interpretation of it, I should not hesitate to say: "Oh yes, I am a Christian." But I know that, at the present moment, if I said any such thing, I would lay myself open to the gravest misinterpretation.[15]

2) The cross, which he confronted once in a crucifix at the Vatican, and later wrote:

What would not I have given to be able to bow my head before the living image at the Vatican of Christ Crucified! It was not without a wrench that I could tear myself away from that scene of living tragedy. I saw there at once that nations, like individuals, could only be made through the agony of the Cross and in no other way. Joy comes not out of affliction of pain on others, but out of pain voluntarily borne by oneself.[16]

To return our attention to the Christianity which Gandhi rejected, there the Christological problem of our time can be posed with reference to that milieu-consciousness which has so often meant capitulation for the Christian conscience. Our Christological problem would then rightly take the form of the same two questions which Jesus asked the disciples in the passage which constitutes the center of the earliest Gospel (Mark 8:27-29), with the difference in fact that in our case we can hardly hear Jesus' decisive second question. The simple preliminary question which Jesus asked the disciples—"Who do *men* say that I am?"—is virtually the only one his modern disciples have recognized. But Jesus' first question concerning himself is the sociological question, the question of current opinion, to which the proper form of answer is simply the descriptive response given by the disciples in Mark: "Some say . . . others say. . . ." Yet the contemporary Christian answer to this question has been, on the one hand, the basis for an irrelevant dismissal, and, on the other, a substitute for faith. On the one hand, Christians have heard this first question as "Who do *secular* men say that I am?" and have dismissed these answers as the expressions of a belligerent unbelief. On the other hand, they have heard the question as "Who do *Christian* men say that I am?" and have accepted those equally milieu-given answers as the form of their own faith instead of recognizing them as the reflections of a popular religiosity. In neither case has the response to Jesus' first question served the purpose he intended, namely to serve merely as the background for an altogether personal confession of faith paralleling that of Peter. As for Jesus' second and decisive question of faith, abruptly divorcing each disciple from the support of his secular-Christian milieu and confronting him with the fearful task of personal decision—"But who do *you* say that I am?"—the Christian of today normally does not even hear it. The question of a deeply personal and therefore self-critical response to Christ does not arise in a Milieu-Christianity. For it is there that Christ is defined for all by consensus, which is to say, by cultural dogma.

In the absence of any real theological recognition of the incessant demand of Christ—"But who do you—you modern disciples—say that I am?"—cultural dogma has easily prevailed. The cultural faith of men in the church-going Jesus who comforts the comfortable and afflicts the afflicted has removed the Church from Christ's urgent demand for a living faith in himself. Christology is today the most neglected area of theology in the Catholic Church because the Church has not yet distinguished herself radically enough from her milieu to be able to hear the critical question of her master: "But who do you say that I am?" The Church is still too absorbed in resisting the answers of secular man and in defending the answers of "Catholic culture" to hear the question asked of her real self by the person to whom she is wedded. Nor can the problem be solved by believers on a deeper institutional level by retreating from the milieu into a properly dogmatic understanding of Christ. While a milieu can never provide the substance of faith, it will always exist as its context. The truth of the Council of Chalcedon is unable to answer Christ's question to the modern disciple. When Chalcedon's formulation is taken as finally definitive for the Church today it will be found in fact, as Karl Rahner has shown at length,[17] that a contemporary consciousness will have overlaid fifth-century concepts so as to revise them into the figure of a mythological Christ.

In a perceptive article, Father John Dunne has stated incisively the Christological problem of our time:

In our culture, where Jesus is the archetypal man, the culture hero, it is necessary to move to a position where he can be seen as truly human. To feel the overwhelming mystery of the incarnation in our time it is necessary to pass from the initial stage in which we find ourselves where Jesus is the culture hero, through an intermediate stage in which he becomes fully and unequivocally human for us, to a final stage in which we can appreciate the unending wonder of the statement "Jesus is the Lord." [18]

That exaltation of Jesus in the Father which Catholic Christianity takes for granted can reveal its shattering truth to the mind and heart of the believer only if he has first known Jesus as man. But if we are to confront Jesus fully as man in the context of a Milieu-Christianity, where Jesus is the culture hero, a special discipline is required: one must "pass over to the subjective standpoint of Jesus." It is only in passing over to the standpoint of Jesus himself and in sensing something of its normal human character—relative, changing, growing in his understanding of God's will—that the humanity of Jesus can be affirmed with a depth which will open us to the truth of his exaltation. While recognizing the uncertainty of our grounds and the consequent risks involved in thus passing over to the standpoint of Jesus, we must still make this attempt if we are to free ourselves from both the cultural Jesus who reveals only the gods of our time and the mythological Jesus, the God charading in human form, who hides beneath our professions of the Chalcedonian formula.

The possibility of such an existential Christology has been recognized cautiously by Karl Rahner: "A Christology using categories appropriate to the description of consciousness need not be false *a priori* or impossible. If there is an ontic Christology, there can also be an existential one." [19]

In view, however, of the popular heresies uncovered by Rahner in his analysis of Catholicism's now almost exclusively ontic Christology, it can be said more truly that if there is to be a living ontic Christology today, then there *must* also be an existential one—to grant new life and clarity to terms which, as they stand now, have to be translated by theologians before the meaning of the Creed is evident. An extended redefinition of "ontological person" and "nature" in an effort to re-create for us their original meaning and vividness will simply not do for a living belief in Jesus Christ today. The glory contained in the ontic meaning of the man-God is dependent on a prior existential perception of his humanity. One can assume that such a perception was present in the ontic categories themselves at a time when they carried far more weight than they do now. But today in a very different idiom there are too many unrecognized heresies already deadening the community of faith for us to avoid trying to do anew what was always necessary from the beginning: to know Jesus fully as man in order then to confess him fully as God. Thus one can only emphasize the truth of Rahner's observation that existential statements on Christ's mind are "extremely useful in filling out the formal emptiness of a *purely* ontic Christological statement, which would otherwise be in danger of being filled out in some other way. . . ." [20]

How, then, can we pass over to the subjective standpoint of Jesus?

Father Dunne suggests that the key for doing so is Jesus' relations to John the Baptist. By analyzing Jesus' life in terms of these relations, we can see certain great turning points in his growing understanding of himself and his work. These turning points confirm the changing character of Jesus' standpoint and underline his humanity. More particularly, they reveal his life as one of receiving and communicating unconditional love.

While following the method of passing over to Jesus' standpoint, we can nevertheless begin to analyze Jesus' life at a different point in the Gospel, which is more interior to Jesus himself than his relations to John and which can perhaps culminate in a deeper insight to his self-understanding. One can begin with the concept of the *ebed Yahweh*, the Suffering Servant of God.

The Suffering Servant of Yahweh is, first of all, a profoundly Jewish concept, rooted in the Servant poems of Isaiah and exemplified in the living history of Judaism. The primary meaning of the *ebed Yahweh* as given in Isaiah is that the Servant of God through his innocent suffering and death takes the place of the many who should suffer instead of him. The truth revealed in the *ebed Yahweh* is therefore that salvation comes through suffering:

He was wounded for our transgressions, he was bruised for our iniquities; upon him was the chastisement that made us whole, and with his stripes we are healed . . . the Lord has laid on him the iniquity of us all. He was oppressed, and he was afflicted, yet he opened not his mouth; like a lamb that is led to the slaughter, and like a sheep that before its shearers is dumb, so he opened not his mouth. . . . Yet it was the will of the Lord to bruise him; he has put him to grief; when he makes himself an offering for sin, he shall see his offspring, he shall prolong his days; the will of the Lord shall prosper in his hand; he shall see the fruit of the travail of his soul and be satisfied; by his knowledge shall the righteous one, my servant, make many to be accounted righteous; and he shall bear their iniquities . . . he poured out his soul to death, and was numbered with the transgressors; yet he bore the sin of many, and made intercession for the transgressors. (Isa. 53:5-7,10-12)

The problem of the Servant's identity in the poems of Isaiah has centered on the question whether an individual personality or a collective one was intended by the unknown author. The problem is resolved by the interpretation of modern scholars based on the corporate personality of Israelite thought, according to which the prophet is thought to have intended the individual in whom the people are recapitulated. So far as the more divisive question goes, of the fulfillment of the Servant figure in history, Christians should be prepared to acknowledge at this point that its corporate meaning has been revealed profoundly in the continuing pilgrimage of the people who gave it birth. A Jewish scholar has put it well: "From Isaiah 53 forward, Jews have thought about the meaning of their anguished history, and have seen their suffering as an atonement for humanity, and themselves as the sin-offering of the world." [21] A Christian interpretation of Jesus in the light of the *ebed Yahweh* must begin by acknowledging the figure's corporate realization in the suffering history of Israel. The Judaism from which Jesus drew his developing consciousness of the *ebed Yahweh* is the Judaism which has lived out the role of the *ebed Yahweh* through the millennia of tears since then.

The beginning of Jesus' consciousness that he had to realize the task of the Suffering Servant can be traced to the moment of his baptism by John in the Jordan (Mark 1:11). In one of the most thorough treatments of Jesus as the Suffering Servant,[22] Oscar Cullmann has emphasized the importance of the fact that at Jesus' baptism the words of the voice from heaven, "Thou art my beloved Son, with thee I am well pleased," are a quotation from the opening line of the *ebed Yahweh* poems (Isa. 42:1). In Isaiah these words are addressed by Yahweh to his Servant. For Jesus to have heard them spoken to him at his baptism must have compelled his recognition that he had to take on the full role of the *ebed Yahweh*, as introduced in Isaiah in terms of God's favor but destining him in the unfolding drama of the poems "to pour out his soul to death." The Gospel of John confirms this interpretation by the words of John the Baptist, "Behold the Lamb of God, who takes away the sin of the world" (John 1:29), which relate Jesus' baptism to his vicarious suffering as "a lamb that is led to the slaughter." Jesus' two subsequent references to his baptism (Mark 10:38 and Luke 12:50) both show that for him to be baptized has come to mean the same as to die. For he has been baptized into a vision and a task of suffering.

The development of Jesus' conscious identification with the *ebed Yahweh* can be followed through the Gospel in terms of his more and more frequent references to his suffering and death as central to the work he must accomplish: the bridegroom who will be taken away (Mark 2:20); the prophecies of death following Peter's confession (Mark 8:31; 9:31; 10:33 ff.); the son of the vineyard owner killed by his tenants (Mark 12:1 ff.). This rising sense of the *ebed's* task as impending is supported by Jesus' direct quotation from Isaiah 53 with reference to himself: "For I tell you that this scripture must be fulfilled in me, 'And he was reckoned with transgressors'; for what is written about me has its fulfillment" (Luke 22:37). Jesus' allusions to Isaiah 52–53 include his sayings at the Lord's Supper, where he announces that he will shed his blood for many. Finally, the one other concept which figures prominently in Jesus' own formulation of his work, that of the Son of Man, is united in his understanding with the theme of the Suffering Servant: "For the Son of man also came not to be served but to serve, and to give his life as a ransom for many" (Mark 10:45). As Cullmann says, "It is as if Jesus said, 'The Son of Man came to fulfill the task of the *ebed Yahweh.*'" [23] While Jesus refers to himself in the Gospel as the Son of Man because the title is more comprehensive with its eschatological overtones, he nevertheless merges this title with the meaning of the *ebed Yahweh* so that the vocation of the *ebed* becomes the main content of the Son of Man's earthly work.

The self-designation of Jesus as the Suffering Servant is so deeply rooted in the Gospel that Father John McKenzie has insisted that "if this theme is not the work of Jesus himself then we know nothing about his words or his person." [24] Its further prominence in the opening chapters of the Acts of the Apostles indicates that the disciples and the primitive community of believers saw this theme of suffering servanthood as the one which revealed the true identity of Jesus.

The decisive question asked of the disciples by Jesus—"But who do you say that I am?"—and which we have described as a question almost unheard by the Church today, was not answered by Peter in terms of the *ebed Yahweh*. His response was instead, "You are the Christ" (Mark 8:29). But what is significant about Peter's profession of faith is that Jesus wasn't satisfied with it. Not only did he go on to identify his own messianic vocation with great suffering, "to teach them that the Son of man must suffer many things, and be rejected . . . and be killed" (v. 31), but he sharply rebuked Peter's contrary suggestion that such suffering was somehow avoidable: "Get behind me, Satan! For you are not on the side of God, but of men" (v. 33). Essential to the definition of the Christ is suffering, rejection, and a sacrificial death. To profess a true faith in Jesus Christ is to profess a faith in Jesus the Suffering Servant.

It is significant that of the four passages in the New Testament which explicitly call Jesus *pais*, or servant, two occur in a speech attributed to Peter and two are spoken in prayers of the Church in the presence of Peter (Acts 3:13, 26; 4:27, 30). Cullmann has suggested that

the author may have preserved the precise memory that it was the Apostle Peter who by preference designated Jesus the "Suffering Servant of God." . . . He, who had wanted to hear nothing of it during the lifetime of Jesus, made Jesus' suffering and death the very center of his explanation of Jesus' earthly work.[25]

But in the great Markan Christological passage, Jesus takes one step further after he fills out Peter's profession of faith with the Suffering Servant and rebukes him for professing a Christ without scandal. At this point the words of Gandhi reassert themselves, "Living Christ means a living Cross, without it life is a living death," and find their foundation in Jesus' statement of what it means to follow him. For a faith in Christ is not possible without the symbol and demanding reality that sums up a Christocentric life: "If any man would come after me, let him deny himself and take up his cross and follow me" (v. 34). Though Gandhi could not claim to be a Christian in the sectarian sense, the example of Jesus' suffering was at the essence of his faith in non-violence and ruled all his actions. For him the suffering of Jesus so defined the law of love that love and suffering were seen as one in a single flame of life. And it is thus, in terms of suffering servanthood, that Jesus defined his own vocation on earth and the vocation of any man who would travel his way. Faith without crucifixion is meaningless. "Christianity" therefore means nothing to Christ: "Not everyone who says to me, 'Lord, Lord,' shall enter the kingdom of heaven, but he who does the will of my Father who is in heaven" (Matt. 7:21). If it is thought that the implications of this are too strong with regard to the Church, then there are also Jesus' words in the presence of his mother: "Whoever does the will of God is my brother, and sister, and mother" (Mark 3:35). If we admit that Jesus loved his mother as much as he loves the Church, we can be safe in assuming that he would not hesitate to identify only those who through their suffering love do the will of God today as "my bishops, my clergy, and my laity."

If the Suffering Servant is the key to Jesus' own growing understanding of his mission on earth, and thus the key to our understanding of his humanity, it is also true that only in passing over to the subjective standpoint of suffering servanthood which constitutes that Christic self-understanding shall we be able to affirm the full truth of Jesus' humanity. And, as we have seen, it is only by passing through Jesus' humanity that we can feel the overwhelming mystery of his divinity. The significance of this task of faith becomes evident in the fact that the essence of his humanity, suffering servanthood, is a reality which can hardly be understood except through an existential commitment to it as such. There can be no theoretical appropriation of the meaning of suffering as it is expressed in the *ebed Yahweh* and in Jesus. Philosophers have not thought such thoughts, nor can they be expected to as philosophers, for reason will refuse to admit the necessity of embracing suffering in love until a committed life has lost itself in that salvific mystery. To follow to its conclusion the Markan Christological passage, we can understand Jesus' explanation of cross-bearing, "whoever loses his life for my sake

and the gospel's will save it" (Mark 8:35), as the description of
an existential passing over to the standpoint of Jesus' humanity—
in suffering servanthood—and thus in this loss of autonomous life
for Christic life a mediation, through the suffering love of Jesus'
humanity, of the overwhelming mystery of Incarnation. This
mystery is complete when the Son of Man "comes in the glory of
his Father" (v. 38), but it is again a mystery whose realization
is dependent on a committed passing over to the standpoint of
suffering servanthood: "For whoever is ashamed of me and of
my words in this adulterous and sinful generation, of him will
the Son of man also be ashamed, when he comes in the glory of
his Father with the holy angels." These words also must have
burned Peter and in retrospect deepened the Servant Christology
in his consciousness. The only way to affirm, and be caught up
in, the glory of Jesus in the Father is to affirm with one's own life
the cross of Jesus' humanity. In this living cross of the believing
community, because Jesus' own cross is now finished, resurrection
is not on the way: it is here.

But in view of the incarnational heresies which deny that living
cross, it is apparent that "this adulterous and sinful generation"
is a permanent phenomenon and that its primary locus today may
be within Christianity. When the Gospel has become a fixture of
culture, and thus been crowned with irrelevance, the discipline
required to pass over to the standpoint of Jesus crucified must
receive its inspiration from beyond that culture. For no Milieu-
Christianity professes a living faith in the cross. To pass over to
the standpoint of the Suffering Servant, one must learn to see
with new eyes, one must be struck by the lightning shock of the
cross. It can be suggested that the kind of shock necessary to pass
over into the suffering love of the man Jesus is contained in the
following report, filed from India by the United Press correspondent Webb Miller on May 21, 1930:

Prayers said as white-clad volunteers knelt in the moonlight and
an impassioned speech by the poetess-leader, Mrs. Sarojini Naidu,
opened the mass attack of 2,500 independence demonstrators . . . on
the Dharasana salt works.

The poetess, wearing a rough, home-spun robe and soft slippers, but no stockings, exhorted her followers to the raid.

"India's prestige is in your hands. You must not use any violence under any circumstances. You will be beaten but you must not resist: you must not even raise a hand to ward off blows."

"Although Gandhiji's body is in prison, his soul goes with you," she cried as she sent the volunteers to the attack.

The cry of "Gandhijiki Jay!" answered her from the dark ranks of volunteers huddled together in the dim light of early morning.

The volunteers formed in columns, with their leaders carrying ropes and wire cutters. They advanced slowly towards the salt works.

Heaps of glistening salt surrounded by the barbed wire entanglements erected by police were the objective of the brief march. About 400 native Surat police stood inside and outside the entanglements. Several British officers directed the police, who had orders to prevent the assembly of more than five persons.

Manilal Gandhi, second son of Gandhi, walked along the foremost of the marchers. As the throng drew near the salt pans they commenced chanting the revolutionary slogan, "Inquilab Zindabad!" intoning the two words over and over.

The columns reached the salt works at 6:30 A.M. There were a few cheers and then the leaders, who had ropes, attempted to lasso the posts holding up the barbed wire, intending to uproot them. The police ran up and demanded that they disperse. The volunteers refused.

The column silently ignored the warning and slowly walked forward. . . .

Suddenly, at a word of command, scores of native police rushed upon the advancing marchers and rained blows on their heads with their steel-shod lathis. Not one of the marchers even raised an arm to fend off the blows. They went down like ten-pins. From where I stood I heard the sickening whacks of the clubs on unprotected skulls. The waiting crowd of watchers groaned and sucked in their breaths in sympathetic pain at every blow.

Those struck down fell sprawling, unconscious or writhing with pain with fractured skulls or broken shoulders. In two or three minutes the ground was quilted with bodies. Great patches of blood widened on their white clothes. The survivors without breaking ranks silently and doggedly marched on until struck down. When every one of the first column had been knocked down, stretcher-bearers rushed up unmolested by the police and carried off the injured to a thatched hut which had been arranged as a temporary hospital.

Then another column formed while the leaders pleaded with them to retain their self-control. They marched slowly towards the police. Although everyone knew that within a few minutes he would be beaten down, perhaps killed, I could detect no signs of wavering or fear. They marched steadily with heads up, without the encouragement of music, of cheering or any possibility that they might escape serious injury or death. The police rushed out and methodically and mechanically beat down the second column. There was no fight, no struggle: the marchers simply walked forward until struck down. There were no outcries, only groans after they fell. There were not enough stretcher-bearers to carry off the wounded: I saw eighteen injured being carried off simultaneously while forty-two still lay bleeding on the ground awaiting stretcher-bearers. The blankets used as stretchers were sodden with blood. . . .

Several times the leaders nearly lost control of the waiting crowd. They rushed up and down, frantically pleading with and exhorting the intensely excited men to remember Gandhi's instructions. It seemed that the unarmed throng was on the verge of launching a mass attack upon the police. The British official in charge, Superintendent Robinson of Surat, sensed the imminence of an outbreak and posted twenty-five rifle-men on a little knoll ready to fire. He came to me, inquiring my identity, and said: "You'd better move aside out of the line of shooting. We may be forced to open fire into the crowd." While we were talking, one of the Gandhiites, a young university student, ran up to Robinson, his face contorted by rage, tore open his cotton smock, exposing his bare breast, and shrieked: "Shoot me, shoot me! Kill me, it's for my country!" The leaders managed to calm the crowd.

The Gandhi men altered their tactics, marched up in groups of twenty-five and sat on the ground near the salt pans, making no effort to draw nearer. Led by a coffee-colored Parsi sergeant of police named Antia, a hulking, ugly-looking fellow, detachments of police approached one seated group and called up to them to disperse under the non-assemblage ordinance. The Gandhi followers ignored them and refused to even glance up at the lathis brandished threateningly above their heads. Upon a word from Antia, the beating commenced coldly, without anger. Bodies toppled over in threes and fours, bleeding from great gashes on their scalps. Group after group walked forward, sat down, and submitted to being beaten into insensibility without raising an arm to fend off the blows.

Finally the police became enraged by the non-resistance, sharing, I suppose, the helpless rage I had already felt at the demonstrators for not fighting back. They commenced savagely kicking the seated men in the abdomen and testicles. The injured men writhed and squealed in agony, which seemed to inflame the fury of the police, and the crowd again almost broke away from their leaders. The police then began dragging the sitting men by their arms or feet, sometimes for a hundred yards, and then throwing them into ditches. One was dragged into the ditch where I stood: the splash of his body doused me with muddy water. Another policeman dragged a Gandhi man to the ditch, threw him in, then belabored him over the head with his lathi. Hour after hour stretcher-bearers carried back a stream of inert, bleeding bodies.

Much of the time the stolid native Surat police seemed reluctant to strike. It was noticeable that when the officers were occupied on other parts of the line the police slackened, only to resume threatening and beating when the officers appeared again. I saw many instances of the volunteers pleading with the police to join them. . . .

By eleven the heat reached 116 in the shade and the activities of the Gandhi volunteers subsided. I went back to the temporary hospital to examine the wounded. They lay in rows on the bare ground in the shade of an open, palm-thatched shed. I counted 320 injured, many still insensible with fractured skulls, others in writhing agony from kicks in the testicles and stomach. The Gandhi men had been able to gather only a few native doctors, who were doing the best they could with the inadequate facilities. Scores of the injured had received no treatment for hours and two had died.[26]

The raid which Miller reported was resumed that evening, and four hundred more volunteers were injured. Two days later in the nearby Satyagraha camp, after the police by similar methods had evacuated it of all but a few of Gandhi's followers, those remaining encountered the police again according to this description by one of them:

The officer returned in the afternoon of the 23rd and looked into with great care all the papers of the inmates of the camp. Some twenty policemen surrounded us. We were going on with our own work. As it was hot we gave our police brethren a drink of cold fresh water. On the mornings of the 21st and 22nd, we had given them our blood as patiently and quietly. When the police came to drive us out of our place on the 22nd morning they helped themselves to some fruits from our larder which we had stocked for our wounded soldiers. If they had only asked us we should have given them the fruits gladly.[27]

Gandhi was once asked if he believed in the verse of the Sermon on the Mount, "If any man would take your coat, let him have your cloak as well." He answered:

In the verse quoted by you Jesus put in a picturesque and telling manner the great doctrine of non-violent non-cooperation. Your non-cooperation with your opponent is violent when you give a blow for a blow, and is ineffective in the long run. Your non-cooperation is non-violent when you give your opponent all in the place of just what he needs. You have disarmed him once for all by your apparent co-operation, which in effect is complete non-cooperation.[28]

Gandhi and his followers disarmed India's oppressors by deliberately offering their bodies and their lives to the British, thus resisting them in spirit and in truth. The scene which took place at the Dharasana salt works was repeated in hundreds of similar incidents across India as the people became aware of the strength of suffering love embodied in non-violence.[29] As Indian casualties rose, British self-justification fell. Louis Fischer, Gandhi's biographer, has described this process succinctly: "The British beat the Indians with batons and rifle butts. The Indians neither cringed nor complained nor retreated. That made England powerless and India invincible."[30] India's assumption of power came through blood and crucifixion, not because the British were particularly kindhearted. It may be true that a different imperialist power, whether communist as in Hungary or capitalist as in Vietnam, would have raised the cost in suffering even higher in an effort to hold off India's independence. But to those who witnessed scenes such as the above, the British seemed brutal enough during their years of oppression to make the confrontation between armed might and the power of suffering love a genuine one. In any event, Gandhi's faith in non-violent resistance was realistic enough not to rest on the presumably civilized sensibilities of the opponent and the hope of an early victory. In his letter of 1930 to the viceroy announcing the beginning of the civil disobedience campaign which was to continue, with intermittent truces, for seventeen years, Gandhi rooted his non-violent faith in voluntary suffering without limit:

According to the science of Satyagraha, the greater the repression and

lawlessness on the part of authority, the greater should be the suffering courted by its victims. Success is the certain result of suffering of
the extremest character, voluntarily undergone.[31]

The logic of non-violence is the logic of crucifixion and leads
the man of non-violence into the heart of the suffering Christ.
The purpose of non-violence is to move the oppressors to per-
ceive as human beings those whom they are oppressing. Men
commit acts of violence and injustice against other men only to
the extent that they do not regard them as fully human. Non-
violent resistance seeks to persuade the aggressor to recognize in
his victim the humanity they have in common, which when recognized fully makes violence impossible. This goal of human
recognition is sought through the power of voluntary suffering,
by which the victim becomes no longer a victim but instead an
active opponent in loving resistance to the man who has refused to recognize him as man. The man of non-violence acts
through suffering love to move the unjust opponent to a perception of their common humanity, and thus to the cessation of violence in the commencement of brotherhood. The greater the repression, the greater must be the suffering courted by its victims; the greater the inhumanity, the greater the power of suffering love necessary to begin restoring the bonds of community.
Suffering as such is powerless. Love transforms it into the kind
of resistance capable of moving an opponent to the act of mutual recognition we have described. The suffering of his victim
must be acknowledged by the oppressor as being human before
he will cease inflicting it, and it is the love manifested in that
suffering undergone openly and voluntarily which will bring him
finally to this acknowledgment.[32]

We can understand then why Gandhi looked to Christ as the
supreme example of non-violence: at the cross suffering love received its fullest expression, even in the eyes of him who could
not affirm Christ as uniquely divine. Gandhi knew that the man
who died on Golgotha understood his entire life and mission as
pointing toward that voluntary end, yet regarded that end, in
spite of its outward character, not as futility but as complete

fulfillment. The man fixed on the cross was self-defined in terms of suffering servanthood. Jesus of Nazareth had no other purpose in life than the cross of suffering love, which is to say, he had no other purpose in life than life itself.

But for the believer, the inner dynamic of redemption can also be understood in terms of non-violence. If it is the purpose of non-violence to move men by suffering love to a recognition of their common humanity; it is the purpose of the cross to move us in the same way to a recognition of all men in Christ. The cross moves us, first of all, to an acknowledgment of Jesus' own suffering humanity. In order to profess a faith in Christ, as Peter and the disciples learned, we must profess him first in the scandal of suffering and rejection which summarizes his humanity. But to identify oneself in faith with the Christ of the cross is to acknowledge that here is the ultimate self-disclosure of God in man, in the action of suffering love unto death and in the words of Christ embracing all men, victims and executioners alike (for with respect to one another and to Christ, all men are both, and Jesus spoke of all): "Father, forgive them for they know not what they do." With these words and with the cross embodying them, Jesus revealed so profound a union between himself and mankind that the crucifixion cannot be seen in isolation from a single injustice in history, nor can it be separated from the personal confrontation of victim and executioner in any single injustice. By the crucifixion violence and injustice have everywhere become *crucial*, cross-centered.

In inflicting violence on one another, men know not what they do, for they know not the sacredness of their brothers' and their own humanity, which at its innermost core is one with the humanity of Christ. The violence of men at any place or time in history is the violence of Golgotha. And the victim, yet by his infinite love no longer victim but redeemer, is everywhere and always the same: the man of the cross. To recognize the humanity of the Christ of the cross is to recognize all men in him, who in his suffering is one with all those by whom he has been murdered. To pass over to the suffering servanthood of the man Jesus is to see, through his forgiveness, his redeeming presence in all men, oppressed and oppressors alike, and to see therefore the possibility of his redeeming mediation through suffering love of any human conflict. To profess a living faith in the Christ of the cross is to affirm the redemptive reality present in every cross of suffering love enacted in history. Christ becomes present everywhere as he was present: in suffering servanthood and crucifixion. In and through this presence he redeems mankind from division and leads it into community.

In thus interpreting the cross from the standpoint of belief, we can again confirm that interpretation best by returning to the witness of one who made no claim to Christian belief. When India finally gained its independence from England in 1947, the Father of India could take no part in the victory celebrations. The partition of India and the creation of Pakistan had been accepted, against Gandhi's plea for unity, as the necessary condition for independence and had intensified a Hindu-Moslem conflict which threatened to inflame both countries. Against the rise of mass violence independence was an empty victory. Instead of celebrating it with the nation, the seventy-eight-year-old Gandhi went to Calcutta, "into a Moslem house in an area where the stones were slippery with fresh blood and the air acrid with the smoke of burning homes," [33] and there he undertook a fast unto death. His fast would end only if and when sanity returned to Calcutta. Dr. Amiya Chakravarty has described the fast and its effects:

To most Indians, as to people outside, Gandhi's decision to fast as a means of changing an acute situation of social or political impasse, seemed remote, irrelevant and based on individual habit and unreason. And yet the challenge was clear; right in the heart of a brutal communal upheaval in Calcutta, resting in a broken house exposed to streets where fighting was going on, Gandhiji had chosen to impose self-suffering and penance upon his aged body, as well as on his mind, which he had put to the test of fire. Everyone knew that within a day or two the sheer physical agony mounted to an hourly and momently torture which nothing could relieve; the toxic processes and tissue destruction would begin, not only bringing death nearer but setting up an intolerable psycho-physical sequence. His face and eyes, made luminous by suffering and controlled suffering, would show little trace of the agony that his will had mastered, but the nature of his ordeal was unmistakable to the millions. Even while repudiating his method and its efficacy, the one question in people's minds would be, "How is Gandhiji?" People would begin to feel uncomfortable; the grocer's boy, the rickshaw-puller, the office clerk, the school and college students would scan the news columns early in the morning and listen to the radio throughout the day and feel more and more personally *involved* in the situation. I remember how University students would come up to us and ask to be excused from attending their classes because they felt disturbed and did not know what to do. But why feel disturbed? They would say that though they did not believe in such methods and in the philosophy behind it all, one thing struck them as curious; after all, if anybody had to suffer for the continued killing and betrayal in the city, it was not Gandhiji. He had taken no part in it. So, while others were engaged in crime, it was he who had to suffer like this. They felt awkward and some wanted to stop his suffering, and even gathered together weapons from streets and homes at great personal risk; they wanted to return them to Gandhiji.

As we know, Gandhiji would look at groups who came with Sten guns and knives and now offered these in return for his promise to break the fast and ask them, "Why?" Why should it matter to them whether one more man, a man of seventy-eight, suffered or died when they had easily allowed hundreds of innocents to suffer and die? If all the agony and shame had not mattered, why should one more individual signify at all in a situation of retaliation, vengeance and crime that they had accepted as being moral, and courageous? So it was to save him, Gandhiji, that they had come; but the saving of Gandhiji, or not saving him, was not the point at all.

So the fast would continue. Men would come back from their offices in the evening and find food prepared by their family, ready for them; but soon it would be revealed that the women of the home had not eaten during the whole day. They had not felt hungry. Pressed further, the wife or mother would admit that she could not understand how they could go on when Gandhiji was dying for their own crimes. Restaurants and amusement centers did little business; some of them were voluntarily closed by their proprietors. Why this total and pervasive suffering for a whole city? Why did it all begin to matter? The nerve of feeling had been restored, the pain began to be felt; the pain of the whole society, because of the pain of its members, whether Hindu, Muslim or others. Gandhiji knew when to start the redemptive process. Involvement did not merely mean pain: it was fundamentally the joy of union, and the acceptance of new responsibility which such glad assurance of united strength makes possible. An immense release filled the atmosphere when Gandhiji declared that now we had all suffered and shared; his fast would be broken. Release turned into rejoicing, the fast actually led up to feasts in which the warring communities joined heartily, while Gandhiji sipped his small glass of orange juice.

One would like to carry the story further; but the meaning of his fast was clear. Suffering was happening in a social and moral vacuum, with no response from peoples whose minds had lost all human sensitiveness. It could only be reciprocated and then redeemed by the process of suffering. Then, out of sharing and involvement would arise a new situation; it would not be merely change but transformation.[34]

The transformation which Gandhi sought and was given through the cross is the transformation spoken of by the angel at the open tomb: "He is not here; for he has risen." Or more pointedly in Luke, "Why do you seek the living among the dead?" The cross raises the dead to the living because the cross itself is living, as Gandhi described and followed it. For Gandhi dared not think of birth without death on the cross. He also said, "God did not bear the Cross only 1900 years ago, but He bears it today, and He dies and is resurrected from day to day." [35] To the Suffering Servant, resurrection is as present a reality as crucifixion, although present only in and through the cross. Only in yielding up one's spirit—"Father, into thy hands I commit my spirit"—is there granted the power to roll back the rock so that the dead can become the living. Only in suffering love unto death is a Calcutta reclaimed from the valley of the dead. Only through the Servant's gift of life in the darkness of death can the violent be returned to life, for it was after Jesus' death that the centurion and those who assisted him in that death confessed, "Truly this was the Son of God."

Does not a full commitment to Jesus' humanity of suffering servanthood necessarily involve an existential commitment to the overcoming truth of his divinity as well? To answer yes with particular reference to Gandhi's witness is not to claim Gandhi for Christianity, but to claim to see the full meaning of Christ through Gandhi, in a living cross and resurrection which would be true to Gandhi's own understanding of what it means to live and to die. The cross is revolutionary not simply because it raises men to another life but because it transforms them into the fullness of that life on this earth. The revolution of peace is realized in Calcutta, not heaven, because only the wounded flesh and spilled blood of Calcutta can provide the matter of a new heaven and a new earth. The spirit of a new earth must also be in Calcutta, as it was in the Christic figure suffering into love the violence of the city, and in the community thus re-created.

Because he envisioned the face of God as Truth, Gandhi experimented with truth in a lifelong struggle to see God face to face. In the course of that struggle, which became in part the struggle of India and finally of the British Empire and the world, Gandhi encountered God as suffering love. In realizing through his experiments that the God of Truth is found through the God of suffering love, Gandhi passed into the redeeming truth of the Incarnation.

NOTES

1. Karl Rahner and Herbert Vorgrimler, "Jesus Christ," *Theological Dictionary* (Herder and Herder: 1965), p. 239.
2. Karl Barth, *The Humanity of God* (John Knox Press: 1966), p. 49.
3. Steven S. Schwarzschild, "A Little Bit of a Revolution?", *The Secular City Debate* (Macmillan: 1966), p. 148.
4. I have read in galleys the two books referred to in this section, *The Capitulation* by Carl Amery and *The Segregated Covenant* by William Osborne (both Herder and Herder: 1967), and can therefore give no precise page references.
5. Other studies which substantiate further the existence of Milieu-Catholicisms in Germany and the United States include *German Catholics and Hitler's Wars* by Gordon C. Zahn (Sheed & Ward: 1962), *The Catholic Church and Nazi Germany* by Guenter Lewy (McGraw-Hill: 1964), and *Nationalism and American Catholicism* by Dorothy Dohen (Sheed & Ward: 1966).
6. M. K. Gandhi, *The Law of Love*, edited and published by Anand T. Hingorani (Bharatiya Vidya Bhavan: 1962), p. 79. Gandhi's views on Christ have been collected in three somewhat overlap-

ping works, two small books and a pamphlet: *The Law of Love; The Message of Jesus Christ,* edited and published by Anand T. Hingorani (Bharatiya Vidya Bhavan: 1963), the most complete source on the subject; *What Jesus Means to Me,* compiled by R. K. Prabhu (Navajivan Publishing House: 1959).

7. Prabhu, *What Jesus Means to Me,* p. 33.
8. Hingorani, *The Message of Jesus Christ,* p. 11.
9. *Ibid.,* p. 111.
10. *Ibid.,* p. 40.
11. *Ibid.,* p. 34.
12. Prabhu, *What Jesus Means to Me,* p. 13.
13. Hingorani, *The Message of Jesus Christ,* pp. 22–23.
14. Prabhu, *What Jesus Means to Me,* p. 16.
15. Hingorani, *The Message of Jesus Christ,* p. 44.
16. *Ibid.,* p. 68.
17. Karl Rahner, "Current Problems in Christology," *Theological Investigations,* Vol. I: *God, Christ, Mary and Grace* (Darton, Longman & Todd: 1961), pp. 149–200.
18. John S. Dunne, "The Human God: Jesus," in the first of the *Commonweal Papers,* a special issue of *Commonweal* on *God* (February 10, 1967), pp. 510–11.
19. Rahner, "Current Problems in Christology," p. 172.
20. *Ibid.,* p. 173.
21. Jacob Neusner, "The Assignment of Guilt," *Continuum* (Autumn 1966), p. 432.
22. Oscar Cullmann, "Jesus the Suffering Servant of God," *The Christology of the New Testament* (The Westminster Press: 1959), pp. 51–82.
23. *Ibid.,* p. 65.
24. John L. McKenzie, S.J., *The Power and the Wisdom* (Bruce: 1965), p. 98.
25. Cullmann, "Jesus the Suffering Servant of God," p. 74.
26. Parts of this report appeared in the *Chicago Daily News,* May 22, 1930, and in Webb Miller's *I Found No Peace: The Journal of a Foreign Correspondent* (New York: Simon and Schuster, 1936), pp. 193–95. Quoted together by Gene Sharp, *Gandhi Wields the Weapon of Moral Power: Three Case Histories* (Navajivan Publishing House: 1960), pp. 138–42.
27. From an account published in *Young India* on May 29, 1930, quoted by Sharp, *Gandhi . . . Three Case Histories,* p. 145.
28. Prabhu, *What Jesus Means to Me,* p. 39.
29. "Despite the repression by the Government, the people displayed a remarkable degree of self-restraint and non-violent discipline. Eventually the number of lathi charges rose somewhere in the hundreds. Then the Government took to firing on unarmed

crowds, and during the campaign hundreds were killed and thousands were wounded in this manner." Sharp, *Gandhi . . . Three Case Histories*, p. 179.

30. Louis Fischer, *The Life of Mahatma Gandhi* (Collier Books: 1962), p. 279.

31. Quoted by Sharp, *Gandhi . . . Three Case Histories*, p. 117.

32. A good description of this process from the standpoint of a sociologist can be found in the pamphlet *Non-Violent Action: How It Works*, by George Lakey (Pendle Hill Pamphlet 129).

33. Fischer, *The Life of Mahatma Gandhi*, p. 472.

34. Amiya Chakravarty, *A Saint at Work: A View of Gandhi's Work and Message* (The Young Friends Movement of the Philadelphia Yearly Meetings: 1950), pp. 23 ff., quoted by Sharp, pp. 258–60.

35. Hingorani, *The Message of Jesus Christ*, pp. 37–38.

TWO

Cross and Church

4

The Non-Violent Power of Pacem in Terris

SOME OF *Pacem in Terris'* most eminent commentators have held that the 1963 papal encyclical is seriously deficient in its understanding of political reality. Few men in the Nuclear Age would want to reject entirely the deep spirit of hope permeating Pope John's encyclical. But many would agree with Father John Courtney Murray's respectful suggestion that "the spirit of confident hope which the Pontiff courageously embraces fails to take realistic account of the fundamental schism in the world today." [1]

The two most distinguished Protestant theologians in America expressed similar criticisms. Reinhold Niebuhr wrote in *Christianity and Crisis:* "The Pope speaks of the 'community of mankind' without making clear that this community is in one sense a reality and in another sense an ideal, since mankind is divided by a multitude of languages, customs, traditions and parochial loyalties. . . . In this spirit John XXIII advocates disarmament but fails to consider the problems of immediate security that confront both sides in the horrible nuclear dilemma. . . . This idealism is a little too easy." [2]

Paul Tillich, at the New York *Pacem in Terris* Convocation held in February, 1965, felt that the encyclical had confused power with authority and that a direct discussion of the ambiguities of power was lacking. "But without it," he added, "a realistic approach to the peace problem is impossible."[3] Paul Ramsey has also charged from time to time that *Pacem in Terris* is characterized by an omission of the problem of power.[4]

The charges that *Pacem in Terris* is unrealistic in its vision of hope, and naïve in its treatment of power, are encountered often enough to merit consideration. Such charges have been made from a close reading of the document and are based on what critics have felt is a facile imposition of principles on problems whose complexity is not granted by the Pope. As another critic, Will Herberg, remarked: "Principles are set forth which, in their *ultimate* bearing, indeed commend themselves to 'all men of good will' for their truth and value; but then, immediately, these principles are made to apply—in a simple unrefracted manner—to *short-range* problems of policy and program." The document, in short, "suffers from a pervasive confusion of perspective," in which principles and policies, the ideal and the concretely possible, have been uncritically merged.[5]

But the perspective of *Pacem in Terris* goes so much deeper than any of these theologically respectable criticisms that one sometimes wonders how the document was read: by entering into the heights and depths of the global vision of Pope John or by trying to shrink that vision into the theological-political framework which corresponds to the American experience, and then because it wouldn't shrink, dismissing it as "unrealistic" and "naive in its treatment of power." The criticism of Murray, Niebuhr, and Tillich cannot be dismissed so lightly, but one can begin to respond to it by seeking in *Pacem in Terris* some key to a reality and a power which, while given a deep response by the world, has somehow eluded our efforts to define it. We feel, despite the distinguished critics, that Pope John *is* realistic and *does* know what power is all about, but we are hard pressed to define what that reality and that power is which is not only treated in but embodied by *Pacem in Terris*. It is clear that we do not find in *Pacem in Terris* the reality and the power of some great men who have served our age well: Murray, Niebuhr, and Tillich. But it can be suggested that the power of Pope John does correspond remarkably to the power of our century's other great man of peace, Mohandas Gandhi. It may be that an age wiser than ours, when trying to come to terms with the problem of power, will look back for help not so much to the theologians of power, nor to the power politicians, as it will to the living experiments in truth of a man whom Winston Churchill referred to as "this seditious, half-naked fakir," [6] and to the brief testimony to peace on earth of a dying Pope. While we have hardly done enough to bring that day about, there is yet hope that power will some day be thought of in terms other than those of nuclear strategy and diplomacy, and that Gandhi and Pope John will be celebrated together as the two great prophets of man's greatest power: that of non-violence.

The non-violence of *Pacem in Terris* is as pervasive as it is undefined. It is found, first of all, in what Pope John called in the encyclical "the sentiment of universal fatherhood which the Lord has placed in Our heart." [7] E. E. Y. Hales has written of *Pacem in Terris* that "in this remarkable new document, published only two months before he died, Roncalli succeeded in lifting himself right out of his political and even out of his clerical environment on to the lofty plane of Father-in-God of all men, irrespective of their creed, their color, their continent, irrespective even of their acceptance of his own fatherhood." [8]

Pacem in Terris is the last will and testament of a father to his children, and it embodies the father's wish for enduring peace and well-being in the entire family of mankind. Even were it not addressed to "all men of good will," there could be no question from the text that *Pacem in Terris* is directed far beyond the visible Church. It is addressed with a father's love and urgency to the deepest problems of the world, which are seen by the Church today only to the extent that she realizes the social mandates of a Savior who was as much man as he was God. But Pope John was not willing to wait until that day when the Church would absorb enough of his Christic love for the world to become an effective medium of that love. Pope John loved the world and he spoke to it directly, not through the cracks in the Church's walls. In his final words to the world he left every wall behind him to embrace the world's needs as a father would his sons', in the hope that the Church in Council would follow him, thus bringing the people of God fully into the family of man.

In December 1959, one year after he had become Pope, John XXIII made the following entry in his *Journal of a Soul:* "Since the Lord chose me, unworthy as I am, for this great service, I feel I have no longer any special ties in this life, no family, no earthly country or nation. . . . Now, more than ever, I see my-self only as the humble and unworthy 'servant of God and servant of the servants of God.' The whole world is my family. This sense of belonging to everyone must give character and vigor to my mind, my heart and my actions." [9]

As Pope John's final message to the only family remaining to him, the whole world, *Pacem in Terris* is a totally non-violent commitment to man. Gandhi had spoken of this connection between a man's sense of the family of mankind and his non-violence: "For a non-violent person, the whole world is one family. He will thus fear none, nor will others fear him." [10] It is not surprising therefore that the repudiation of force is a constant theme in *Pacem in Terris.* It could be no other way. The degree to which a person will justify violence and war is in inverse proportion to the depth of his awareness of the unity and bonds of the human family. Pope John felt those bonds of worldwide community at the very center of his being in an age of possibly ultimate conflict and destruction. He wrote: "It is hardly possible to imagine that in the atomic era war could be used as an instrument of justice." [11] But he did not reject violence simply because he lived in an age of nuclear weapons, but because no loving father can tolerate the threat of murder among his sons, and nuclear weapons made that murderous threat more massive and more likely. Thus it is "the immense suffering which the use of those armaments would bring to the human family" [12] which he cites as the immediate grounds for his judgment on war in the atomic era. The human family is the essence of the Johannine vision. For Pope John to justify war in any form would have been a denial of his communion with his family. The justification of war demands the division of mankind into just and unjust killers, into one's own, on the one hand, and the enemy to be driven out, on the other. What father can so divide his sons, especially in an age when battle would kill them all? Pope John embraced them all.

Two other passages in his *Journal of a Soul* provide insight into the universal spirit behind and within *Pacem in Terris*. As the papal representative in Turkey and Greece, Archbishop Roncalli wrote in 1940: "The world is poisoned with morbid nationalism, built up on the basis of race and blood, in contradiction to the Gospel. In this matter especially, which is of burning topical interest, 'deliver me from men of blood, O God.' Here fits in most aptly the invocation: 'God of my salvation': Jesus our Saviour died for all nations, without distinction of race or blood, and became the first brother of the new human family, built on him and his Gospel." [13]

John XXIII hated nationalism as much as he loved mankind. He could acknowledge no fundamental divisions in the family of man, and he thought that to do so would be in contradiction to the Church he represented, which called itself "catholic." He wrote in 1942: "It is one thing to love Italy, as I most fervently do, and quite another to display this affection in public. The holy Church which I represent is the mother of nations, all nations. . . . We are all more or less tainted with nationalism. The Apostolic Delegate must be, and must be seen to be, free from this contagion. May God help me." [14]

It was when he had reached the summit of his life that the man who no longer had "any special ties in this life, no family, no earthly country or nation" and for whom the whole world was a family, was moved to write his encyclical on peace. At that point the world-embracing ecumenism and catholicity of Pope John had carried him to the same non-violent love of all men that was manifest in Mohandas Gandhi.

Gandhi said that "belief in non-violence is based on the assumption that human nature in its essence is one and therefore unfailingly responds to the advances of love." [15] *Pacem in Terris* is based on the same assumption. The encyclical states that "even though human beings differ from one another by virtue of their ethnic peculiarities, they all possess certain essential common elements, and are inclined by nature to meet each other in the world of spiritual values, whose progressive assimilation opens to them the possibility of perfection without limits. They have the right and duty therefore to live in communion with one another." [16]

For Pope John, as for Gandhi, a repudiation of force was based on the dignity of man, whose nature is above the rule of violence. It is in the encyclical's section on justice that Pope John stated most clearly this opposition between force and human dignity: "Disagreements [among nations] must be settled, not by force, nor by deceit or trickery, but rather *in the only manner which is worthy of the dignity of man,* i.e., by a mutual assessment of the reasons on both sides of the dispute, by a mature and objective investigation of the situation, and by an equitable reconciliation of differences of opinion." [17] (Italics added.)

In the Johannine vision of man, non-violence is a natural-law imperative. Only a non-violent solution of conflicts, through reason and reconciliation, corresponds to the demands of human nature as they can be perceived by reason alone. It is true that there is a faith involved in non-violence, but it is a faith first of all in the human person as such, hence a faith in all persons, including one's opponent. The faith of non-violence is a faith in the human spirit's permanent capacity to open itself to truth. It is therefore a faith proper to reason, not revelation, although revelation offers an enormous resource for its further development. Reason demands man's faith in man, so that human conflicts can be settled by human means.

Thus it is in *Pacem in Terris* that "justice, right reason and humanity urgently demand that the arms race should cease." [18] But while reason demands of man the step of disarmament, he can take that reasonable step only if "the fundamental principle on which our present peace depends," namely "equality of arms," can be replaced gradually by another, "which declares that the true and solid peace of nations consists not in equality of arms but in mutual trust alone." [19] Reason can fulfill itself here only by learning a faith in man, a faith sufficient to carry man, step by step, from an irrational law of fear to a reasonable law of love.

The opposition between fear and mutual trust is the root of man's choice between war and peace. One of the most beautiful expressions of this fear-trust, war-peace polarity is found in John Knowles' novel *A Separate Peace,* in which a boy causes the death of his closest friend by failing to meet him on the level of their faith in each other's friendship. As a man looking back, he testifies to his friend's faith in man and indicates the division between war and peace at a point closer to home than any battlefield: "My war ended before I ever put on a uniform; I was on active duty all my time at school; I killed my enemy there.

"Only Phineas never was afraid, only Phineas never hated anyone. Other people experienced this fearful shock somewhere, this sighting of the enemy, and so began an obsessive labor of defense, began to parry the menace they saw facing them by developing a particular frame of mind. . . .

"All of them, all except Phineas, constructed at infinite cost to themselves these Maginot Lines against this enemy they thought they saw across the frontier, this enemy who never attacked that way—if he ever attacked at all; if he was indeed the enemy." [20]

Albert Einstein stated the same truth in the following words: "In the last analysis every kind of peaceful cooperation among men is primarily based on mutual trust and only secondarily on institutions such as courts of justice and others. This holds for nations as well as individuals. And the basis for trust is loyal give and take." [21]

The movement of states from fear and arms toward mutual trust is, according to Pope John, an objective demanded by reason because "there can be, or at least there should be, no doubt that relations between states, as between individuals, should be regulated not by the force of arms but by the light of reason, by the rule, that is, of truth, of justice and of active and sincere co-operation." [22]

Or as Gandhi put it, in terms of the human dignity with which Pope John began: "Non-violence is the law of our species as violence is the law of the brute. The dignity of man requires obedience to a higher law—to the strength of the spirit." [23]

Pope John's combined repudiation of what may seem to be very different realities, force on one hand, and deceit and trickery on the other ("disagreements must be settled, not by force, nor by deceit or trickery"), indicates the deep relationship between truth and non-violence. Violence is as much a sin against truth as are deceit and trickery. And truth is set forth in *Pacem in Terris* as being "first among the rules governing the relations between states." [24] The subtitle of *Pacem in Terris* is "On establishing universal peace in truth, justice, charity and liberty." On the other hand, it has been said rightly that the first casualty of war is truth. To take the point a level deeper than the lie of propaganda, one can affirm that it is the truth of man himself which is violated in war, that truth within man which has the power to achieve justice without violence.

The term which Gandhi coined to describe the power of non-violence is *Satyagraha,* whose root meaning is "holding on to truth," hence truth-force. Satyagraha, truth-force, can also be described as love-force or soul-force. It is only from a total adherence to truth that one can understand and use the full power of non-violence. At the same time truth demands non-violence. As Gandhi explains his doctrine, "In the application of Satyagraha I discovered in the earliest stages that pursuit of truth did not admit of violence being inflicted on one's opponent but that he must be weaned from error by patience and sympathy. For what appears to be truth to the one may appear to be error to the other." [25]

The victory sought by non-violence is not a victory over one's opponent but rather the victory of truth, a truth which cannot be identified simply with one's own position in the conflict. Gandhi was totally committed to truth, as he understood it, and was prepared to sacrifice his life for it, as he did progressively up to the moment of his assassination. But Gandhi identified Truth with God so completely that he preferred the formulation "Truth is God" to the usual "God is Truth." He was therefore acutely sensitive to the fact that no man could claim to possess the final truth. That is a Truth to which man must commit himself with all his power but without claiming it prematurely.

The practical consequence Gandhi drew from man's relative knowledge of an absolute Truth was that a serious conflict situation always involved two truth-claiming parties, each in possession of a truth it believed deeply enough to do battle over. But Gandhi's insight was that the proper growth of both parties toward the final Truth each sought could only be frustrated by violence. A mutual progression in truth takes place not through coercion, but through persuasion. To force the opponent to yield to our own truth is only a confession of its inherent impotence to convince him in mind and heart. Or rather, it is a confession of our failure to employ the force of truth, which force alone can effect the conversion we are in reality seeking through the blind desperation of violence. We have evidence enough in Vietnam of the complete futility of seeking to win a people to our truth through armed force and the tactics of a police state. Real truth is not our side victorious in any sense, but the mutual victory of both opponents over the conflict between them. It is the truth of Americans and Viet Cong reconciled, with each of them having recognized that truth in the other's claims which was valid from the beginning.

Gandhi always began a non-violent campaign with an exhaustive inquiry into the concrete facts and truth of the conflict situation as presented by both sides. He sought to understand equally the opposing points of view and for that reason would go to extreme length to enter sympathetically into the position of those he naturally differed with most. His insistence on the mutual presence of truth and on the possibility of the opponents' reconciliation at a higher level of understanding led him to ac-

cept compromises which partisans always found wanting. A report which he helped draft and agreed to in ending his first
campaign in India, the campaign in 1918 for the planter-domi-
nated peasants of Champaran, has been described in terms of
such partisan disappointment:

"The report was essentially a compromise. Gandhi was unwill-
ing to yield on questions of principle but was willing to compromise on matters of detail. . . . When the report was issued
many felt that Gandhi had yielded too much. . . . But the planters'
prestige was gone forever, and it was their prestige which had
sustained them." [26]

Gandhi knew that the power of truth would always break the
back of injustice, whether or not its details could satisfy the
partisans of either side.

Gandhi said that the opponent "must be weaned from error by
patience and sympathy," and that no opponent, however oppressive, can resist the force of Truth if we draw enough of its
power into our resistance to his injustice.

Pope John wrote in *Pacem in Terris*: "In every human being,
there is a need that is *congenital to his nature* and *never becomes
extinguished*, compelling him to break through the web of error
and open his mind to the knowledge of truth. And God will
never fail to act on his interior being, with the result that a person, who at a given moment of his life lacks the clarity of faith
or even adheres to erroneous doctrines, can at a future date be
enlightened and believe the truth." [27] (Italics added.)

This passage adds to the natural-law foundation of non-violence
a theological substructure, and is as biblically sound as it is
socially revolutionary. It states the permanent ontological relationship between God and man in truth. From the human standpoint, man is open to truth by his very nature, so that his need
for truth *cannot* be extinguished. From the divine standpoint, God
will *never* fail to act on the interior being of a person, so that at
any point in a man's life, however deeply and perversely he may
be involved in error, there is the definite possibility of his opening himself to the light of truth. Thus there is affirmed an absolute
faith in the person's capacity *for* truth, corresponding to the un-

ceasing divine power involved *in* truth. The power of truth is the power of God responding to the openness of man's being. Prior to death, man as man does not have the power to seal himself definitively from truth, because truth is a divine force pressing on the permanent potentiality of man's openness. While he may be morally (i.e., immorally) resistant to that force, he remains ontologically open to it. There is therefore a profound agreement between Gandhi's assertion that Truth is God and Pope John's principle that man by his very nature as man cannot surrender his need for truth, nor build an impenetrable barrier to the divine power in truth.

In short, to take the classic case, Hitler was not unredeemable, and the power of Truth on which Gandhi relied was *in principle* just as applicable to Nazi Germany as it was to South Africa and India. To deny this ontological or permanent capacity of man for Truth is to assert a premature death in man which would give him the moral character of Satan. A theology of redemption can admit *no* human exception to the permanent possibility of salvation. However much Hitler, Stalin, or any current devil figure may be in the power of evil, we should be wary of sacrificing a belief in man's openness to God for the sake of our righteousness against any enemy or for an easy skepticism concerning man's spirit. The classic case-argument against the power of Truth and non-violence can be admitted as absolute only at the deeper expense of a biblically rooted anthropology. If the price is felt to be too great, then we can go no farther than the historically based assertion that the power of Truth and non-violence sufficient to overcome Hitler would have had to be enormous.

But again, it would be poor history to deny that a similar perspective of powerlessness was the reasoned argument and very real obstacle to any possible success of Gandhi in South Africa and India. The English were not such gentlemen as to close up shop before having inflicted on India hundreds of lathi charges and beatings, years of military occupation, and the political imprisonment of thousands. Nor are Americans such gentlemen as not to be committing worse crimes in Vietnam. The two-sided realism of Gandhi and Pope John would affirm that all men, whether Germans, British, or Americans, are capable of profound evil at the same time as they remain permanently open to the redemptive power of Truth. On the other hand, the optimism of non-violence is not a blindness to the evil present in man but a recognition of the power of his spirit to overcome it.

It should be noted carefully that a theology of such openness to Truth's power in man does not assert that Satyagraha *will* always be effective in practice. In fact it will not be. But a theology of redemptive truth does assert that Satyagraha *can* always be effective. Its failures must be attributed neither to the divine power of Truth, which is infinite, nor to human nature itself, which is open, but failure must be attributed rather to the practitioners of non-violence, whose mediation of Truth is insufficient in terms of its full power in God and in terms of the immediate need of unredeemed man to be struck by it. It is in this context that Gandhi's assertion that he never committed a wholly non-violent act should be placed. And it is in this context also that the crucifixion of Jesus becomes more and more significant: If one asks why the power of Truth in even the man-God was insufficient to turn Pontius Pilate from the order of execution, the answer may be that it was only in and through that execution, as suffered by Jesus, that the fullness of God's power could actually become manifest. The ongoing and mysterious working-out of that crucified power in history is the redemptive process which places us simultaneously both after and before the resurrection. Christians do not really know what they mean when they demand that non-violent love be "effective" in order that they embrace it, because they have already embraced in faith the meaning of a cross whose "effectiveness" was questionable to those standing beneath it. The effectiveness of non-violence is ultimately an open tomb which few men seem able to envision as the culmination of the suffering history in which they are now involved.

The conclusions Pope John drew from his faith in the divine power of truth and the openness of man's spirit were the same as Gandhi's: non-violence in every sector of life—for truth alone would achieve the victory—and a constant coming together in dialogue with the opponent. Hence his "opening to the left," his encouragement of the Christian-Marxist dialogue, and his own meeting with Khrushchev's son-in-law, Alexis Adzhubei. During his meeting with Adzhubei and his wife, Pope John recalled the biblical passages on the creation of the world and commented on them as follows: "The first epoch was that of light: *fiat lux.* We are at present in the first era, that of light: the light of my eyes has met with the light of your eyes. May the Lord assist the progress of good if it so pleases Him." [28]

The light of truth would widen through such dialogue. For, as Gandhi had said, "what appears to be truth to the one may appear to be error to the other," and it is only by testing both truths in the conflict proper to them, that of dialogue in a confrontation of love, that a genuine resolution, and growth in truth, can be achieved.

If it seems true, as the critics have claimed, that *Pacem in Terris* lacks a realistic methodology for achieving peace on earth, it may be because we have been trained to recognize only one methodology in the international order: that of military power. Whatever passing homage we pay to foreign aid and the Peace Corps, we remain possessed by that belligerent and unrecognized nationalism which Pope John so feared and which rests heavily, in our case, on the proposition that peace *is* the profession of the Strategic Air Command. Any other means of preserving peace is precisely that, "other," and is considered no substitute for the megatons which keep our country free. The means of peace are the means of war, cocked and aimed at the eye of the enemy. Vietnam is said to be the price of peace in our land, a price we pay in murder and oppression. There is no more terrible symbol of technological man gone wild than the daily effort to count bodies into a victory of the spirit. When it comes to peace, this is the realism and the methodology we believe in, a realism of the sword and a methodology of blood.

But just as he rejected outright force as being beneath the dignity of man, Pope John rejected the "peace" methodology of nuclear deterrence because he could not betray the natural unity of the human family, whose only real basis for peace can be love and the collaboration that goes with it. The law of fear which the deterrent rests on cannot ensure peace because it is opposed to the natural unity of man. To divide man in fear as a means of keeping him from war is self-defeating. Fear and division are the roots of war. For this reason a constant purpose of Gandhi in his campaigns had been to free the oppressed from their fear of their oppressors. Any peace built on fear is not only false but threatens the worst consequences to man.

The peace methodology Pope John chose instead of violence and fear was that of the human family's convergence in love and collaboration in the task—to use Teilhard's phrase—of building the earth. Teilhard has also said that "we must believe without reservation in the possibility and the necessary consequences of universal love." [29] Pope John did so believe, and encouraged the spread of that belief as the true basis for peace on earth.

For the tremendous power of *Pacem in Terris* is not the destructive power of man aspiring to be God, but the loving power of God revealing Himself in a servant of man. God speaks through his prophets, and *Pacem in Terris* is the love of God expressed through his human instrument, John XXIII. The encyclical charts the social expression of love in today's world, a love manifested in total non-violence and total service to man. *Pacem in Terris* has the power to move men because it embodies the power of a man who surrendered all power to God.

Non-violence, or Satyagraha, is truth-force, and in *Pacem in Terris* we see this force of truth making its impact on the conscience of man. It is the force that comes from one man's lifelong adherence to divine Truth, and moves men in conflict to bring together their warring truths and grow in the truth of peace. Non-violence is a force so powerful in truth and so creative in love that it can transform conflict into reconciliation. *Pacem in Terris* is such a force. The power of its testimony provides a fittting measure for our understanding of power.

It must be admitted, however, that there is an element essential to Gandhi's Satyagraha which is apparently not found in Pope John's encyclical. When Gandhi said that the opponent must be weaned from error by patience and sympathy, he went on to develop the meaning of patience, self-suffering, so that his doctrine came finally to mean the vindication of truth by the infliction of suffering not on the opponent but on one's self. Non-violence is, first of all, as we find it in *Pacem in Terris*, love and the reasoned resolution of conflict; but it is a love which resolves conflict at its worst by the specific method of suffering the full injustice of the opponent. The acceptance of suffering in love for the sake of a higher good is the absolute weapon of Truth. It reveals man's dignity as no other action can. And it opens the eyes of the oppressor to the sacredness of the man before him. If there is a concrete methodology which would grant to *Pacem in Terris* a missing link in its argument, it is Gandhi's techniques for suffering away injustice.

At the same time, in turning to Gandhi for the techniques of non-violence based on self-suffering, we are simply recognizing the Johannine spirit and vision being given its concrete expression. In a pre-Johannine theology of war and peace, the *ultima ratio*, or last resort, for man's prevention of injustice was the waging of war. In the Johannine view of man, which rules out war as beneath man's spirit and insists on his permanent capacity to grow in love and truth, the last resort could only be the resistance of self-suffering love, as practiced and perfected by Gandhi. The truth of *Pacem in Terris* is completed in Gandhi's experiments in truth.

But *Pacem in Terris*, while containing no reference to the techniques of suffering love, is itself the fruit of such suffering. Commentators have often remarked on the extraordinary purity and serenity of the encyclical's voice, whose doctrine expands like the sea of God's love. Reading *Pacem in Terris* is like gazing to the bottom of a mountain pool. It is pure and clear. Yet this godlike purity can be understood fully only if one reads Pope John's final testimony to the world in the context of the spiritual diary which Angelo Roncalli kept for sixty-seven years, his

Journal of a Soul. It is there that one finds the hidden methodology of the Johannine non-violence. The vision of peace in the
encyclical can then be seen as corresponding to a personal unity
and integrity which was the fruit of a life of self-suffering. The
deep unity of mankind which is felt by the reader in every passage of *Pacem in Terris* is a reflection of the spiritual unity of
the man Roncalli. The harmony and integrity of life which the
Pope counsels in *Pacem in Terris* was one he knew intimately.
The non-violence he expresses was the personal non-violence he
had suffered gradually into a global vision of peace. The purity
of his words came from a daily fire of self-purification. The
serenity of his voice was the serenity of one crucified to the world
through Christ. The power of his love was the power of one who
sought always the lot of the powerless.

In short, the self-suffering of the experiments in truth which
underlay Gandhi's doctrine has a deep parallel in the life and
doctrine of Pope John. The Johannine vision of peace cannot be
divorced from the Johannine cross. Pope John's idealism was not
easy at all. It was the culmination of a lifelong agony of love. The
peace and joy of John's doctrine was the joy of a man who had
left himself behind. He wrote of this peace of selflessness in a
letter to a friend in 1934:

"Let me tell you with the heart of a brother that now more
than ever it is a case of closing your eyes and hands, or ridding
yourself completely of the baggage of your selfhood and of plung-
ing into the sure and tranquil sea of God's holy will where alone
will you find a measure of peace." [30]

If it is asked how man can possibly attain that peace on earth
which we find described in the encyclical, we might answer: in
the same way that Pope John did. As he said on June 1, 1963,
two days before his death: "I suffer very much, but with love." [31]
The power of non-violence is the power of suffering transformed
by love. Peace on earth is achieved by men who know how to
suffer injustice away. Only if enough men choose such a path
can *Pacem in Terris* begin to be realized.

The conclusion of *Pacem in Terris* is not the last page of the document, but Pope John on his deathbed. It was a conclusion foreseen by John in recurring passages of his *Journal of a Soul* which speak of the realities of cross and death in terms of fulfillment. Before the Council John had told Cardinal Suenens: "Once the Council has begun, I know well the task that will be reserved for me: to suffer." [32]

In the hours before his death, John held his arms in the form of a cross on his bed. He said to friends:

"In my vigils at night, I have always kept before me Jesus Crucified with his arms outstretched to receive the whole world. It is the role of the Catholic and Apostolic Church, of the Roman Church, to work for the realization of the prayer of the Divine Master: *Ut unum, ut unum sint.*" [33]

Pope John died fearing that his family would experience the agony of another war. "I am afraid, I am afraid," the Pope said on his deathbed, "I fear that my children might become involved in a new war." [34] After a requiem Mass for John, Monsignor Loris Capovilla, his private secretary, quoted these words as among his last. He recalled that the Pope had been in the Italian Army medical corps during the First World War and carried from that experience a permanent "horror of massacres and tortures of so many young lives." Pope John had spoken himself of this battlefield inspiration for *Pacem in Terris*:

"I shall never be able to forget the screams of an Austrian whose chest was torn apart by a bayonet during the war and who was carried to the hospital at Caporetto where I was an attendant. His image became ever more vivid within me as I worked on the encyclical *Pacem in Terris*." [35]

According to his secretary, "that one avoid war was the thought that assailed the dying Pontiff."

The profound union which the dying John felt with his family, the world, provoked his fear and concern for its peace. And to this union with mankind and care for its future was joined Pope John's final effort to make peace among his children, the suffering he underwent in love. Unlike Gandhi's, the public suffering of Pope John for peace came only at the end of his life and lasted

but a few days. But its intensity and its power to draw men together recall the Mahatma's suffering. In the last days of Pope
John there was suddenly manifested to the world the full power
of what even his voice in *Pacem in Terris* could convey only im-
perfectly: the power of selfless love and the reality of suffering
offered in sacrifice for the human family. At one stage in this
final agony, which drew the world into John's heart, a New York
newspaper headlined: "Pope John Powerless to Raise Arm." But
as one believer commented: "The world knows nothing of power.
He is raising far more than his arm."

The resurrection of the human spirit which *Pacem in Terris*
represents has only just begun in the family to which Pope John's
letter was addressed. The Church is still bewildered by the legacy
of John, and the world simply knows that someone holy passed
through. But to know that much, and to have felt the non-violent
love of his message, is to begin to learn the lesson of power
which Pope John gave us. At a time in history when our material
power has become a blasphemy against creation, it is time to
learn the power of the spirit.

NOTES

1. John Courtney Murray, "Key Themes in the Encyclical," commentary in the America Press edition of *Pacem in Terris* (New
   York: 1963), p. 63.
2. Quoted in "In the Magazines," *worldview* (June 1963), p. 3.
3. *To Live As Men: An Anatomy of Peace* (Center for the Study of
   Democratic Institutions: 1965), pp. 15–16.
4. See, for example, Ramsey's article "The Uses of Power," *The
   Perkins School of Theology Journal* (Fall 1964), p. 24, fn. 6.
5. Quoted in "In the Magazines," *worldview* (June 1963), p. 4.
6. When Gandhi was finally granted an interview with the Viceroy
   of India in 1931, Churchill expressed his revulsion at "the nause-
   ating and humiliating spectacle of this one-time Inner Temple
   lawyer, now seditious fakir, striding half-naked up the steps of
   the Viceroy's palace, there to negotiate and to parley on equal
   terms with the representative of the King-Emperor." Louis Fischer,
   The Life of Mahatma Gandhi (Collier Books: 1962), p. 281.

7. Pope John XXIII, *Pacem in Terris* (Vatican Polyglot Press: 1963), p. 27.
8. E. E. Y. Hales, *Pope John and His Revolution* (Doubleday: 1965), p. 63.
9. Pope John XXIII, *Journal of a Soul* (McGraw-Hill: 1965), pp. 298–99.
10. M. K. Gandhi, *The Law of Love*, edited and published by Anand T. Hingorani (Bharatiya Vidya Bhavan: 1962), p. 85.
11. Pope John XXIII, *Pacem in Terris*, p. 32.
12. *Ibid.*
13. Pope John XXIII, *Journal of a Soul*, p. 251.
14. *Ibid.*, p. 260.
15. M. K. Gandhi, *My Non-Violence* (Navajivan Publishing House: 1960), p. 81.
16. Pope John XXIII, *Pacem in Terris*, p. 27.
17. *Ibid.*, p. 25.
18. *Ibid.*, p. 29.
19. *Ibid.*
20. John Knowles, *A Separate Peace* (Dell: 1961), pp. 255–56.
21. *Philadelphia Inquirer*, March 22, 1950, p. 2. Quoted by Culbert G. Rutenber, *The Dagger and the Cross* (Fellowship Publications: 1958), p. 133.
22. Pope John XXIII, *Pacem in Terris*, pp. 29–30.
23. Gandhi, *My Non-Violence*, p. 4.
24. Pope John XXIII, *Pacem in Terris*, p. 24.
25. M. K. Gandhi, *Satyagraha (Non-Violent Resistance)* (Navajivan Publishing House: 1951), p. 6.
26. Gene Sharp, *Gandhi Wields the Weapon of Moral Power: Three Case Histories* (Navajivan Publishing House: 1960), p. 33.
27. Pope John XXIII, *Pacem in Terris*, p. 41
28. *Wit and Wisdom of Good Pope John*, collected by Henri Fesquet (Signet: 1965), p. 86.
29. Teilhard de Chardin, *Building the Earth* (Dimension Books: 1965), p. 97.
30. Fesquet, *Wit and Wisdom of Good Pope John*, p. 118.
31. *Ibid.*, p. 125.
32. *Ibid.*, p. 102.
33. *Ibid.*, p. 124.
34. This story was an Associated Press dispatch from Vatican City which appeared in the New York *Herald Tribune* (European edition) on June 7, 1963.
35. Fesquet, *Wit and Wisdom of Good Pope John*, p. 83.

5

Toward a New Perspective on War: The Vision of Vatican II

ONE FACTOR IN particular weighed heavily against the Vatican Council's bearing a satisfactory witness to peace in the nuclear age. The Council lay heir to the Johannine legacy on peace, which while providing an enormous impulse and resource to the Council on the issue, making silence virtually impossible, at the same time invited a comparison which could only end unfavorably for the body Pope John called into being. For there was never more than a faint hope that 2300 bishops in assembly would equal the witness to peace of a single man whose power of reconciliation calls to mind Gandhi, St. Francis, and the Prince of Peace Himself. The following of prophets is always a hard task for the Church, but never so hard as when the prophet is Pope. When the chair of Peter was filled by the spirit of Pope John, there were times when Rome itself was the voice of one crying in the wilderness, especially on the issue of peace on earth. The same has been true of Pope Paul's appeals for peace in Vietnam as far as American Catholicism is concerned. Prophetic encyclicals on hard-line subjects leave a respectful but scandalized Church only one attitude: devout deafness. As for the Bishops in Council echoing the voice of *Pacem in Terris* in its most prophetic emphases, Robert McAfee Brown has put it well: "Prophetism does not thrive on majorities." [1]

One comes then to the treatment of war and peace in the *Pastoral Constitution on the Church in the Modern World* with both a yearning for the word on that issue which most needs it today and a fear of inevitable failure. But if *Pacem in Terris* highlights what is lacking in the final text of Schema 13, it also illuminates what is present: the Council Fathers' genuine effort to bear the Johannine burden well and to speak powerfully the words of peace to man in his most serious crisis.

Peace is the last of the "problems of special urgency" which are treated in Part II of the Constitution. Chapter V of Part II, entitled "The Fostering of Peace and the Promotion of a Community of Nations," begins in Article 77 by placing "the human family's hour of supreme crisis" [2] in a Teilhardian perspective, which recalls also Pope John's opening speech to the Council with its soaring vision of "a new order of human relations which, by men's own efforts and even beyond their very expectations, are directed toward the fulfillment of God's superior and inscrutable designs." [3] The Constitution testifies to the human family's gradual movement together and ever-increasing consciousness of unity at the same time as it underlines the threat to it of a final global war.

The significance of the Fathers having chosen this context for their discussion of the problem and for a continuing emphasis in the text should not be missed. Peace today is seen in relation first to mankind's struggle upward in history toward unity and a global love, thus disclosing the profoundly inhuman threat of global self-destruction. The dynamism of history suggests what no just-war theology can with respect to nuclear war: the eschatological overtones of the threat and the theological revolution necessary to comprehend it. The importance of such a context can be grasped best by noting in contrast the small place given the question of man's global suicide by so eminent a just-war theorist as Paul Ramsey. Ramsey's analyses [4] (and the earlier efforts of

Father John Courtney Murray [5]) are carefully confined to the prospect of a strictly limited nuclear war, whose possibility (or "moral imperative," as Father Murray put it) is treated as if it were the only morally significant issue. To grant theological significance to the larger perspective of a global holocaust, which is recognized as the deepest moral issue by every thinking non-theologian, would be to shut the just-war door permanently. "Eschatological war" and man's common good do not mix well. While the Council does take the extremely significant step of admitting the history-threatening *nature* of the problem, the *quaestio facti*, whether or not it goes on to give the kind of theological response thus demanded, must be considered further.

The Council Fathers are clearly aware that a spiritual revolution of some kind is necessary. The Constitution emphasizes the horror and perversity of modern war, which is "immensely magnified by the increase in the number of scientific weapons." [6] Basing itself on a recognition of the "almost total and altogether reciprocal slaughter" now threatened, the Council acknowledges the degree of moral imagination required in such a crisis: "All these considerations compel us to undertake an evaluation of war *with an entirely new attitude*." [7] (Italics added.)

This acknowledgment of the Council's task of moral imagination prefaces its condemnation of total war, which is deliberately set off from the rest of the text and must be counted as the most solemn declaration of Vatican II:

All these considerations compel us to undertake an evaluation of war with an entirely new attitude. The men of our time must realize that they will have to give a somber reckoning of their deeds of war for the course of the future will depend greatly on the decisions they make today.

With these truths in mind, this most Holy Synod makes its own the condemnations of total war already pronounced by recent popes, and issues the following declaration:

Any act of war aimed indiscriminately at the destruction of entire cities or extensive areas along with their population is a crime against God and man himself. It merits unequivocal and unhesitating condemnation. [8]

In calling this statement "the central declaration of the Vatican Council," Paul Ramsey has noted further:

The fact that this is the most important statement of the Council is signalized by its use of the word "condemnation" this once among few if any other such usages in any of the sixteen promulgated Constitutions, Decrees, and Declarations, running to 103,000 words, issued by Vatican II. The Council did not even formally condemn atheism; yet, in language freely used at all previous councils but rarely by Vatican II, it condemns acts of war aimed indiscriminately at the destruction of entire cities with their populations.[9]

Although the Council's declaration is introduced by a reference to the condemnations of total war pronounced by recent popes, none of the texts referred to is so clear on the issue as the Council itself. Prior to the Council, the most precise text on total war was found in Pope Pius XII's address to the World Medical Association in 1954:

When putting this method [ABC warfare] to use involves such an extension of the evil that it entirely escapes from the control of man, its use must be rejected as immoral. Here there would no longer be a question of "defense" against injustice or a necessary "safeguarding" of legitimate possessions, but the pure and simple annihilation of all human life within the radius of action. This is not permitted for any reason whatsoever.[10]

Pius employed a criterion to total war, that of controllability, which made his statement subject to the casuistry of weapons technicians and theologians of a like inclination, who could deny that even the worst of thermonuclear devices "escaped from the control of man." [11] Thus when a very similar statement against nuclear weapons appeared in the first draft of Schema 13, which was discussed during the Council's third session (fall 1964), it was quickly challenged by Auxiliary Bishop Hannan of Washington, D.C. (now Archbishop of New Orleans), on these same grounds. "There now exist," said Bishop Hannan, "nuclear weapons which have a very precise limit of destruction. . . . It may be permitted to use these arms, with their limited effect, against military objectives in a just war according to theological principles." [12]

A critique of Schema 13's statement prepared by several Catholic weapons specialists from Washington, D.C., and submitted to the Council in its third session, made much the same point: that since Pope Pius XII's statement in 1954

there has emerged no consensus as to the distinction between what man can "control" and what he can reasonably *expect* and *intend* to happen in an extreme situation . . . Moreover, the best technical opinion is that the effects of nuclear weapons is [sic] certainly not "absolutely" incalculable.[13]

In the face of such criticism, grounded in the technical expertise of defense specialists and responding to the weakness of Pius XII's categories, it seemed possible that the Council would be forced to avoid any pronouncement at all against modern war, given the apparent loopholes in the Church's traditional just-war criteria. A Council Father representing the other major nuclear power in the West, Archbishop Beck of Liverpool, exploited another hole in the morally defined limits of the just war:

There may well exist objects which in a just war of defence are legitimate targets of nuclear weapons even of vast force. To attack a ballistic missile or a satellite missile in the outer atmosphere would, for example, be a legitimate act of defence and with just proportion duly preserved, it might require the use of a weapon of vast power.[14]

With such theoretical avenues of escape available to the nuclear-power theologians, it began to seem unlikely that the Council would or even could speak any strong word against a threatened nuclear holocaust in the context of the theology accepted by the great majority of the Fathers present. It is this dominant theological background of the just war which made almost irrelevant the stirring plea by Patriarch Maximos of Antioch in the third session that the Council Fathers issue a solemn and clear condemnation of all ABC warfare. [15] The real question, ignored by Maximos, was how such a condemnation could be formulated and defended in terms of the traditional criteria for the just war and in the face of the nuclear technicians' claim that nuclear weapons could be controlled. Maximos had called for the solution without coming to terms with the problem. However deeply convinced a Council Father might be of the globally murderous character of modern war, he would have to do more than issue a call to action in order to speak out effectively for peace. The problem was to show the Council exactly how to condemn nuclear genocide in the precise framework of the categories controlling the Church's traditional approach to war. Anything less was irrelevant to the possibility of a fruitful convergence between the world's crisis, on the one hand, and the Church's deeply rooted (but apparently inadequate) theology of war on the other.

A response to this problem was made in a critique of the Schema and a proposed amendment submitted to the Schema's redrafting committee by Bishop John Taylor, the American bishop of Stockholm, Sweden. Bishop Taylor's intervention on the subject was drawn up too late in order to be delivered orally at the third session and was therefore not made public. It was supported and signed, however, by Archbishop George Flahiff of Winnipeg and English Bishops Gordon Wheeler and Charles Grant, and was due at least equal consideration by the redrafting committee as were the spoken interventions. Bishop Taylor proposed a shift in the declaration from the technically controverted criterion of "controllability" to the morally defined criterion of "discrimination" whose bases are the distinction between combatant and non-combatant and the moral rights of the innocent in war. He offered an amendment to the text which would substitute for "incalculable" and "uncontrollable" the terms "indiscriminate weapons" or "weapons of total war," which convey in themselves the moral notion of massive or indiscriminate killing at which the text was aiming yet without leaving an opening for "the best technical opinion" of defense experts eager to attack such a declaration in their own frame of reference. Such a substitution of moral for technical terms, grounded in the rights of non-combatants, would be decisive in permitting the Council to condemn total war in the traditional theology more definitively than Pius XII ever did and in a way that could be understood as referring directly to the nuclear crisis confronting mankind.

Bishop Taylor recommended further that in order to be relevant to the world's actual moral situation this condemnation of total-war methods would have to be extended to the even more immediate problem of nuclear deterrence, the public threat and instant readiness by the major powers to wage total war. The declaration on the *execution* of total war would have to be supported by a similar declaration on the *intention* to wage total war present in the deterrent. In this connection, he proposed a text following the total-war condemnation which would read:

Moreover, a nation's public threat of the methods of total war, as manifested in their preparation for ready execution, must be condemned equally with the act of execution, inasmuch as citizens called on in advance to support such a policy could only judge it on its public evidence as grossly immoral in intention.[16]

Bishop Taylor's amendment went on to emphasize the point which Archbishop Roberts stressed repeatedly through the Council, the right of conscientious objection, and concluded by making a transition from the just-war framework of the total-war condemnation to the Gospel of Jesus Christ with which the Church had once begun:

As total war is now a war against God's plan and against mankind itself, the actuation of the spirit of Christ the Lord is more imperative than ever: the spirit of meekness and humility, renouncing violence, opposed by nature to force even in its just use, seeking by a love embracing enemies to overcome evil with good. In order therefore to respond to the needs of our age, Christians should cultivate a deeper awareness that violence is the natural expression of hatred and should undertake a fuller exploration of the non-violent love and teaching of Christ.

The revised text of the Schema, which was presented to the Council for discussion in its fourth session (fall 1965), followed the Taylor recommendation for a shift to the criterion of discrimination as the key to a strengthened concept concerning total war. The Schema was therefore able to condemn definitively any act of mass murder by modern weapons, whether nuclear or not, without inviting the charge of technical incompetence. In article 98, titled "Modern warfare, and in particular so-called 'total' war," the September 1965 Schema declared:

Any act of war aimed at the indiscriminate destruction of entire cities and their inhabitants, and a fortiori at the practically total destruction of a whole area is, of its nature, objectively, a crime against God and against man himself; it is to be vigorously and unhesitatingly condemned.[17]

This condemnation of total war was absorbed into the final text of the *Pastoral Constitution on the Church in the Modern World* in the form quoted earlier and thus became "the central declaration of the Vatican Council." It was there challenged again by Bishop Hannan, who in an eleventh-hour appeal (December 2, 1965) to the bishops in charge of the Schema argued, with the support of nine other bishops, that total war had never been condemned in such a manner by "recent Popes," as the final draft of the Schema claimed. [18] In their reply of December 5, Archbishop Garrone and Bishop Schroffer of the drafting committee cited Pius XII's statement to the World Medical Association as just such a condemnation. [19]

Bishop Hannan had a valid point but one which he could not very well develop or pursue further. By shifting the criterion of the total-war condemnation from Pius' notion of controllability (which only implies discrimination) specifically and emphatically to that of discrimination alone, the Schema had, on the one hand, nullified the kind of technical criticism Hannan had been able to make earlier and, on the other hand, had greatly strengthened the Church's position against total war while retaining a definite continuity with papal teaching. What Bishop Hannan's final challenge amounted to, therefore, was an effort to draw back into the Schema's definition the earlier and more vulnerable concept which he had already effectively criticized and which, one can presume, would have been dismissed summarily after the Council by all "the best technical opinion."

But in the Constitution passed and promulgated, the Council rests its total-war condemnation instead on the criterion of discrimination, thus reaffirming the absolute character of non-combatant immunity, and is so concrete in its references to cities, areas, and population that the issue is brilliantly clear. A Polaris commander or a United States President should have no difficulty understanding it. [20]

In response to Archbishop Roberts' question to the Council, "Could not the failure of Christian efforts of so many years past be due in part to emphasis on weapons rather than on persons?" [21] the Constitution upholds strongly the rights and duties of individual conscience. It recommends that legal provisions be made for conscientious objectors and commends in the highest terms possible "those who fearlessly and openly resist" any military command in conflict with natural law. [22] The "praesumptio juris" clause contained in the September 1965 draft of the Schema, which presumed the duty to obey lawful authority until its injustice was "manifestly clear," was dropped from the final text in recognition of the barriers to conscience this principle had produced in the past. Instead of buttressing military authority, the text affirms the primacy of conscience in war and repudiates the way of blind obedience: "actions which deliberately conflict with these same principles [of universal natural law], as well as orders commanding such actions, are criminal, *and blind obedience cannot excuse those who yield to them.*" [23] One's mind wanders back over the past crimes which could have been avoided, or at least resisted with dignity, had the Church spoken so clearly then.

It is evident then that the Council has spoken powerfully on the peace issue. Its achievements in certain areas are outstanding: its clear and unqualified condemnation of total war; its support of the legal right of conscientious objection; its affirmation of the primacy of conscience in every action of war.

Nor does the Council fail to mention the use of non-violent resistance as an alternative to war:

We cannot fail to praise those who renounce the use of violence in the vindication of their rights and who resort to methods of defense which are otherwise available to weaker parties too, provided this can be done without injury to the rights and duties of others or of the community itself.[24]

The qualifying phrase tends to weaken the statement and indicates fear where there should be faith, but the Council has at least taken the step of endorsing a way of resistance consistent with the Gospel. The Constitution bases its praise of non-violence on the reconciliation of all men through the Cross of Christ, by which He slew hatred in his own flesh and poured forth the spirit of love into the hearts of men (Eph. 2:16; Col. 1:20-22). It is both inspiring and reassuring to see the Cross that was raised over Constantine's army, and over the crusades and pogroms of succeeding centuries, being returned finally to its Gospel meaning of reconciliation.

But despite these genuine achievements and the resurrection of the non-violent Cross, the Council has not seen fit to divorce the Cross completely from the sword. *The Church in the Modern World* maintains a government's right to a military defense in the nuclear age:

As long as the danger of war remains and there is no competent and sufficiently powerful authority at the international level, governments cannot be denied the right to legitimate defense once every means of peaceful settlement has been exhausted.[25]

The question of whether a military rather than a non-violent defense can long remain "legitimate" for a modern nation, and will not become instead that total war which "merits unequivocal and unhesitating condemnation," is a question left open by the Council. It does point out that "through a certain inexorable chain of events" modern warfare can catapult men into the most atrocious decisions. [26] But the Constitution does not draw the conclusion from this fact which Cardinal Alfrink, for example, did in a post-conciliar address to the international board of Pax Christi: that in the world of today there is a natural incompatibility between the Gospel and war. Nor does it more than hint at the more basic conclusion still, which a deepening awareness of

Scripture is forcing the Church at large to consider: that there is an incompatibility between the Gospel *as such* and war.

The most frequently cited failure of the Council's statement, however, is its omission of an explicit condemnation of the total-war deterrent. In fact not only did the September 1965 draft of the Schema not follow Bishop Taylor's recommendation for such a condemnation but it actually sanctioned the deterrent. At that stage the text had included the statement: "As long as international institutions give no adequate guarantee of peace, the possession of these armaments, exclusively as a deterrent for an enemy equipped with the same weapons, cannot be said to be in itself illegitimate." [27]

It is this clause upholding the nuclear deterrent which was so vigorously challenged in the fourth session debate by the English Bishops Wheeler and Grant, who had earlier supported the Taylor proposals, and by Abbot Butler of Downside (now Auxiliary Bishop of Westminster). Of the three critics, Bishop Grant posed most sharply the moral question raised by the draft:

It seems that our schema condemns as a crime against God and man himself the destruction of entire cities with their inhabitants; and at the same time to condone the balance of terror, and especially it appears to condone the intention to use present-day arms in the last resort. . . . If, however, we declare such use to be a crime against God and man, then according to the rules of Moral Theology in which we were all born and brought up, it follows that all intention to commit such a crime, whatever may be its purpose, whatever may be the provocation, is in itself illegitimate.[28]

Although as a result of such criticism the final text of the Constitution has dropped the sanctioning clause, neither does it contain a declaration on deterrence corresponding to the one on total war. It does indict the deterrent strongly for secondary reasons: "The arms race is an utterly treacherous trap for humanity, and one which ensnares the poor to an intolerable degree." [29] But regarding the central question of the relation between the deterrent and the intention to do what the Council has already condemned as "a crime against God and man himself," the Constitution is silent.

Some critics of the Council's statement have construed this silence as itself a sanction of the deterrent, regardless of the removal of the explicitly justifying clause. Robert Tucker has argued, for example, that "the substance of this position is that the means that may never be employed and the evil that may never be done may nevertheless be threatened." [30] Paul Ramsey has agreed "that in its analysis of deterrence and the morality of deterrence the Council leaves standing the assumption that we may intend to do evil that good may come." [31] Ramsey adds immediately in defense of the Council that "in the matter of the actual conduct of war the Council has clearly declared . . . that the nations ought never, in the actual prosecution of war itself, to do evil that good may come." But if it is true that the Council accepts the notion that we may *intend to do* that "crime against God and man himself" which we may never *actually carry out,* it can hardly be denied that the total-war condemnation has been emasculated by the condoning of what constitutes the essence of the crime, namely the intention to do it and the preparation for it. Whatever contribution the Constitution might have otherwise made toward peace would be dissipated by an acceptance, implicit or not, of the intention to commit the crime it claims to have rejected.

In order to understand more deeply the thinking which went into the final draft of this statement, it is helpful to consider the contribution of one Council Father in particular, the then Abbot Christopher Butler. After the Council's third session, Abbot Butler was a key member of the subcommission which revised the section of the Schema dealing with war and peace. The term "key member" is chosen deliberately because it was Abbot Butler who not only formulated much of the thinking which went into the relevant section of the Constitution but who more than any other member of this commission, and perhaps any other conciliar commission, opened himself to the views and criticisms of others. Abbot Butler told one critic of the Schema: "On the question of peace you have to be very patient with us. We have had to come a long way in a short time." [32] The profound strength and humility behind these words can be witnessed to by those who saw their speaker struggling constantly toward new insights on an issue concerning the gravity of which he had no doubt. But if Abbot Butler was always a man of peace, he was equally a man of truth, and he demanded that the truth of peace be shown to him at every step by the Schema's critics.

In September 1965, at the beginning of the fourth session, an exchange of letters took place between Abbot Butler and this writer which I feel are significant enough for the light they throw on the final Constitution to be quoted here at length. In response to an essay on the Schema which I had sent him, Abbot Butler commented in his letter on the specific content of the Schema's section on peace as it stood on the eve of the Council's debate:

As it stands, it does not condemn any sort of weapons in se. It does, however, impressively and in grave language, reiterate the Christian teaching that "indiscriminate acts of war" are immoral, and points out that, while this is true in general, it is particularly relevant when thinking of "atomic weapons." It insists that new, more ample efforts, be made (to avoid such war), and that no nation has the right to make the destruction of another enemy its aim. It points out that the "balance of terror" is something "omnino deforme," and that the expense of modern armaments could be better used to help the needy. It says that the situation created by this balance of terror is very precarious, and that the best that can be said for it is that it gives us a short time in which to settle our disputes in a way worthy of man.

It condemns the "free use of modern weapons," and says that the tendency must be towards their suppression.

But it does not say that the possession of such arms "simply for deterrent purposes," is in se illicit—indeed, as the text stands, it says that it cannot be called illicit.

And here is a point on which I disagree with you. You argue that the present deterrent involves a hypothetical intention to resort to this (immoral) use of such arms. I deny that the deterrent *necessarily* involves such a (hypothetical) intention. It *can* co-exist with the mere intention to deter the adversary. There is a moral difference, I hold, between the "ruse de guerre" of pointing your revolver at your enemy's innocent wife, and the actual intention to shoot her. I would add that, in my view, it is not the task of the Council to judge of the interior intentions of President Johnson and his Russian opposite number(s).[33]

My reply to Abbot Butler's defense of the sanctioning clause argued as follows:

As you point out, there is a serious point at issue where the text goes on to assert that "the possession of these armaments, exclusively as a deterrent for an enemy equipped with the same weapons, cannot be said to be in itself illegitimate." I do think, however, that there is a significant difference between my argument on this point and your representation of it, so that a condemnation of total war in execution can indeed be held to involve as well a moral repudiation of the "balance of terror."

Both you and the Schema link the notion of deterrence, "solum ad deterrendum adversarium," with that of "the *possession* of these armaments." With regard to those terms and specifically "possession," I would agree that you are quite right in denying that deterrence *necessarily* involves an intention to resort to the immoral use of such arms. "Possession" is comprehensive enough to avoid being identified with the intention of immoral use. But it is also too comprehensive to meet truly the moral question at issue, which is not the "possession of these armaments" for the purpose of deterrence, but rather their "preparation for total war" for the purpose of deterrence.

My point is that a nation's public threat of the methods of total war, *as manifested in their preparation for ready execution,* does involve a conditional (if "provoked"; if "attacked"; if "driven to it") intention to wage total war—and in fact could involve no less from the standpoint of public policy and of the government's, the military's, and the citizens' corporate responsibility for such a "preparation for total war." This is not a question of a single moral agent pointing a revolver at the enemy's innocent wife (knowing that he will not in fact pull the trigger) but rather of a mass of government officials, military personnel, and a nation's ordinary but (in varying degrees) responsible citizens called on in advance to support such a public policy, with the publicly manifested intention of pulling the trigger "if necessary." These moral agents are all necessary to support and prepare the enormous machinery involved in a nation's threatening total war as a deterrent. But these responsible agents could nevertheless only judge such a policy on its public evidence as grossly immoral in the manifest intention to execute total war "if necessary." If it is held that such an intention is not made manifest in public policy, then we are no longer even considering a total-war "deterrent," because no enemy can be deterred by an unknown threat—the intention to execute the threat must be manifest, in public policy and in the "preparation for total war," for it to succeed in deterring. . . .

There is no need, or even point, in judging the inner intentions of government leaders on a question of public policy. Deterrence as a public policy demands the manifest intention of a nation to do finally what it threatens to do. Nor would such a statement as is here being suggested involve a judgment on any political leaders. It would simply extend the condemnation of total war to *a total-war deterrent,* defined in terms of a "preparation for total war"—without judging whether any particular deterrent is of a total-war character.

But to define "deterrence," as the present text of the Schema does, in so comprehensive a way ("the possession of these arms") as to avoid the issue of *a total-war deterrent* ("the preparation for total war") is both to interrupt the flow of the text from the principles already laid down in section 98 on total war, and to fail to meet the actual moral problem (again not "possession" but "preparation"). Hence, to put a more precise statement in a single sentence: "A nation's public threat of the methods of total war, as manifested in their preparation for ready execution, must be condemned equally with the act of execution, inasmuch as citizens called on in advance to support such a policy could only judge it on its public evidence as grossly immoral in intention." [34]

In the subsequent conciliar debate on the Schema, Abbot Butler took the unusual step of criticizing the section in which he had been one of the principal drafters and over the revision of which he continued to have authority. The statement he made to the Council concerning the clause sanctioning the deterrent was as follows:

According to our text, so long as international organizations are inadequate for peace-keeping purposes, it cannot be said to be, in itself, illegitimate to possess "modern arms" for the sole purpose of deterring an adversary similarly equipped. I suggest that this passage be omitted from the document. No one thinks that the great powers merely *possess* such arms. The fact is that, on both sides of the Curtain, there is a system of preparation for the use of these arms—and for their illegitimate use in indiscriminate warfare. It might be said: If we think such preparation is legitimate, we had better say so openly, and not hide behind a reference to the mere possession of the arms.

But then should we not have to go on to say clearly that not only would it be illegitimate to put such preparations into effect in actual war, but the very intention so to use them, even a "conditional intention," would be gravely immoral? This is so, whether we are speaking of the intentions of the heads of state, or of those of their subordinates and the general population.

It would be an awkward question whether such preparations are conceivable without an at least conditional intention of using the nuclear weapon. We should do well to avoid such questions. We should not speak about the possession of nuclear arms, because the question is unrealistic; and we should also not speak about the legitimacy of preparations for nuclear war. It is obvious enough that the intention of waging war unjustly is itself unjust.[35]

Several points are of particular importance in the position Abbot Butler took in his speech and presumably brought to bear on the Constitution in his further contributions to the final text. The first is that in arguing for the omission of the sanctioning clause he identifies the deterrent not with the possession of massive weapons, as does the Schema, but with their preparation for indiscriminate warfare. "Possession" is therefore beside the point and its use in the Schema to describe innocuously the deterrent, thereby giving grounds for sanctioning it, should be dropped.

Secondly, Abbot Butler is clear in identifying the immorality of an act of indiscriminate warfare with its conditional intention. Execution and conditional intention are both immoral. "This is so, whether we are speaking of the intentions of the heads of state, or of those of their subordinates and the general population."

Abbot Butler does not, however, go on to adopt the position that the preparation for indiscriminate warfare itself necessarily involves the conditional intention to carry out such preparations. He simply says that "it would be an awkward question" to decide. Apparently he continues to see this point as involving to some extent elements on which the Council can make no competent judgment, namely "the interior intentions of President Johnson and his Russian opposite number(s)."

His final position therefore lies between a sanctioning of the deterrent, which he rejects because it would be based on a wrongly innocuous characterization of the deterrent as possession only, and a condemnation of it, which he is drawn toward but cannot accept finally because of a continuing inability to see a necessary logical connection between that preparation for total war which does characterize the deterrent and the actual intention to carry it through. Abbot Butler expresses his certainty, however, on the immorality of a conditional intention to wage total war. His only question, and one he apparently found insoluble, is whether or not the preparation can be proven to involve necessarily such an intention. That final link in the argument was never made in his mind, and as a result, his final position on the Schema was that it should remain silent both on the possession of nuclear arms, which was irrelevant, and on the legitimacy of their preparation for nuclear war, which was not clear to him. He did not feel that silence at these points was an evasion of any kind because the essence of the strictly moral position taken was clear, whatever the facts concerning actually existent deterrents: "It is obvious enough that the intention of waging war unjustly is itself unjust." It was the Council's task to set down the relevant norms on the question, and the individual Christian's task to apply them in his specific political context. To Abbot Butler a condemnation of the deterrent seemed to enter too deeply into the contingency of political fact to be able to retain the general strength of a norm.

In the conclusion of his speech Abbot Butler returns to this point in a way which illuminates both his clarity and his uncertainty:

The weapons of the gospel are not nuclear but spiritual; it wins its victories not by war but by suffering. Let us indeed show all sympathy for statesmen in their immense difficulties; let us gratefully acknowledge their good intentions. But let us add a word of reminder that good ends do not justify immoral means; nor do they justify even a conditional intention of meeting immoral attack with immoral defense. *Our help is in the name of the Lord, who made heaven and earth.*[36] (Italics in original.)

Abbot Butler will not have the Council make negative judgments on the actual intentions of statesmen, which he sees as being involved in any normative condemnation of deterrence. But neither will he grant to statesmen the right to "even a conditional intention" to an immoral defense, which intention he identifies with the act of execution condemned in the Council's declaration. The conditional intention to wage total war, he feels, is obviously murderous and covered in theory by the declaration; the actual intentions of statesmen are too contingent and obscure to allow the concept of deterrence to be drawn into a formal condemnation.

The importance of the Butler position, and the reason for this extended exegesis of it, lies in the fact that it is duplicated in the final text of the *Pastoral Constitution on the Church in the Modern World*. First of all, the clause sanctioning the deterrent has been omitted from the text. The recommendation that it be omitted was not made by Butler alone but by Grant, Wheeler, and other Council Fathers as well. Some of these Fathers recommended, however, that the Council go on to condemn the notion of deterrence in terms of its preparation and manifest intention for total war.[37] In fact Cardinal Joseph Ritter, in what is both his most remarkable and his least-known statement at the Council, asked that the very *possession* of total-war arms be clearly condemned.

Cardinal Ritter made his statement in a written intervention submitted during the fourth session. Some of the biggest questions in Rome during the final session arose from Cardinal Ritter's prolonged deliberation over whether or not to present this particular intervention on the Council floor or in writing. After the intervention had been prepared, the question of its mode of presentation was debated at length by different theological advisors to the Cardinal. Cardinal Ritter finally submitted the intervention in writing, preferring not to speak, according to one report, because he feared provoking a scandalous opposition from some of the more nationalistic American bishops. The most significant passages of the Ritter intervention dealt with the draft statement's clause upholding the nuclear deterrent in terms of "possession." In view of their importance and little-known character, they deserve to be quoted here in full:

My dear brothers! The possession of those arms which actually constitute the "balance of terror," even those which are aimed exclusively at deterring an adversary, already involve the intention—conditional perhaps but effective—of using those arms: for possession without any intention of use would deter no one, would effect nothing. From the very nature of these arms, their enormous quantity and distribution, it can be seen what kind and how great a destruction is already projected. How then are we able to condemn every intention of destroying cities and at the same time at least in part approve the balance of terror?

What therefore should be done?

First: it is impossible to be silent in this matter. We have already promised the world the result of our deliberation.

Second: We must genuinely deliberate in order to produce some result. But we must deliberate, we must debate about actual situations and conditions. What must be said about the morality of possession of those arms which actually exist, which constitute the very problem of the balance of terror, and what do we believe about those weapons which are already prepared for use?

We must admit that the present situation involves some elements which are good in themselves. Nations have accumulated arms with a primary intention not of waging but of avoiding war; at the same time national leaders are examining various plans for eliminating arms; and finally as long as international institutions are not able to guarantee peace satisfactorily and mutual trust among nations is lacking, other means of defense must seem inadequate. Nevertheless, in my judgment, the possession of arms which we must now consider should be condemned as wrong because it already includes the intention of total war and apart from that intention constitutes its very danger.

I believe, therefore, that there should be an absolute condemnation of the possession of arms which involve the intention or the grave peril of total war. After a careful consideration of the concrete situation, I believe there should be a clear and distinct declaration that the moral law requires that all urgently and without delay collaborate in the elimination of the possession of such armaments, no matter how great the difficulties are which are feared and must be overcome.

As is evident, I propose this almost unwillingly. I would willingly listen to and consider contrary arguments. But the demands of sincerity urge that we struggle with reality. We have already said much about the renewal of the Church, about manifesting Christ more clearly to men and rendering the witness of our faith. "Now is the acceptable time" as it seems to me, "now is the day of salvation." Setting other considerations aside, we must become "true preachers of the faith of things to be hoped for—unhesitatingly joining our profession of faith to a life springing from faith" (Constitution on the Church, n. 35).

Joseph Cardinal Ritter [38]

These words, published posthumously, stand as a fitting memorial to one of the greatest Christians of our time. One's only regret is that they were never spoken, as originally intended, in St. Peter's before two thousand other Council Fathers, thus making their full impact on the Council and the Church as a whole rather than only on the members of a conciliar subcommission which finally decided against them.

For although the clause upholding the deterrent was deleted (as many Fathers recommended), the final Constitution rather than making "an absolute condemnation of the possession of arms which involve the intention or the grave peril of total war" (as Cardinal Ritter recommended) is silent on the morality of deterrence. Moreover, at the precise point in the text where such a judgment would be appropriate—in section 81 immediately following the condemnation of total war and after an opening paragraph introducing the question of deterrence—this peculiar statement is made:

Whatever be the facts about this method of deterrence, men should be convinced that the arms race in which an already considerable number of countries are engaged is not a safe way to preserve a steady peace, nor is the so-called balance resulting from this race a sure and authentic peace.[39]

How can the Council disavow any knowledge of "the facts about this method of deterrence," yet go on in the same sentence to declare that "men should be convinced that the arms race . . . is not a safe way to preserve a steady peace"? Robert Tucker has expressed the critic's bewilderment at so apparent a contradiction between an abstention from fact and an appeal to it:

Why should men be so convinced, whatever be the facts? Again, the

Council implies that "this method of deterrence" prevents war while aggravating the causes of war, that deterrence both lessens and increases the dangers of war . . . how can the Council know all this without also knowing the facts about "this method of deterrence"? [40]

What is the further reason for the immediate shifting of focus from the concept of deterrence, with its overriding moral question relative to total war, to the arms race, which while essential to deterrence raises only secondary moral questions?

The only answer which can prevent our reading the statement as an absurd contradiction and which would at the same time explain the text's quick shift in focus is that by "the facts about this method of deterrence" the writers of the text had in mind a special brand of facts whose nature and obscurity rendered the Council incompetent to pronounce a moral judgment on deterrence itself, yet without disabling it with regard to the arms-race judgments immediately following. The concluding statement on the arms race is in fact so strong as to constitute a de facto repudiation of deterrence: "The arms race is an utterly treacherous trap for humanity, and one which ensnares the poor to an intolerable degree." [41]

What "facts about this method of deterrence" are too obscure to permit a direct moral pronouncement on deterrence, yet do not impede a second-hand rejection of it through the arms race? What facts if not "the interior intentions of President Johnson and his Russian opposite number(s)" which Abbot Butler regarded as essential to the moral question of deterrence and at the same time beyond the competence of the Council? On the other hand, the objective character of the arms race need leave no critical observer in doubt as to its eventual outcome if continued, quite apart from the immediate intentions of any of its participants.

In short, the Constitution reflects the Butler position by going as far as it can toward a normative rejection of modern war and deterrence based on their objective moral character. It stops short of condemning deterrence, except obliquely through the arms race, because the intentional factor was here felt to have become so central as to involve directly the attitudes of practicing states-

men. There is no suggestion, however, that statesmen have thereby
been granted immunity to commit or to intend to commit the
"crime against God and man" which the Council states "merits
unequivocal and unhesitating condemnation." On the contrary,
the total-war condemnation which is at the center of the Council's
statement on war and peace so establishes the character and tone
of what follows that "government officials and military leaders"
are reminded pointedly and at various places in the text "to give
unremitting thought to their tremendous responsibility before
God and the entire human race." [42] The Constitution affirms with
Butler that "support should be given to the good will of the very
many leaders who work hard to do away with war, which they
abominate." [43] But again the final emphasis is not on the evident
good will of certain leaders but on the enormity of their responsibility before God and man:

Today [the work of building peace] certainly demands that they extend their thoughts and their spirit beyond the confines of their own
nation, that they put aside national selfishness and ambition to dominate other nations, and that they nourish a profound reverence for
the whole of humanity, which is already making its way so laboriously
toward greater unity.[44]

The text is also careful to underline the positive responsibility
of each individual, leader or not, in this task and his corresponding obligation to disobey any orders commanding actions contrary to "universal natural law and its all-embracing principles." [45]

There is no foundation in the Constitution for the opinion that
man may intend to do the crime he may never actually do.
Cardinal Ritter in his written intervention thought the text's
central declaration had already outlawed the intention of total
war equally with its execution:

Quite rightly the document proceeds to condemn total war both in
execution and intention—and it does so absolutely, making no distinction between atomic warfare and conventional warfare. For every
action which is aimed at or accomplishes the destruction of whole
cities with their inhabitants "is of itself objectively a crime before God

and man himself which must be condemned forthrightly and without delay" (n. 98). This condemnation must be pronounced so clearly and distinctly that no one will be able to hide or twist its meaning! [46]

Cardinal Ritter's emphatic recommendation that the statement be so clear as to prevent any distortion whatsoever stands out ironically today in view of critics' denial of the very meaning he himself attached to the statement.

We have already seen that Bishop Butler, one of the principal authors and revisers of the text, also felt that the intention to wage total war was in fact already condemned by the Constitution: "It is obvious enough that the intention of waging war unjustly is itself unjust." It must be kept in mind that this interpretation of the total-war condemnation by Council Fathers who were as prominent as anyone in guiding it to its conclusion was made *before the final debate on it and the Council's subsequent adoption of the condemnation in the form they had so interpreted.* For later critics to interpret the same text *after the Council* in an opposite sense is to fail to observe the primary canon of the exegete, namely, to seek critically the intentions of the authors in the context in which they wrote. The factor which makes this failure more understandable is that none of these critics possessed the background and information on the Council we have presented here. But even a straight reading of the text, apart from its sources, should have obviated any such misinterpretation.

The wording of the Council's declaration is precise: "Any act of war *aimed indiscriminately* at the destruction of entire cities or extensive areas. . . ." (Italics added.) In interpreting this text, most commentators have drawn their controlling emphasis from the term "act of war" and have virtually ignored the qualifier "aimed indiscriminately." It has usually been simply assumed that by "act of war" the declaration meant the immediate execution of such an act, and that by "aimed indiscriminately" it *must therefore mean* the simultaneous targeting implicit in the act.

But the text itself gives grounds for a more comprehensive understanding of the act being condemned if the qualifier, "aimed indiscriminately," is given a weight and meaning proper to itself as it is in Cardinal Ritter's interpretation—"every action which is *aimed at or accomplishes* the destruction of whole cities with their inhabitants." (Italics added.) It is clear on reflection that the indiscriminate aiming designates the intention of the agents involved, and that this intention need not be—in fact, if one is true to the act being described, should not be—confined to an intention simultaneous with the actual execution of the "act of war." For it is well known that the indiscriminate aiming of thermonuclear missiles has now been in effect for years in the hardened underground silos and patrolling submarines which contain the weapons to destroy "entire cities or extensive areas along with their population." Nuclear missiles are not "aimed indiscriminately" as a last-second measure. Their indiscriminate aiming has long been proclaimed publicly as the essence of national defense policies, awaiting only the word of command and the pushing of buttons. The act of war which the Council condemns as a crime against God and man is today "aimed indiscriminately," by both the East and the West, in the form of thousands of already targeted thermonuclear weapons.

In the Council's declaration, the intention to total warfare is explicitly condemned in terms of its "indiscriminate aiming." The notion of deterrence is presumably left separate from the condemnation of this intentionally defined act of war because deterrence was thought to involve the particular intentions of practicing statesmen. If the Constitution is therefore read carefully in the context of the conciliar debate which led up to it, the Council is clearer than its critics on the morally "un-do-able" character of modern war, in both execution and intention.

One is still left nevertheless with the questions raised by a final amendment to the Constitution whose ambiguity seems studied:

Since peace must be born of mutual trust between nations and not be imposed on them through fear of the available weapons, everyone must labor to put an end at last to the arms race, and to make a true beginning of disarmament, *not unilaterally indeed*, but proceeding at

an equal pace according to agreement, and backed up by adequate
and workable safeguards. (Italics added.)[47]

Walter Stein, whose pre-conciliar writing provides a helpful
perspective in evaluating the Council's statement, has charged
that this conclusion

renders the declaration as a whole radically equivocal, hesitating, and
inexorably caught in the chain of thought-forms which precipitated,
and sustain, the nuclear crisis. For, though it is certainly true that
peace can finally be secured only through international agreements,
backed up by true and workable safeguards, is it not also true that
withdrawal from sin is always a unilateral obligation?[48]

But to put this particular amendment in the context of its conciliar development, as we have tried to do with the statement
as a whole, we can do no better than to cite a final letter from
Abbot Butler. The letter was addressed to this writer on December 12, 1965, four days after the closing of the Council, and
is concerned almost entirely with a clarification of the amendment in question. After referring to the NCWC translation of
the Constitution, a copy of which he was sending me, Abbot
Butler wrote:

There is one passage (I have not read the whole translation) where
it may be worth while to have the exact Latin. It is in num. 82, and
relates to bilateral disarmament. The Latin (I cite from memory) is:
"Omnibus elaborandum (or collaborandum) est ut diminutio
armorum re incipiat, non unilateraliter quidem sed pari passu ex
condicto progrediatur. . . ."[49]
You will see that the English says, roughly: "That disarmament
should really begin, not indeed unilaterally but proceeding by equal
steps and by agreement."
If you find that this passage is being used either to exclude unilateralism or to justify the possession of nuclear arms, I offer the following observations:
(1) The passage is an almost-last-minute modification of the previous text. The final discussion of the chapter took place in Joint
Commission on a Saturday evening, at the end of a most gruelling
week, and in great haste. Otherwise, I think this passage would have
come under heavy criticism, or might have done.
(2) Its wording is curious. One would expect the word "et" after
"re incipiat," and before "non unilateraliter quidem."

(3) The NCWC translation does not appear to take account of the fact that "progrediatur" is not a participle but a subjunctive; and it appears to link "non unilateraliter quidem" as a qualification of "re incipiat."

(4) So far as I have been able to determine, the bishop who was chairman of the revising subcommission did not intend to broach the issue of "retention of nuclear arms" or to condemn unilateralism.

(5) I offer the following translation: "That disarmament should really begin, (and) proceed not indeed unilaterally but by equal stages and by agreement." The inserted "and" seems necessary for the meaning of the passage.

(6) If my translation can be accepted, then it could be argued that the summons to a start in disarmament is unqualified and could be met by at least partial unilateral disarmament.

(7) I suggest that the real purpose of the passage is, to point out the urgent desirability of the *most* desirable solution, viz., mutual progressive disarmament.[50]

Abbot Butler's explication of the text is not only decisive in rendering invalid its use to exclude unilateralism, as has already been done on several occasions. It is also valuable in the perspective it adds to the Council statement as a whole, in view of Abbot Butler's anxiety lest the text be used "to justify the possession of nuclear arms." From the standpoint of the subcommission which revised the Council's statement on war and peace, there was clearly no intention to justify anywhere the possession of nuclear arms. It is only later critics and commentators, failing to take into adequate consideration the nuances of the conciliar debate and revision of the text, who have read such meanings into it.

What we must admit in the last analysis is that the Council both succeeded and failed in its statement on war and peace. Its success and its failure must be measured, however, by standards different from those of critics whose interpretations of the text are divorced from the background of the Council or whose own final judgments are drawn from a just-war ethic rather than from the Gospel of Peace. To fail to interpret the text in its conciliar context is inevitably to misread it, as its harshest critics have done. To fail to measure it finally by the Gospel is to grant it an achievement which is illusory in view of the radical witness to peace demanded by Christ Himself.

What the Council succeeds in doing in effect, by way of any rigorous application of its total-war condemnation to current conditions, is to bring down the curtain on the just-war doctrine. All war in our time has been shown to involve "acts aimed indiscriminately at the destruction of entire cities or extensive areas along with their population." Only the aiming of such acts of total war can keep a modern war limited in the context of a world dominated by nuclear powers. The intention to wage total war is therefore at the root of even those defense policies which seem to resemble most a just-war ethic. Moreover, even apart from the major powers' commitments to wage total war "if necessary," every conflict risks escalation into total nuclear war by accident or miscalculation "through a certain inexorable chain of events." To transpose a moral principle traditionally applied to sexual conduct, one can characterize all modern war as a thermonuclear occasion of genocide.[51] Judged by the Council's declaration, modern war itself is a crime against God and man and merits unequivocal and unhesitating condemnation. If we wish to take the Council seriously in its central declaration, in spite of the Council's own evident hesitancy to face that declaration squarely throughout its statement, we must declare the just war dead.

What the Council fails to do in lieu of the death of the just war, or does only slightly and hesitantly, is to reopen that scripturally founded tradition of non-violence which has remained largely unexplored since the early age of the Church but which now has Gandhi's, Dolci's, and King's experiments in truth as proof of its untapped power. As we noted earlier, the Council praises "those who renounce the use of violence" and relates that praise specifically to the cross of Christ. But the Council hardly draws the conclusions from that relationship which would be warranted by a closer investigation of it.

It is significant therefore that, whereas in *Pacem in Terris* Pope John spoke of the settling of disputes by negotiation and reconciliation of differences as "the *only* manner which is worthy of the dignity of man," [52] *The Church in the Modern World* refers to such means as a "manner *more* worthy of man." [53] While Pope John found it hardly possible to imagine that war today could be an instrument of justice,[54] the Johannine Council has been careful to include a paragraph in praise of the military profession as "a genuine contribution to the establishment of peace." [55] Moreover, the non-violent methodology of Pope John's approach, resting on an absolute faith in each person's capacity for truth, is given little stress in the Constitution's section on peace, although it is evident in the document's earlier encouragement of the Christian-Marxist dialogue.

It is not only by the standards of *Pacem in Terris* that the Council can be seen as having fallen short of the witness demanded by Christ. The Council's momentous task on war and peace, as described in its own words, "to undertake an evaluation of war with an entirely new attitude," is precisely where the Council has in the end been able to do no more than look beyond itself. The theology with which the Council began was simply too far removed from the goal it set for itself and yet came close to achieving. The doctrine of the just war is not a fit instrument to measure the meaning of the threat of world destruction. Nor can it prescribe a form of Christian witness and power which can begin to respond to a human crisis of such magnitude. The urgent rhetoric and appeals with which Chapter V is filled, and which give ample evidence of the Fathers' deep concern, are not matched, nor could they be, by norms drawn from the scholastic ethic. The highest point to which that ethic could go in the present crisis is the point which the Council reached: a resounding condemnation of total-war methods in both intention and execution which, as Bishop Hannan sensed correctly, should mean a wholesale withdrawal of Catholic support from every nuclear arsenal in the world. But that point is not high enough, as can indeed be seen by the Council's own failure to draw the explicit conclusions on deterrence and military defense demanded by its norm—a failure small in comparison to American Catholics' support of technological terror in Vietnam and their involvement in thermonuclear genocide. The norm is there but logical objections and national loyalties continue to bury it beneath the priorities of state.

But if it is the Council's just-war theology which blocked the total realization of its purpose, what are we to say of Pope John, whose just-war roots were no different but whose document offers a deeper testimony to peace on earth? Perhaps simply that, unlike 2300 bishops, Pope John knew where to keep silent. Where his theology didn't correspond to his moral sense, as on the absolute injustice of war in the Nuclear Age, Pope John simply offered a suggestive phrase, in the knowledge that men of good will would understand him and in the hope that theologians would follow him. The fact that theologians have not done so, with the kind of intensive reconsideration of war in the light of the Gospel so urgently demanded, is reason enough for the Council's inability to speak the fullness of the Word it felt.[56]

The revolutionary awakening of conscience and transformation of man which the Council saw as necessary, and which Pope Paul pointed to in his United Nations address, demands more of the Church herself than the laying down of an admirable norm whose application is quickly obscured by national loyalties. It will be said, of course, and rightly to some extent, that it is not the role of the teaching Church to make all the concrete applications demanded by her norms. But what is being suggested here is that there is a further norm which would in itself make such obscurity impossible and would bring the full weight of a worldwide Christian conscience to bear on the crisis of man's preservation in time: namely, the direct antagonism between the Gospel of Jesus Christ and the deliberate killing of one's neighbor. The Church's laudable effort to come to terms finally with war, at the point where war has brought man to the edge of global disaster, suggests that the reckoning should have come earlier, at that point where war first challenged the salvific meaning of accepted crucifixion. The threat of thermonuclear war is the end of a long and bloody road. The Church has traveled that road. To bear a powerful witness to peace at the end of it she must be willing to retrace her steps humbly and in penance for the blood of past centuries.

There are suggestions elsewhere in the *Pastoral Constitution on the Church in the Modern World* of the kind of moral imperative which the Council is calling for in its statement on peace without itself fully attaining. In Chapter II of Part I, for example, on "The Community of Mankind," one finds these words:

> Coming down to practical and particularly urgent consequences, this Council lays stress on *reverence for man;* everyone must consider *his every neighbor without exception as another self, taking into account first of all his life.* . . .
> In our times a special obligation binds us to make ourselves the neighbor of *every person without exception,* and of actively helping him when he comes across our path, whether he be an old person abandoned by all, a foreign laborer unjustly looked down upon, a refugee, a child born of an unlawful union and wrongly suffering for a sin he did not commit, or a hungry person who disturbs our conscience by recalling the voice of the Lord, "As long as you did it for one of these the least of my brethren, you did it for me" (Matt. 25:40).[57] (Italics added.)

The deliberate citing of examples to drive home the obligation to love and actively help "every person without exception" leaves one wondering why a more scandalous example could not have been included. If the exceptionless character of Christian love is indisputable, then the advancing enemy soldier merely raises this special obligation anew. If it is suggested that he raises it in a more complicated way, because there are women and children at our sides, then we must begin to recognize the precedents in the Church and in history for the protection of one's own without surrendering our reverence for man's life.

The Constitution returns to this theme on its final page: "Now, the Father wills that in all men we recognize Christ our brother and love Him effectively, in word and in deed."[58] Yet the possibility is left open in Chapter V for the word of battle and the deed of blood.

The prospect of "eschatological war" summons the Church

from a just-war doctrine whose highest word is not high enough to "an evaluation of war with an entirely new attitude." War in our time discloses the inherent powerlessness of matter at its most powerful to resolve the injustices of man's spirit. Thus the dead end of war forces the Christian conscience into a confrontation with the issue of war itself, and into a growing recognition of that gap between the intention of peace and the execution of the sword which in the light of the Gospel reduces the notion of a just war to legalized fratricide. To a Christian the most embarrassing fact about the just-war doctrine, yet one which even saints have glossed over, is its apparent opposition to the cross of Christ, which Gandhi perceived as the essence of non-violence. The sword and the cross have never been easy companions but never have they been so obviously at war with each other as in that century when a nuclear sword has been raised over the world and the cross has been borne by a Hindu for the freedom of man's spirit. What the Christian owes to Gandhi is his unparalleled testimony to the power of the cross.

The revolution of conscience which the Council calls for on war can only begin where the Council ended. If the Church at large goes no further than the Council's conclusions, then not only will she have failed to understand the spirit of the Council but she will have failed man's spirit. Not until the condemnation of total war has become in the Church merely the background for the emerging Gospel mandate for total peace will the revolution of conscience be assured. What the Council said about the primacy and power of conscience will prove to be of far more significance than the total-war condemnation once the Church has gone beyond the tradition which sustains that condemnation. Abbot Butler's concluding words to the Council provide the key to what must be the Church's future teaching on war and peace: "The weapons of the gospel are not nuclear but spiritual; it wins its victories not by war but by suffering. . . . Our help is in the name of the Lord, who made heaven and earth." Or as Cardinal Ritter wrote, " 'Now is the acceptable time' as it seems to me, 'now is the day of salvation.' "

It is true to say finally, then, that the Council has done much more than to bring down the curtain on the just war. It has taken some faltering steps of its own toward an assertion of the power of non-violence, and much more important, it has urged a transformation of man's mind and spirit on war which can be fulfilled only through non-violence. It may happen that such a deepening commitment to non-violence, by believer and non-believer alike, will resemble nothing so much in essence as that community of love described as just born in the Acts of the Apostles and as the dying sign of victory in the Apocalypse.

NOTES

1. Robert McAfee Brown, "A Response to the *Pastoral Constitution on the Church in the Modern World*," *The Documents of Vatican II* (America Press: 1966), edited by Walter M. Abbott, p. 309.
2. *Pastoral Constitution on the Church in the Modern World* (National Catholic Welfare Conference), p. 84. All quotations from the Constitution used here are taken from the NCWC translation.
3. *The Documents of Vatican II*, pp. 712–13.
4. See especially Paul Ramsey, *War and the Christian Conscience* (Duke University Press: 1961), and his later pamphlet, *The Limits of Nuclear War* (The Council on Religion and International Affairs: 1963). Ramsey deals with the question of global suicide in chapter nine of *War and the Christian Conscience*, "The Politics of Fear," but the issue is left there and does not enter significantly into any of his later analyses of the "just nuclear war."
5. John Courtney Murray, "Theology and Modern War," *Morality and Modern Warfare* (Helicon Press: 1960), edited by William J. Nagle, pp. 69–91. Father Murray's essay appeared in a number of publications in somewhat varying forms.
6. *The Church in the Modern World*, p. 87.
7. *Ibid.*
8. *Ibid.*, pp. 87–88.
9. Paul Ramsey, "Tucker's *Bellum Contra Bellum Justum*," a commentary on *Just War and Vatican Council II: A Critique*, by Robert W. Tucker (The Council on Religion and International Affairs: 1966), p. 68.
10. Harry W. Flannery, ed., *Pattern for Peace: Catholic Statements on International Order* (Newman Press: 1962), pp. 236–37.
11. Even Father John Courtney Murray in commenting on Pope Pius' statement argued with the weapons technicians:
    "Around this time (1954) there was a lot of loose and unin-

formed talk about weapons that really would go beyond human control; there was talk, for instance, of the so-called 'cobalt bomb' and its 'unlimited' powers of radioactive contamination. It is impossible to know what were the sources of the pope's scientific information. To my knowledge, he never adverts to the qualitative distinction and radical discontinuity between low-kiloton and high-megaton weapons. The former are not necessarily weapons of mass destruction. Even the latter do not 'escape from the control of man'; their blast and fire effects, and their atmosphere-contamination effects, have been fairly exactly measured." "Theology and Modern War," p. 81, fn. 7.

Murray's position was used to support the argument of a West German theologian that the Pope's statement could be so interpreted as to admit the destruction of the entire world:

"In an article in *Stimmen der Zeit*, G. Gundlach, S.J., throws some light on the meaning of this statement. According to Fr. Gundlach the Pontiff was not speaking of the controllability of the weapons. He was referring rather to the *use* of these weapons. It was not the uncontrollable weapon that he was condemning but the uncontrolled use of such a weapon, that is, a use which would not be aimed at self-defense but annihilation of the enemy. This is more consistent with the information about atomic weapons which Fr. Murray refers to in the note cited above. . . .

"Fr. Gundlach goes on to argue that the cause to be defended can be so important that the right and duty to defend it is conceivable even if the only accomplishment of such a defense were a manifestation of the divine order and majesty. Even should the world be destroyed in the process, it would not affect the morality of the defense. The world is not eternal and there are greater values than the continuation of the world. Moreover, in the event that it should be destroyed in a just defense, it would not be the responsibility of the defender but of the unjust aggressor." John R. Connery, S.J., "Notes on Moral Theology," *Theological Studies*, XX (1959), 608–609.

This kind of theologizing deserves no comment.

12. "Intervention of Bishop Philip M. Hannan on Paragraph 25 of the Schema *De Ecclesia in Mundo Huius Temporis*," November 10, 1964. Distributed at the American Bishops Press Panel.

13. "Critique of Paragraphs on Nuclear Warfare in 'De Pace Firmanda.'" This critique was written by William V. O'Brien of Georgetown University, who said in a covering letter to an American bishop that he had been assisted in the preparation of his comments by Dr. Alain C. Enthoven, Deputy Assistant Secretary of Defense; Dr. Charles M. Herzfeld, Department of Defense; Dr. William J. Nagle, Department of State; Dr. John E. Moriarty, Department of State; Dr. James E. Dougherty, St. Joseph's Col-

lege. Nagle and Moriarty have said since then, however, that the O'Brien paper does not reflect accurately their own views. A confirmation of this lies in the fact that Moriarty wrote to the same American bishop during the fourth session to urge the adoption by the Council of an unequivocal statement condemning total war. I am indebted to both Nagle and Moriarty for their encouragement of my own efforts at the Council and in print.

14. "Speech Given by the Most Reverend George Andrew Beck, Archbishop of Liverpool, in the Discussion on Paragraph 25 of the Schema *De Ecclesia in Mundo Huius Temporis*." Distributed at the American Bishops Press Panel.

15. On November 10, 1964. "The voice of 2,000 Bishops assembled in Council should be able to change the course of history and save the human race from disaster. Absolutely nothing can justify a world-wide cataclysm. If the souls of future generations are to be destroyed, then why is the Church so concerned about developing its pastoral life? National sovereignties must absolutely be subjected to certain limitations. Because the whole human race is watching us, we cannot afford to be silent for any consideration. . . . We should issue a solemn and clear condemnation of all A-B-C warfare. The billions thus saved could be used for the relief of poverty." From a summary of Patriarch Maximos' speech distributed at the American Bishops Press Panel.

16. Bishop Taylor's proposed amendment to the Schema was published in the July-August 1965 issue of *The Catholic Worker* under the title "Whether the Human Family Will Live or Die (Statement by an American Council Father)."

17. *Schema of the Pastoral Constitution, The Church in the World of Today* (Vatican Polyglot Press: 1965), p. 96.

18. The other bishops who signed the letter were Francis Cardinal Spellman, New York; Patrick L. O'Boyle, Washington; Miguel D. Miranda, Mexico; Denis E. Hurley, Durban; Joseph Khoury, Tyr Maronitarum; Lawrence Cardinal Shehan, Baltimore; Guilford Clyde Young, Hobart; Adolfo Servando Tortolo, Parana; Felipe Cueto Gonzalez, Tlalnepantla. Bishop Hannan had also tried to have the Schema amended on the floor of the Council through a number of "modi" which he proposed on November 17, 1965, but these did not receive the support they needed to be incorporated into the Constitution. Bishop Hannan's efforts at an NCWC meeting to get the entire American hierarchy to back his "modi" drew the warning from another bishop that if such a step were taken the American bishops would invite the same kind of critique by future historians as the German Catholic bishops of Hitler's era were then receiving. The "modi" were therefore given the active support of only a few American bishops and were defeated by the Council's vote when they reached the aula of St. Peter's.

19. Archbishop Garrone and Bishop Schroffer commented on the text of the Constitution: *"De textu, prouti post diligentissimum examen nunc iacet, non exsistit diversitas opinionum inter theologos; indiscriminatam enim destructionem, qualis hic intelligitur, nullus theologus catholicus moraliter licitam esse admittit vel admittere potest."*

20. The ambiguity present in the Church's previous stand against total war can be seen in the fact that at the same time as Schema 13 was being debated by the Council Fathers, a doctoral dissertation at the Gregorian University *defending the justness of total warfare in Catholic teaching* had reached its final stage of research and writing. (The dissertation had already been approved by a faculty adviser, had been defended successfully before a committee of Gregorian professors, and its author had completed his studies in Rome and returned to the United States for some final research and writing.) This dissertation was not written by a seminary student but by a professor of philosophy who had already written an ethics textbook widely used in American Catholic colleges and who was making use of a sabbatical to obtain his second doctorate in Rome. His dissertation (which drew much of its documentation from the writings of Herman Kahn) would likely have been published in the United States, thereby giving ecclesiastical sanction to total war in the climate of American public opinion. After the Council's statement defining total war precisely and condemning it as "a crime against God and man himself," the dissertation was dropped.

21. In his third-session intervention. Archbishop Roberts devoted his fourth-session intervention, also in support of conscientious objection, to the case of Franz Jagerstatter. See Gordon Zahn, *In Solitary Witness: The Life and Death of Franz Jagerstatter* (Holt, Rinehart and Winston: 1964).

22. *The Church in the Modern World*, p. 86.

23. *Ibid.*

24. *Ibid.*, p. 85. The inclusion of this reference to non-violence is no doubt a direct result of the tireless lobbying at the Council of Jean and Hildegard Goss-Mayr of the International Fellowship of Reconciliation.

25. *Ibid.*, p. 87.

26. *Ibid.*, p. 88.

27. *Schema of the Pastoral Constitution, The Church in the World of Today*, p. 98.

28. Bishop Grant's intervention was published in the November 1965 issue of *The Catholic Worker*.

29. *The Church in the Modern World*, p. 89.

30. Tucker, *Just War and Vatican Council II*, p. 48.

31. *Ibid.*, p. 71.

32. In an interview with the writer during the fourth session.

33. Abbot Butler to James Douglass, September 18, 1965.
34. James Douglass to Abbot Butler, September 21, 1965.
35. "Christian Citizenship" by the Rt. Rev. Christopher Butler, O.S.B., Abbot of Downside (intervention in the debate on *The Church in the World Today*). *The Catholic Worker* (October 1965), p. 1.
36. *Ibid.*, p. 3.
37. Among these were Archbishop George Flahiff of Winnipeg and Bishop Reginald Delargey of New Zealand, both of whose interventions were submitted in writing and therefore received no publicity.
38. Cardinal Ritter's fourth-session intervention on war and peace (he submitted at least three other written interventions on the same subject earlier in the Council, according to his peritus and secretary, Msgr. Joseph W. Baker) was published shortly after his death, in the diocesan weekly, the *St. Louis Review* (June 23, 1967). It was reprinted in *The Catholic Worker* (July-August 1967), p. 5.
39. *The Church in the Modern World*, p. 88.
40. Tucker, *Just War and Vatican Council II*, pp. 47–48.
41. *The Church in the Modern World*, p. 89.
42. *Ibid.*, p. 88.
43. *Ibid.*, p. 90.
44. *Ibid.*
45. *Ibid.*, p. 86.
46. Ritter intervention, *The Catholic Worker* (July-August 1967), p. 5.
47. *The Church in the Modern World*, p. 89.
48. Walter Stein, *Peace on Earth: The Way Ahead* (London: Sheed & Ward Stagbooks, 1966), p. 14.
49. Abbot Butler's memory of the Latin was correct, with the exception of the one word he felt uncertain about and whose correct variant does not change the text's meaning. The Latin text reads: "*omnibus adlaborandum est ut diminutio armorum re incipiat, non unilateraliter quidem sed pari passu ex condicto progrediatur. . . ."* Schema Constitutionis Pastoralis De Ecclesia in Mundo Huius Temporis: Textus et Correctiones Admissae Necnon Expensio Modorum (Partis Primae) (Typis Polyglottis Vaticanis: MCMLXV), p. 77.
50. Abbot Butler to James Douglass, December 12, 1965.
51. For a documentation of these theses in terms of current American defense policies, see my two articles: "Modern War and the Just War" (*worldview*, September 1963); "The Morality of Thermonuclear Deterrence" (*worldview*, October 1964).
52. Pope John XXIII, *Pacem in Terris* (Vatican Polyglot Press: 1963), p. 25.
53. *The Church in the Modern World*, p. 89.
54. Pope John XXIII, *Pacem in Terris*, p. 32.

55. *The Church in the Modern World*, p. 87.
56. Where John wrote, "It is hardly possible to imagine that in the atomic era war could be used as an instrument of justice" (a direct translation from the original Italian and as given in the Vatican Polyglot translation of the encyclical), the just-war theologians have invariably imposed a minimal and legalistic interpretation which would have the Pope referring exclusively to a war of aggression (thus leaving open the possibility of a nuclear war of defense, according to this logic). How this interpretation can be brought into harmony with the mind of Pope John as revealed in the whole of *Pacem in Terris* or in any of his public pronouncements on peace (where he never once justified any kind of war) has never been explained nor even suggested. Such an interpretation clashes besides with the immediate context of the statement, where the Pope has just finished referring at length to "the immense suffering which the use of those armaments would bring to the human family." Is it reasonable to suppose that Pope John would then make a tentative statement about war in the atomic era which is in fact reducible to a legal category defined by Pope Pius XII in 1944 (when he first outlawed the war of aggression regardless of justifying causes)? *The Church in the Modern World* footnotes its moral imperative "to undertake an evaluation of war with an entirely new attitude" with precisely this statement by Pope John, which again is no new attitude if it does no more (as Paul Ramsey and others have claimed) than refer back to Pius in the early forties.

A more general (and contrary) way of ignoring Pope John's initiative has been to dismiss him *because he made no legal pronouncements* in the tradition of Pius XII. Thus in a book titled *Peace and Modern War in the Judgment of the Church* (Newman Press: 1966), Dr. Karl Hormann grants to *Pacem in Terris* a commentary of one sentence: "In this Encyclical the Pope instructs all the faithful as well as all people of good will that they abide by the principles of peace in a world-wide domain" (p. 7). The remainder of his exposition is devoted to the "more effective" teaching of Pius XII. Dr. Hormann writes: "No doubt his successor, Pope John XXIII, was not less interested in peace; however, he exercised his vigorous love for it in a different way, namely, by simple exhortations . . ." (pp. v–vi).

57. *The Church in the Modern World*, p. 25.
58. *Ibid.*, p. 100.

6

André Schwarz-Bart and Vatican II

THE QUESTION OF peace is larger than war and peace, and the question of conscience greater than conscientious objection. It was not only on the subject of nuclear war that the Second Vatican Council was presented with an enormous mandate of conscience for the attainment of peace in the modern world. The prospect of thermonuclear genocide and the Vatican Council's struggle to return to a Gospel of Peace are deeply related to another question of conscience: the Church's role in that crime of genocide which is not a threat, but a fact.

There is only one perspective in which to consider the Council's treatment of the relations between Christians and Jews, and that is the perspective of a past that extends into ghettos, box cars, and gas chambers. It is impossible for a Christian to speak of these things with the kind of feeling demanded, for the Christian is not only outside the tradition of suffering that has borne them, but he stands within the tradition that inflicted them. The best the Christian can hope to do is to learn through eyes that have seen them, and through a heart that has felt them. In this respect, there is no more important experience for a Christian than a reading of André Schwarz-Bart's *The Last of the Just*.[1] It is within the perspective of *The Last of the Just* that the Vatican

Council's treatment of the relations between Christians and Jews can be seen in terms of the burden of conscience put upon the Church.

Yet how does one respond to *The Last of the Just*? What word is there that can be spoken without a sense of the futility of words themselves? What kind of analysis of this book is not itself a kind of blasphemy? Because there are certain sights and sounds, experiences and dreams, and certain revelations of the immensity of evil and of love in men's lives which are not subject to analysis, and which serve us best only to the extent that we can manage to serve them. *The Last of the Just* belongs to that category of experiences—for "experience" describes it better than "book"—which draw us so deeply into the possibilities of human existence, in two diametrically opposed directions, that for a few moments we know, because we feel, the terror and the beauty of this earth as it is shaped by men. Such an experience acts on one with the power of darkness and of light, blacking out all the slogans of self-assurance which mask the evil in oneself, yet in the midst of this terrible night which is man, exposing a tiny core of such intense light that we can begin, even in that profound darkness, to believe again—or perhaps to believe for the first time. For it is only such a belief, suffered in darkness with one's eye on the core of light, which can truly bring life.

How, in particular, does a Christian respond to *The Last of the Just*? Does not the overwhelming shame and anguish rising in him make silence the best response—not the silence of indifference and inhumanity which made the writing of such a book necessary, but the silence of a recognition which shatters speech because it shatters the self, the recognition of oneself and one's Church as the guilty?

"I am so weary that my pen can no longer write," wrote André Schwarz-Bart as he neared the end of Ernie Levy's story at the edge of the gas chamber. He quotes: "Man, strip off thy garments, cover thy head with ashes, run into the streets and dance in thy madness. . . ." But for even the scene that followed, the failure of words was overcome, and we are blessed with the beauty of that final page with its incredible litany, a drop of pity, and a presence. One has to speak.

What, then, does a Christian learn from *The Last of the Just*?

He learns, first of all, what it has meant for Jews to live in a Christian universe, beginning in Schwarz-Bart's account with that day in the year 1185 when Rabbi Yom Tov Levy and several Jewish families were driven by a most Christian mob, inspired by its bishop, into an abandoned tower in York, and were there offered the mercy of conversion for six successive days. After which, to the scandal of the Benedictine chronicler, the Jews took themselves, at the point of the rabbi's knife, to God rather than to the Church that beckoned.

The Christian begins to see and to feel, through Schwarz-Bart, what it has meant to live *in* the world of Christendom, but not of it. The reader is confronted at every page in *The Last of the Just* by a Christian world, by a Western world which has been molded, nourished, and sustained by Christian institutions. But he is made to see and feel this world no longer from the inside, his side, where King Louis is a saint, but from the outside, Rabbi Solomon Levy's, for whom King Louis is the Inquisition.

It is a profoundly disturbing experience to discover the seeds of Nazi Germany in a venerated past. "Our eyes register the light of dead stars," says Schwarz-Bart, and the roots of Ernie Levy's agony are clearly discernible not in the age of Hitler, where Christians conveniently isolate anti-Semitism, but in that of Aquinas, and even earlier, as early as Christians designated Jews as God's outcast people. *The Last of the Just* begins therefore with the shock of the continuum between "the thirteenth, greatest of centuries," as a once-popular Catholic book put it, and certain strains of the fascism of the thirties. This is not to suggest that St. Thomas Aquinas was a fascist, nor Adolf Hitler a scholastic. They would have had little sympathy for each other. But in keeping with his time Aquinas was one of many willing to tolerate and encourage, on theological grounds, the kind of anti-Semitic premise which Hitler drove, centuries later, to a terrifying conclusion. To deny this is to do no particular justice to St. Thomas, who, as all men do, labored within the limitations of his tradition and would doubtless have repudiated that aspect of his doctrine long before the Vatican Council did.[2] Still, it is a new kind of revelation given the Christian as he follows the concrete pilgrimage of the Levy family through their Christian universe, and witnesses the inversion, in their eyes and in reality, of symbols he draws on as life-giving. To Ernie Levy, at the end of this pilgrimage, the Christian universe and the Nazis' world are the same. While a Christian of any real faith must believe that they are in fact contradictory, he would do well to recognize the hate-building history which made such an identification quite natural to someone in Ernie Levy's phase of the process.

If a Christian learns from Schwarz-Bart what his world has meant to those crushed by it, he also learns in depth the violence which has characterized Christendom in itself. There is a strong polarity in *The Last of the Just* between suffering and violence. From the patience and suffering of the Jews the Christian reader is thrown back on the extraordinary violence of his own tradition. Christians have been fighting wars and conducting pogroms and inquisitions, all in the name of God and justice, since the time of St. Augustine, but perhaps never has the antinomy between the Gospel of Peace and Christian action been revealed so poignantly as it is in several passages from *The Last of the Just*.

There are two in particular. The first concerns the Rabbi Solomon Levy who was called before St. Louis, King of France, in the year 1240. According to custom, the rabbi was to be questioned concerning the divinity of Jesus to determine the precise nature of the torture to which he would be subjected. It is said that, slender and slight in his black gown, the rabbi stepped irresolutely before the saintly king's tribunal.

"If it is true," he whispered in a forced tone, "if it is true that the Messiah of which our ancient prophets spoke has already come, how then do you explain the present state of the world?" Then, hemming and hawing in anguish, his voice a thread, "Noble lords, the prophets stated that when the Messiah came sobs and groans would disappear from the world—ah—did they not? That the lion and the lamb would lie down together, that the blind would be healed and that the lame would leap like—stags! And also that all the peoples would break their swords, oh, yes, and beat them into plowshares—ah—would they not?"

And finally smiling sadly at King Louis, "Ah, what would they say, sire, if you were to forget how to wage war?"

How does a Christian explain the present state of the world, and specifically the enormous range of warfare prepared and conducted by Christians under the guise of Christian principles? This is not simply the problem of a theology of history, but it is a profound moral problem in view of the two-thousand-year-old existence of a Gospel of Peace which, in terms of the Church preaching it, has had control over a sizable number of the institutions of the world. But why have Christians *not* forgotten how to wage war? Where has the message of peace fled? Why has it been so necessary to defend what men call Christianity at every step of the way with weapons of a constantly increasing barbarity? If Christians are truly repentant for their deep involvement in the Third Reich's policy of genocide, why then are they today so solidly in support of thermonuclear genocide? What made it so impossible for St. Louis to feel and act on the full power of a question like the Rabbi Solomon Levy's, and perhaps one formed in his own conscience, nurtured as it was by the Gospel? Has the tradition of violence, and of the just war which every warring country claims, arisen in Christianity because the Gospel supports the wars of Christians, or because Christians' wars have been introduced into the Gospel?

A second passage in *The Last of the Just* brings this same question into a tighter theological focus. It occurs when Ernie and Golda have met, found an incredibly beautiful love for each other, and are hours away from deportation by the Nazis:

"Oh, Ernie," Golda said, "you know them. Tell me why, *why* do the Christians hate us the way they do? They seem so nice when I can look at them without my star."

Ernie put his arm around her shoulders solemnly. "It's very mysterious," he murmured in Yiddish. "They don't know exactly why themselves. I've been in their churches and I've read their gospel. Do you know who the Christ was? A simple Jew like your father. A kind of Hasid."

Golda smiled gently. "You're kidding me."

"No, no, believe me, and I'll bet they'd have got along fine, the two of them, because he was really a good Jew, you know, sort of like the Baal Shem Tov—a merciful man, and gentle. The Christians say they love him, but I think they hate him without knowing it. So they take the cross by the other end and make a sword out of it and strike us with it! You understand, Golda," he cried suddenly, strangely excited, *"they take the cross and they turn it around, they turn it around, my God. . . ."*

It is one of the beautiful paradoxes of *The Last of the Just* that in the inhuman Christian world that one meets there, the person of Christ is treated with such reverence by Schwarz-Bart. For, in Ernie Levy's eyes, Jesus Christ is not that Christianity of the sword which has pursued the Jews for centuries. Jesus is a Jew, a simple Jew like Golda's father, a merciful man and gentle. His sign is a cross of suffering love, not its perversion in the sword of violence that Christians have fashioned. And here one meets with a thought whose purity and simplicity cuts straight through centuries of persecution: If Jesus is to be loved, he must be loved as a Jew, not as a Christian. For Christians didn't exist in Jesus' time. The Church's persecution of Jesus' own people has rested on a denial of his humanity.

Thus in Ernie Levy's death camp, a Catholic infirmary attendant of vaguely Jewish ancestry is profoundly right in the confusion he confesses to Ernie concerning the person of Christ:

"To tell the truth, I don't know any more whether I'm Catholic or not. When I found out a year ago that I was one-eighth Jewish, at first I was very ashamed. It was stronger than I was—I had the feeling that I'd crucified Our Lord, that . . . you understand, don't you? I was still on *the other side*. And then I came here and I began to be ashamed of the part of me that isn't Jewish. Terribly ashamed. I kept thinking of those two thousand years of catechism that prepared . . . the ground . . . that allowed . . . You understand, don't you?" His face was even more open. "Two thousand years of Christology," he said dreamily, as if to himself. "And yet—I know it's absurd but I still believe, and I love the person of the Christ more than ever. Well, except that he's not the blond Christ of the cathedrals any more, the glorious Saviour put to death by the Jews. He's—" Gesturing at the infirmary, he leaned forward above Ernie's suppurating elbow and said, his face altogether open, "He's *something else*," in a suddenly Jewish tone, the miserable tone of a prisoner.

Schwarz-Bart makes the Christian recognize that to love Jesus as a kind of Aryan Christian, and not as the Jew he was, "a merciful man and gentle," is not to love Jesus at all.

But the distance is terribly far from the Jew, Jesus, to the Christ depicted in the children's passion play in which Ernie Levy is beaten for the crime of deicide. There is an agonizing truth, unknown to the speaker, in the cry uttered by the child who knocks down Ernie with a rock: "For Jesus!" And Schwarz-Bart concludes the episode of deicide with the telling words: "It was the year 1933 after the coming of Jesus, the beautiful herald of impossible love."

A Christian, then, can learn from André Schwarz-Bart the beauty and purity of the man, Jesus.

An enormous question is raised in *The Last of the Just*. It is raised again and again, it torments Ernie Levy until the moment of his death, and it torments any man of conscience who can begin to feel in his spirit the life and death of Ernie Levy multiplied 6,000,000 times. It is a question which Schwarz-Bart often poses by way of the sky, an inscrutable sky, unreasonably blue, serene and impenetrable, as row upon row of God's children are taken from the earth. For the young Ernie Levy, schooled by his grandfather in the visible revelation of God's providence, the question is, first of all, an answer. When the crowd of worshiping Jews leaves the synagogue and is confronted in the courtyard by the Nazi troops, Ernie Levy knows the answer before the question, for "Ernie had a staggering intuition—that God was hovering above the synagogue courtyard, vigilant and ready to intervene. . . . Ernie felt that God was there, so close that with a little boldness he might have touched him. 'Stop! Don't touch my people!' he murmured as if the divine voice had found expression in his own frail throat."

But the moment arrives later, with the attack upon him by the Nazi youth before the indifferent gaze of a golden-haired girl, when the answer becomes no answer, for "he knew that nothing would answer his call, for that call was born of nothing: God could not hear it." The total annihilation of a universe of love leaves only the certainty of nothingness: "I was not a Just Man, I was nothing."

Yet the question remains, even if Ernie Levy is too dead in spirit to raise it to a conscious level. Where is the Lord of Creation when creation has given way to annihilation? What hole in the universe has so swallowed God's love that such crimes can occur like clockwork beneath a cloudless, blue sky?

In view of such anguish, what God could pronounce judgment on that other Jewish boy whose vision of the holocaust, like Ernie Levy's, forced the death of his faith?

> Never shall I forget that night, the first night in camp, which has turned my life into one long night, seven times cursed and seven times sealed. Never shall I forget that smoke. Never shall I forget the little faces of the children, whose bodies I saw turned into wreaths of smoke beneath a silent blue sky.
> Never shall I forget those flames which consumed my faith forever.
> Never shall I forget that nocturnal silence which deprived me, for all eternity, of the desire to live. Never shall I forget those moments which murdered my God and my soul and turned my dreams to dust. Never shall I forget these things, even if I am condemned to live as long as God himself. Never.[3]

Who can give the definitive answer to the question of God's presence in the holocaust? A Jew in Ernie's death camp continues to affirm his faith but only through the strength of contradiction: "One of my friends used to tease me by asking if God, in his omnipotence, could create a rock so heavy that he couldn't lift it. Which is my position—I believe in God, and I believe in the rock."

André Schwarz-Bart does not pretend to know the answer to the question of God and the rock. But he raises a parallel question about man.

When the Jews were helpless before the Nazis in the courtyard, an unhoped-for event occurred: windows above opened and the heads of men, women, and children appeared, heads whose eyes refused to be averted from whatever crime was to be committed by the Nazis. Driven by those eyes back into a shamed sense of humanity, the Nazis began to retreat from the Jews. In that brief pause, the blue sky responded with the heads of men.

But a question occurs to the grandfather, Mordecai: "What will happen, my God, on the day when German windows no longer open upon Jewish suffering?" Perhaps the answer which history has given to that question—that when men's eyes were averted, inhumanity struck with the full power of darkness—is a kind of response, too, to the mystery of an untroubled sky. For God acts through men, and when men retreat behind closed shutters, or sit in silence behind the walls of a privileged Church, then God has no voice to speak with or hands to act with. The sky above Jewish suffering was blue and empty because the windows of the world, and of the Church, were shuttered.

To raise such questions as these is to come finally to the words of Mordecai in response to his grandson's question on the ultimate meaning of suffering: "That which is far away, that which is profound, profound, who can reach it?"

Yet short of that final mystery of meaning, there are signs which can move men to faith and to a love which resurrects. One such sign is the living testimony of the last of the Just Men, Ernie Levy.

The question of whether Ernie believes finally in a divine solution, in the midst of the most impenetrable darkness, is given no clear answer. Probably he does not, if one is judging in terms of a conscious biblical faith. It is of no matter. His belief cannot be the belief of the mind, in a mindless world. The insanity of such events destroys the last hold of reason on faith. Ernie Levy lives by no secure formulations of God's will and way, but only by the way of the Just Man, surviving through love beneath the suffering of men. The Just Man senses all the evil rampant on earth, and he takes it into his heart. The size of his heart is great enough to hold the world, and thus the world itself continues to live through the love of the Just Man absorbing the suffering of mankind. If the Just Man were lacking, the sufferings of mankind would poison even the souls of the newborn, and humanity would suffocate with a single cry. As Mordecai says, when he sees his grandson crying out against the beating of an old woman and stumbling forward into the shadow of a Nazi uniform, "He is the lamb of suffering; he is our scapegoat." And Mordecai again, to his wife, Judith: "The Lamed-Vovnik takes our suffering upon himself. And he raises it to heaven and sets it at the feet of the Lord—who forgives. Which is why the world goes on . . . in spite of all our sins."

It is at this point that the Christian can learn from André Schwarz-Bart the meaning of that redemptive suffering which, in the Christian's belief, is identified with the person of Jesus.

There is a great power revealed in *The Last of the Just,* a power which confirms the glory of man even at those times when men in general have collaborated in the building of hell. By all appearances it is a modest power, and may excite little religious interest. The miracles it works are not of a sensational nature. But the Just Man possesses it in such abundance that its redemptive character becomes visible, and we know something of what it means for man to have the power of tears.

The power of tears is man's capacity to allow a world of terrible suffering to enter his heart, and there to be transformed through love into a world of growth and beauty. It is his power to assume in his own spirit the awesome weight of sorrow which men inflict on one another, and in taking on their pain, to turn them and himself in the direction of joy. The power of tears is a total openness to life which overcomes death not by hardening oneself to it, but by absorbing its full blow in peace. It is said that when a Just Man smiles at a baby, there is as much suffering in him as in a Just Man undergoing martyrdom. The Just Man, as the man who makes our humanity real, has the power to accept our burdens as his own—and suggests by his life that it may be in our power to accept his.

The power of tears, or the power of suffering love, is man's deepest claim on life. When, under the shock of a Nazi outrage, Ernie Levy seems to lose it at one point, as if "the organs of suffering were abolished in him," he passes into the shadow of death, first by attempting suicide and then by living as a dog. The transition from life to death in the boy Ernie reveals again the polarity between the nihilistic power of violence and the creative power of suffering. For as Ernie becomes numb to the world he had formerly embraced, he staggers about a meadow instinctively crushing insects in his fingers until his hands are gummy with vermin. For a moment he joins the rebellion against creation expressed earlier in the novel by another anguished spirit: "I say it and I proclaim it—in this world of iron the sword is the best answer to the sword!" With the organs of suffering abolished, the will to annihilate takes over. Love is by nature non-violent, because love suffers away man's evil.

These are some of the truths which a Christian can learn from André Schwarz-Bart. And it can be put more strongly: These are the truths which a Christian *must* learn from Schwarz-Bart if his own Christian faith is to live, and not die amidst diseased misapprehensions and unrepented sins. To a Christian *The Last of the Just* preaches a message of salvation: the salvation of the Christian faith from the Christian world, and its renewal in that rich soil of Israel which can teach the Church finally the meaning of "Shalom," a meaning so evident in the person of Jesus and so lacking in much of the Church's history. *The Last of the Just* presents a program of renewal for the Church every bit as demanding as—and in its stress on peace, unity, and non-violence, very similar in character to—the program Pope John XXIII had in mind when he called together the Second Vatican Council.

It is no accident that an Italian writer was moved, in his eulogy to Pope John in 1963, to compare Papa Giovanni to the Just Man. He wrote as follows:

What has Pope John done to arouse such world-wide expressions of love and gratitude? In one of the most arresting books of recent years a Jewish child asks the Elder what the Just Man must do. The Elder, without hesitation, replies: "Do you ask the sun to do anything? It

rises, it sets, it rejoices your soul." This is what Pope John did: he
was born, he died, he rejoiced our souls. Perhaps someone will feel
tempted to repeat about the Pope what André Schwarz-Bart has written about Christ, the "beautiful herald of impossible love." The Pope
of pentecostal mind has indeed inspired irresistible impulses of love.
Elijah has gone and only an Elisha can wear his clock. Pope John, I
kiss your hand that can never cease to bless, I would kiss your heart
that no heavy tombstone can stifle.[4]

One does well then to place the Council Pope John called
into being, but did not live to see completed, in the perspective
of *The Last of the Just*. If we are moved to compare Pope John
to the Just Man, we should be struck as well by a possible
parallel to Schwarz-Bart's title: that for the Catholic Church
Pope John is the Last of the Just. The Church will be judged
in terms of her response in history to that man sent from God,
whose name was John, just as we shall all be judged in terms of
our continuing response to "Ernie Levy, dead six million times,
yet still alive somewhere."

The Council was certainly aware of the issues raised by André
Schwarz-Bart, regardless of how many of the Council Fathers
read *The Last of the Just*. The same issues are, of course, raised
elsewhere, and it is well known that Jules Isaac, one of Schwarz-
Bart's main sources, had a personal meeting with Pope John
which provided the background for the Council's treatment of
the relations between Christians and Jews. But Pope John did not
live to guide the Council through on that concern which once
moved him to embrace a Jewish guest with the words "I am
Joseph, your brother." Whether or not the document which resulted from the Council's following of Pope John's initiatives is a
proper response to the Church's centuries-old teaching of contempt is open to serious question.

The first thing one is struck by in the Council's *Declaration on
the Relation of the Church to Non-Christian Religions* is its
brevity. The document is five pages long, and within those five
pages eight paragraphs are devoted to the bonds between Christians and Jews.[5] In itself such brevity need not be a failing. Con-

cise rhetoric is a virtue which the Council might well have practiced more often.

The content of Article 4, on Christians and Jews, leaves one grateful in certain respects. It seems almost certain that had a conciliar document of this nature appeared in the thirteenth century it would have revolutionized Jewish-Christian relations, with the effect that we would never have experienced the darkness that came to pass in the twentieth. It is therefore a reason for genuine gratitude that a Council today, before the darkness of tomorrow, is on record as saying that "the Church, mindful of the patrimony she shares with the Jews and moved not by political reasons but by the Gospel's spiritual love, decries hatred, persecutions, displays of anti-Semitism, directed against Jews at any time and by anyone." The explicit direction to Christian catechists and preachers never to present the Jewish people "as rejected or accursed by God, as if this followed from the Holy Scriptures," is further reason for gratitude, coming finally as it does after centuries of the Church's official toleration of theologians' teaching and preaching of contempt. Nor in evaluating this document must one forget to pay tribute to those men in the Church, and especially the American bishops, who fought hard for the strongest statement possible on the ties between Jews and Christians, and whom we must thank for the fact that Auschwitz can never again occur with the silence of Rome.

But the fact is that Auschwitz has already occurred, and Maidanek, Treblinka, Buchenwald, Mauthausen, Belzec, Sobibor, Chelmno, Ponary, Theresienstadt, Warsaw, Vilna, Skarzysko, Bergen-Belsen, Janow, Dora, Neuengamme, Pustkow. . . . It is to be wondered at, therefore, how the Church, in her conciliar condemnation of anti-Semitism, forgot to mention that she herself has been profoundly guilty of this same sin for centuries and thus prepared the seedbed for the most inconceivable crimes in man's history. The element lacking in the Council's declaration is not clarity in its repudiation of anti-Semitism—the condemnation is quite clear, despite the substitution of the word "decry" for "condemn"—but a simple acknowledgment of the Church's immense guilt for this sin and a humble begging of forgiveness, beyond any imaginable human mercy, from the people of Israel. It would seem obvious at this point in history that the biggest obligation of Rome to Israel is penance.

For this reason and in the context of Christian guilt, the Council's unnecessary reminder that "the Jews did not, in large number, accept the Gospel" neglects the far more important fact that Christians have not, in large numbers, accepted the Gospel, especially in their relations with Jews. A full acceptance of the Jewish Jesus, and of his message of love, is a criterion that serves the Church only in measuring herself, and certainly not the people she has most sinned against by the same criterion.

Moreover, the Council's omission of an explicit proscription of the term "deicide," so as to ban it utterly from the Christian vocabulary, cannot be dismissed with the argument that a false theological interpretation might have been attached to the word's use in the declaration. The fact is that Ernie Levy has already been attacked and beaten for centuries under the charge of "deicide" from an avenging Christianity. The false interpretation already there needed to be recognized as such.[6]

On the responsibility for Christ's death, the Council has stated instead: "True, the Jewish authorities and those who followed their lead pressed for the death of Christ; still, what happened in His passion cannot be charged against all the Jews, without distinction, then alive, nor against the Jews of today."

It is here, with regard to the first phrase, that silence *would have* been preferable for the Council. It is difficult to see what point there is, at this point in history, in mentioning the traditionally distorted fact that a few Jews were involved in the death of Christ—as were also the unmentioned Romans and whoever else in Jerusalem at the time cooperated in the conspiracy that brought Jesus to the cross. The declaration's "still" is not strong enough to blow away the lingering odor of past pogroms suggested by the attribution today of *any* responsibility to *any* Jew for Jesus' death, even "the Jewish authorities and those who followed their lead" two thousand years ago. It is no disservice to truth to avoid returning to a theologically insignificant fact (a truly redemptive death would implicate *all* men in the Christ event), which has nevertheless served as a centuries-old cover for the hatred of the Gentiles. The sensitivity demanded of Christian minds to Jewish hearts is not found in such words.

It has been pointed out often that the Council's declaration is addressed not to Jews, but to Catholics, and the suggestion made that its bad press and incredible headlines—"Catholics Absolve Jews of Crucifixion"—have been due to a misunderstanding as to whom the Council is here speaking. This is true enough. The Council was addressing Catholics, and there is no suggestion in the document itself that the Church has any thought of absolving Jews for a non-existent guilt. But even when speaker and audience have been clearly specified, the missing element of guilt where guilt belongs, in the conscience of the Church, remains missing. The bad press is not so much the fault of reporters, for writing as if the document were addressed to Jews, as it is the Church's, for not including and stressing those factors which would have made any such misinterpretation irrelevant. Had the Church humbly acknowledged and repudiated her own role in anti-Semitism, it is certain she would not have been mistaken as a condescending judge.

Rabbi David Panitz has pointed out in this connection that "the need for atonement through the admission of the facts of history is an established Hebraic, and Christian, doctrine. Until you admit you have been wrong, you cannot begin a reconstruction of your life."

The Church in Council did not confront the history of her own enormous guilt against the Jews. The question remains, therefore, as to how the Church can begin a reconstruction of her life which will lead finally to that deep appreciation of Israel which was always due her, not "for the sake of the fathers" held in common esteem by the Church, but for the sake of herself, living and present as a testimony to God's word and love.

If the Church by her very nature is on pilgrimage, as the Council's Constitution *De Ecclesia* affirms, she must learn to acknowledge the immense power of spirit manifest in the pilgrimage of Israel, yesterday and today, a pilgrimage whose end Ernie Levy yearned to see as he walked in the midst of trembling children along the final corridor to the gas chamber:

"O God," the Just Man Ernie Levy said to himself as bloody tears of pity streamed from his eyes again, "O Lord, we went forth like this thousands of years ago. We walked across arid deserts and the blood-red Red Sea in a flood of salt, bitter tears. We are very old. We are still walking. Oh, let us arrive, finally!"

The pilgrimage is old, and at Ernie Levy's stage of the journey it moves forward in total darkness, but even here in the night of Auschwitz there has come a kind of grace, as another Jewish writer has affirmed:

No people has come to know as we have how deeply man is an insubstantial nothingness before the awesome and terrible majesty of the Lord. We accept our nothingness—nay, we even rejoice in it—for in finding our nothingness we have found both ourselves and the God who alone is true substance. We did not ask to be born; we did not ask for our absurd existence in the world; nor have we asked for the fated destiny which has hung about us as Jews. Yet we would not exchange it, nor would we deny it, for when nothing is asked for, nothing is hoped for, nothing is expected; all that we receive is truly grace.[8]

May the Church have the grace to acknowledge the grace of Israel.

But the Church's response to André Schwarz-Bart is not confined to a conciliar document which conveys inadequately the great love and desire for atonement which many Christians feel today toward their Jewish brothers. It is in the very nature of a conciliar declaration as a compromise document not to go far enough, and the deep failure of the Church in Council to acknowledge her sins as a basis for a new beginning in Jewish-Christian relations is prompting the Church at large to do so. The Church has begun to seek, however slowly and painfully, that comprehension of our common past which will one day move her to feel in an agony of love the full impact of Schwarz-Bart's final words:

"Yes, at times one's heart could break in sorrow. But often too, preferably in the evening, I can't help thinking that Ernie Levy, dead six million times, is still alive somewhere, I don't know where. . . . Yesterday, as I stood in the street trembling in despair, rooted to the spot, a drop of pity fell from above upon my face. But there was no breeze in the air, no cloud in the sky. . . . There was only a presence."

NOTES

1. Bantam Books: 1961 (translated from the French by Stephen Becker). All quotations from *The Last of the Just* are drawn from this edition. Because of the nature of this chapter I have not seen fit to give page references to the numerous quotations from Schwarz-Bart.
2. Aquinas' teaching concerning the Jews can be found in his letter to the Duchess of Brabant, "On the Government of Jews," *Aquinas: Selected Political Writings*, edited by A. P. D'Entreves (Oxford: Blackwell, 1959), pp. 84–95.
3. Elie Wiesel, *Night* (Hill and Wang: 1961). Quoted by James Finn in his review of the book in *Commonweal* (January 6, 1961).
4. Giulio Bevilacqua, "Il Morte di Giovanni XXIII" (*Humanitas* XVIII, June 1963, 559–60). Quoted in Bevilacqua's "Meditation" prefacing Pope John's *Journal of a Soul* (McGraw-Hill: 1965), p. xxix.
5. All quotations from the *Declaration on the Relation of the Church to Non-Christian Religions* are drawn from the National Catholic Welfare Conference edition, pp. 4–5.
6. In this connection an American Jewish scholar has written movingly:
    "When I was a boy, I was more than once described as Christ-killer, especially by gangs of boys. I recall a few occasions when such gangs chased me; I don't recall if they ever caught me. Most Jews my age have had at least the former experience.
    "My two oldest boys belong to a Boy Scout troop which has its headquarters at the near-by Episcopal Church. Not one of my sons has ever spoken to my wife or me about 'Christ-killers.' Apparently none of them has experienced what for me was no unusual occurrence. Will they some day experience it? And if they have children, will those children experience it?
    "This is in the hands of Christians, not of us Jews."

Samuel Sandmel, *We Jews and Jesus* (London: Victor Gollancz, 1965), pp. 141–42.

7. In a discussion on "The Council's Statement on the Jews," *Jubilee* (April 1966), p. 40.

8. Richard L. Rubenstein, *After Auschwitz* (Bobbs-Merrill: 1966), pp. 128–29.

7

Anatomy of the Just War

THE STATE OF the just-war doctrine in contemporary Catholic thought is roughly equivalent to that of the prohibition against contraception: it has lost its cogency in terms of current theological thought and continues in use primarily as a point of reference for those who wish to go beyond it. In contrast, however, to the question of birth control, in which new theological perspectives have already come into acceptance, the thinking on war has remained in a post-Johannine limbo. The mind of the Church, as expressed in *Pacem in Terris* and *The Church in the Modern World*, has gone beyond the just war; yet the Church has hardly begun to formulate an ethic of reconciliation based on the Gospel of Peace. We are therefore confronted by some moving forms of Christian witness which nevertheless indicate an inner ethical tension, by a Pope who cries out to the nations, "let the arms fall from your hands," but who feels compelled to add, "defensive arms will, unfortunately, be necessary," [1] and by Catholic intellectuals moved by reason to justify their assent in conscience to the way of peace by means of an ethic of war.

For those few Catholics who speak and write on the subject, the just-war doctrine today serves the primary function of condemning as unjust all warfare in the Nuclear Age, as it has, for example, in talks given by Cardinal Alfrink and Cardinal Lercaro and in the writings of Walter Stein and Justus George Lawler.[2] This may seem a traditional use of a doctrine whose theoretical purpose has never been to justify war as such but rather to provide those norms by which particular wars could be judged justifiable or not. The contemporary application of the doctrine would therefore seem unique only in the increasingly negative answers derived from it by a few writers and prelates. But the traditional, normative use of the doctrine has also become more and more functional: the just-war doctrine today serves the Christian conscience less as a norm commanding assent in its own right than it does as a tool whose weight of tradition carries some remaining authority in the argument to reject all modern wars.

In short, in the Nuclear Age the pacifist conclusion is clearly more important than the just-war premise by which it is reached, or at least argued. This is partly because the norm, in the process of being declared a definitive judgment against any *possible* use of modern weapons, has thereby been surpassed; to think further on the subject of war and peace one has to seek out other norms. But the pacifist conclusion has eclipsed the just-war norm primarily because the Catholic conscience, in the age of Pope John and Vatican II, has begun to think once again on this question in other terms: in terms not of the just war but of the Gospel of Peace. By reason of its current reformation on a host of questions, the sensitive Catholic conscience is in the position today of wanting to affirm a truth on war and peace more profound than its immediate theological tradition and in response to a global moral crisis which itself demands a more profound truth. The Christian conscience knows that it must begin its witness in the world today by saying "No!" to modern war, and it can do this logically on the basis of the just-war doctrine. But for that "No!" of conscience to be granted the strength to transform men, it must be derived from and constantly renewed in the "Yes!" of the Gospel, so that conscience will be not only purged of the nuclear sword but reformed in the strength of the non-violent cross.

Because of this continuing tension between a just-war ethic which holds less and less conviction for the Catholic conscience and a non-violent ethic in the process of being formulated, it is helpful to anatomize the just war in an effort to determine precisely its inadequacies as well as whatever strength it possesses and which might fruitfully be absorbed into non-violence. One has several possible choices in undertaking such an analysis: to survey critically and in detail the theological development of the just-war doctrine from St. Augustine to the present; or to idealize that doctrine into what one feels are its most constitutive elements; or to analyze the doctrine as it is set forth today by one of its most persuasive theorists. The latter is our choice here, because the first method is too comprehensive (besides being beyond the competence of this writer) and the second too prone to distortion and oversimplification, whereas an analysis of the work of a contemporary just-war theorist has the merit of explicating the doctrine in its most vital form for the modern mind with its strengths and weaknesses thereby heightened. As for the particular subject of such an analysis, the obvious choice is the work of Paul Ramsey. Ramsey is not, of course, a Catholic. But neither is the just-war doctrine, and its failure in our age to convince the Catholic mind deeply enough of its verity to produce a single Catholic theorist within range of Ramsey's elaboration of the doctrine underlines the just war's moribund state in the Church. It is to the writing of the Protestant Paul Ramsey that we must look today for the just-war doctrine's most vital presentation and for confirmation of the fact that it no longer carries a central truth for the modern Christian conscience, Protestant or Catholic.

In his book *War and the Christian Conscience* Ramsey sets forth a doctrine of the just war characterized by the concept of non-combatant immunity. The book's subtitle, *How Shall Modern War Be Conducted Justly?*, indicates the direction of Ramsey's thought. His question is not (as it would be were he to follow St. Thomas Aquinas) *whether* modern war *can be* conducted justly, but rather *how shall* it be conducted justly. From the beginning Ramsey's focus is on the means of just warfare, defined in terms

of the inviolability of noncombatant immunity, and his premise is
that such moral means are realizable in modern war.

While Ramsey recognizes that for almost two centuries of the
early Church Christians were universally pacifists, he argues that
the change-over to just-war doctrine and practice was not a "fall"
from the original purity of Christian ethics. It was a change of
tactics only. "The basic strategy remained the same: responsible
love and service of one's neighbors in the texture of the common
life." [3] Christians simply came to recognize that the same Christlike love for neighbor, now given a more responsible setting by
reason of their acceptance into Roman society, could demand
their participation in warfare to defend the public order. The
limits then placed upon the just conduct of war, especially the
prohibition of indiscriminate killing stressed by Ramsey, were
also a creation of the Christian love ethic: "the conscience
schooled by Christ which first compelled Christians to justify
warfare at the same time proscribed for them its moral limits." [4]

In contrast to his emphasis on discrimination, Ramsey virtually
rejects the doctrine's traditional criterion of a just cause so far as
it would bear on a personal moral decision:

My contention is that Christian ethics may attribute to ordinary men,
and to their political leaders, a capacity to know more clearly and
certainly the moral limits pertaining to the armed action a man or a
nation is about to engage in, than they are likely to know enough to
compare unerringly the over-all justice of regimes and nations.[5]

For this reason, in a later review of Gordon Zahn's *German
Catholics and Hitler's Wars*, Ramsey is not prepared to admit
that massive German-Catholic participation in the Nazi war effort
is proof of an ineffective just-war doctrine: "It is tragically but
truly possible for participants on both sides to *believe* they are
justified in fighting. Zahn wants deliverance from the agony of
irremediably uncertain decision and historical action." [6]

Men will continue to believe themselves justified on both sides
of every war, but what the just-war doctrine can and must do is
to establish in men's minds the meaning of the principle of discrimination in warfare.

Regarding Ramsey's application of his theory of justly discriminate war to the realities of nuclear war, his work can be
divided into two phases. The first phase, represented by *War
and the Christian Conscience* and a few early essays, can be
characterized as one of technological innocence. The second
phase of his applied theory, represented principally by his contributions to a series of pamphlets published by The Council on
Religion and International Affairs, shows a degree of technological sophistication on nuclear weapons requiring a more and more
elaborate theory to contain their moral implications.

In 1961, in *War and the Christian Conscience*, Ramsey believed
that the upper limits of justly discriminate counterforce warfare
were barely within the effects of a kiloton nuclear weapon:

Kiloton and fractional kiloton weapons range from the dream of a
nuclear bullet that can be fired with extreme accuracy at a target,
all the way up to explosions of as great and greater power than the
A-bombs dropped on Hiroshima and Nagasaki. I tend to think that
rational nuclear armament would need to be confined *more to the
lower range in such firepower, i.e., closer to the conventional weapons
they will replace.* (Italics added.)[7]

At this stage in his thinking a succinct judgment could be
made on megaton bombs: "It requires no extraordinary morality
on the part of the present generation of men to recognize that
no good or reasonable purpose can be secured by means of megaton bombs." [8]

It is safe to say that in the eyes of a defense specialist looking
in on Ramsey's applied theory these particular judgments, and
Ramsey's argument that the United States should reduce its
nuclear capability accordingly, would have betrayed an idealism
and ignorance of political reality equal to that of any pacifist.
What Ramsey's evaluation of the moral requirements of discrimination then amounted to was a call for the dismantling of United
States nuclear forces to a pre-Hiroshima level. In the early 1960's
multi-megaton weapons were the rule in all Strategic Air Command bombers, whereas a *single*-megaton weapon containing fifty
times the explosive power of the Hiroshima bomb Ramsey felt

would likely be too great.[9] As a moralist Ramsey was recommending limits which the defense technicians had gone beyond
fifteen years before. This is not, of course, to infer that the moral
limits he then discerned were wrong—simply that his just-war
counsel was unlikely to be heeded.

Such is not the case, however, with Ramsey's 1963 pamphlet,
The Limits of Nuclear War, where his more contemporary perspective is indicated by an opening statement:

So far public opinion in this country seems to ignore the difference
between 25,000,000 dead as the probable result of all-out counterforce
warfare and 215,000,000 dead as a result of all-out countercity warfare between the great powers. We seem to turn away from any effort
to make counterforce nuclear war, if it comes, fall far, far short of
all-out.[10]

In *The Limits of Nuclear War* Ramsey is concerned with
arguing the moral case for 25,000,000 discriminately dead against
the prospect of 215,000,000 indiscriminately dead. Here his ab-
sorption of the strategic literature is evident in his own escalation
of the Nuclear Age meaning of "discrimination." Whereas in
War and the Christian Conscience the references to thermonuclear strategist Herman Kahn were extensive, the book's particular conclusions on pre-Hiroshima limits indicated Ramsey's continuing critical distance from Kahn's mode of thinking. In *The
Limits of Nuclear War*, on the other hand, Ramsey has adopted
Kahn's framework by accepting the prospect of thermonuclear
war with all its attendant policy structures as the context for his
own moral analysis. The moralist can begin to dwell on the
distinction between the war of 25,000,000 dead and the war of
215,000,000 dead only when megaton bombs (once denied any
place in the morality of "the present generation of men") are
granted the recognition of a "good or reasonable purpose." In its
fusion of morality and current defense strategy, *The Limits of
Nuclear War* leaped the several weapons revolutions after Hiroshima and made Ramsey relevant to the sixties.

Having agreed with Kahn to "think about the unthinkable" (and thus by conceding to thermonuclear war a definite moral possibility, having justified in men's minds its further preparation), Ramsey makes his most significant step within the context of the Pentagon by his analysis of the justice of deterrence. Ramsey had argued previously that the only reasonable, and therefore moral, deterrent to war was one made up of instruments a government is actually willing to fight with, and he refused to admit that thermonuclear weapons could be intended for such purposeful use. The only truly effective deterrent was the threat to wage counterforce warfare with conventional or low-range kiloton weapons. In this early view a perfect correspondence between deterrent reasons of state and a moral use of weapons made any conflict between nation and conscience politically unnecessary. For the nation, effective nuclear politics consisted simply in choosing and professing publicly a policy of clearly discriminate defense.

In *The Limits of Nuclear War* the relation between public morality and effective politics is not so clear-cut. Complicating factors have been introduced into the analysis. In the first place, Ramsey has escalated tremendously the destructive potential of a "discriminate" weapon into the thermonuclear category, thus straining reason's efforts to keep permissible power within reason. Secondly, he has been forced by his reading of the strategists to recognize that it is the shadow of wide-scale thermonuclear war which today provides the primary limiting factor in all smaller wars. The question is therefore raised, whether actual discrimination on any level is not itself dependent on the constant threat of total war, thereby establishing an essential conflict between the apparently moral acts of deterring or limiting warfare and their fundamentally immoral means in the Nuclear Age: the intention to wage thermonuclear genocide. Ramsey wants deterrence, but he recognizes the moral fact that "if deterrence rests upon intending massive retaliation, it is clearly wrong no matter how much peace results." [11]

His way out of his strategically imposed dilemma is both brilliant and tortuous. Despite its complex casuistry, it is worth considering for the light it throws on the function of moral reason in the world of military technology.

Ramsey sets forth three types of deterrence designed to be both politically effective in deterring the enemy's use of nuclear weapons and morally permissible in avoiding any intention on our part to kill the innocent. The first deterrent is based on the enemy's fear of the "collateral civilian damage" which would result as an unavoidable indirect effect from our waging counterforce warfare in its maximum form. On this first "deterrent without murderous intention," after a challenge from Walter Stein which forced him to revise his formulation, Ramsey claims that deterrence is "a direct effect of the foreseeable indirect effects of legitimate military conduct." [12] He has therefore derived his morally wanted deterrent from those morally unwanted deaths (the 25,000,000) which would be "unavoidably connected" with destroying important military targets.

The subtlety of this position lies in its ability to make prior political capital out of threatened effects whose admitted evil on a massive scale can still be claimed as "unintended." Stein charged originally that this is "a radical abuse of double-effect categories." [13] We would prefer to say that it testifies eloquently to the irrationality of reason in the Nuclear Age, where truth has been reduced to a component of technique. Just as our weapons are said to "work" if they can carry out their particular tasks efficiently, so the solutions of the nuclear moralist "work" when they fulfill their immediate technological function: to justify those making the weapons work. Reason has become the servant of technique, and the moralist the good conscience of the warfare state. The basic question being raised here is not whether Ramsey's reasons for a discriminate holocaust work in the context of his own elaborate theory but whether or not they testify to a higher kind of reason. But we have not yet finished explaining his theory.

Ramsey's second deterrent is based on the enemy's fear of the action we may never morally do or intend, the destruction of cities, but which action is threatened nevertheless by the very size and nature of the weapons themselves. Apart from our pure intention, the weapons' capacity to deter through their inherently murderous capabilities canot be removed from them. "No matter how often we declare, and quite sincerely declare, that our targets are an enemy's forces, he can never be quite *certain* that in the fury or in the fog of war his cities may not be destroyed." [14] (Italics in original.) Nor, needless to say, can *we* be quite *certain* that our deterrent machine won't destroy a few cities "in the fury or in the fog" of war. We are again in the position of deriving our desired deterrence from a factor which threatens to pass beyond our control and do enormous evil but which can be distinguished fortunately from our own subjective intention, thus leaving us blameless.

The third "moral deterrent" cuts the distinction between pure intention and threatened evil even closer by introducing a further distinction "between the *appearance* and the *actuality* of being partially or totally committed to go to city exchanges." [15] (Italics in original.) Ramsey here takes the reluctant step of justifying a government's *declared* policy to do what must never be done, destroy population centers. But he fears that effective deterrence might require it: "If the first two points above do not seem to the military analyst sufficiently persuasive, *or able to be made so,* then an *apparent* resolution to wage war irrationally or at least an *ambiguity* about our intentions may have to be our expressed policy." [16] (Italics in original.) The final saving element here as before is our *actual intention not to do* what must never be done, in spite of our having gone so far as to embrace a public policy declaring the contrary.

The third deterrent tends to threaten our moral security by raising difficult questions regarding deception in politics and the citizen's responsibility for a policy of apparent genocide. As for the deception of the enemy involved in a "thermonuclear bluff," Ramsey argues that the enemy has no right to the truth of our officials' innocent intentions, so that a bluff policy of massive retaliation constitutes no lie to the enemy (apparently regardless of the fact that a massive bluff would provoke further tensions and could lead to nuclear war itself). On the other hand, to the citizen who together with the enemy must judge the policy of his government in terms of its public statement, a serious question is raised by his joining in an outwardly genocidal policy whose presumed innocence is known only by his leaders. How can the citizen support such a publicly hostile but inwardly benevolent (only 25,000,000 dead) policy and retain his innocence together with the Joint Chiefs of Staff?·

Ramsey confesses that he is "most troubled" over this question of a government's leading its own subjects into a gravely sinful consent. In response to it he simply counters with some questions of his own regarding the citizen's degree of responsibility for such a declared policy, "without asserting that the points I will make, which I believe are valid, add up to the entire removal of the objection." [17] In any event, he is convinced finally of the military effectiveness of his first two "moral deterrents," thus freeing himself from any reliance on the third with its further complications.

Ramsey's case for the just deterrent illustrates the strains placed on even the most brilliant effort to maintain the justice of war in the nuclear era. It is a case dependent at every step on a distinction between the threat of a massive evil and the saving possibility of an opposite or moral intention by those judged to be making the threat. The first deterrent preserves our good conscience because the millions of civilian deaths threatened by our counterforce policy are beyond our intention: simply "collateral civilian damage." The second deterrent preserves our good conscience because the city-destruction threatened by our weapons is beyond our intention: "the dual use of the weapons themselves." The third deterrent, if we find it necessary, preserves our good conscience because the genocide threatened by our policy of massive retaliation is beyond our good intention: "our leaders' bluff." At no point in the theory is our intention permitted to correspond with the substance of the threat attributed to us by the enemy. The moral dissociation made by Ramsey between the evident direction of our actions (with the deterrent benefits that follow from them) and our personal responsibility for those actions is as absolute as possible. Populations, cities, and societies are threatened with enormous destruction, but from a moral point of view there is no one threatening them: just indirect effects, the inherent ambiguity of the weapons, and a policy of bluff. Responsible agents are nowhere in sight. And if by chance "in the fury or fog of war" the worst should somehow come to pass and a world should be buried in flame, we would at least have the dying consolation of knowing that we weren't responsible. No one was. It just happened.

Ramsey's moral theory of non-responsible deterrence recalls the pattern of decisions behind the World War II bombing atrocities at Dresden and Hiroshima, as analyzed in the works of David Irving and Robert Batchelder.[18] A single theme is common to the decision-makers' memories of these events: No one seems to have been directly responsible for them. In retrospect we are confronted by a bewildering trail of confusion and apparent misunderstandings so that the chain of responsibility behind each slaughter seems to dissolve. Ultimately, of course, the Prime Minister and the President made the decisions, but they, too, seem to have been controlled by the speed and confusion of events, with little apparent power to stop the technological forces which took charge from the beginning and converged on the two cities.

However clear Ramsey is on the principle of no city-destruction, his theory of non-responsible deterrence gives the moralist's blessing to all the decision-making, or lack of it, necessary to destroy the world. The deterrent machine is prepared to move into action at a speed far greater than the processes which seemed to overtake men's capacity for decision during World War II. The possibility of a global Hiroshima is present on the control board of the Pentagon's "War Room." To justify the continuing existence of that possibility by distinguishing it from the good intentions of everyone connected with it is to baptize once again the kind of moral vacuum which lies behind all the atrocities of our century. Such crimes have occurred not so much through the presence of any clear intention to do them as through the absence of any moral force working strongly against them. The question of intention is beside the point for anyone who does not commit himself unalterably against the poised deterrent machines which threaten not only the enemy society, but the existence of man. When the concept of intention, which controls Ramsey's understanding of "discrimination," is so ambiguous that the act of killing defined by it as justifiable can be expanded to include 25,000,000 persons, and when the act of deterrence justified by it can invite "the fury or fog of war" to do what it will so long as our "intention" remains inviolate, then we had better begin to look for a less spiritualized and more human concept. For the world cannot long survive such spiritualized slaughters. In this case Christ urges us to choose the world. To save one's soul in the deterrent state through a good intention is to lose the world, which can be preserved and developed in the image of the Son only through enough men's committing themselves totally against war and totally to peace on earth.

It is at this point that a deeper question concerning Ramsey's theory asserts itself, one which touches on the just-war doctrine itself: Where exactly does the just-war standard compel the Christian to accept the cross in suffering resistance to the injustice of his own nation? Or to enlarge the scope of the question: At what stage in its defense is the nation itself obliged to embrace the cross—to accept apparent defeat rather than wage war unjustly? Do such critical points even exist? If they do not, or if their practical recognition seems impossible, what in the last analysis distinguishes the just war from total war? Where, in short, does the doctrine raise the cross against personal and national self-interest? These questions can help us test the just-war doctrine concerning its claims that it belongs to the natural moral law and reflects the revelation of Christ.

From the beginning of his doctrine's development in *War and the Christian Conscience* Paul Ramsey's attitude toward the propriety of just-war conscientious objection has been ambiguous. On the one hand, he has consistently supported the citizen's moral right to object in conscience to participation in a war which he judges unjust. On the other hand, Ramsey has just as consistently questioned the wisdom of the exercise of that right, or of even granting it legal recognition.

In *War and the Christian Conscience* he discusses at length the possibility of seeking a change in the Selective Service Act to allow for religious objection to particular wars on just-war grounds, but turns away from recommending such a step:

I do not necessarily advocate this. It may be that a searching examination of the problems which would be raised by the just-war doctrine, if it became operative at all as a matter of private judgment, would cause us to draw back on the ground that this would seriously impair the government's power and right to repel injury (also the heart of the just-war theory). . . .[19]

Ramsey feels that after considering such problems we might think it necessary to return to that pre-democratic understanding of the just-war doctrine which held that it was addressed primarily to the leaders of nations, and that it required the private citizen to serve in a war in which unjust means were used, provided that just means were also used. In any event, all he wishes to do is to raise the question of granting legal status to the just-war objector, and to encourage its debate in the churches. [20]

A comparison of *War and the Christian Conscience* with a 1967 article on "Discretionary Armed Service" reveals no change in Ramsey's position on just-war conscientious objection except a further retreat from its reality, mainly from the impact on him of the popular dissent over Vietnam, which he regards as unfounded and chaotic. The position remains in essence a theoretical/practical split, a theoretical support of the moral right but a practical rejection of its exercise or recognition in law, at least until America manages to achieve "a considerable upgrading of the level of political discourse" [21] (at which time we can assume there would then be little or no need to exercise the right Ramsey would finally grant legal recognition).

In *War and the Christian Conscience* Ramsey also recognized in theory a point at which national cross-bearing becomes an obligation, that point where "we as a people are willing, if war comes, to accept defeat when our fighters cannot win the hoped-for victory rather than venture more and exact more than the nature of just endurable warfare requires." The test is "whether we can mount the resources for action with at most small effect and plan surrender when none is possible." [22]

The transition of "discriminate warfare" in Ramsey's thinking to the megaton range has put "action with at most small effect" far behind us. Yet Ramsey has continued to affirm in theory the existence of a border of limitation beyond which surrender imposes itself as a moral imperative. In *Again, the Justice of Deterrence* (1965) he declares that

justifiable resort to arms by either side in the nuclear age must proceed under an overarching policy that may be called "preemptive surrender." . . . That is to say, either side should be prepared to stop if it seems likely that war will escalate into a purposeless use of violence. [23]

But his own escalation of the practical meaning of "discrimination," together with the various saving distinctions made between action and intention, suggest that the just war remains elastic enough to push the critical point for the nation's conscience beyond any practical recognition. "Preemptive surrender," just as conscientious objection, is acknowledged in theory but its elusive meaning in practice makes it a cross without takers.

Is there no place then in Ramsey's theory for conscience to take a definitive stand, for it to refuse to do "the un-do-able," on the basis of the discrimination which defines his understanding of justice in warfare?

There is a single tentative effort to define a dissenting role for conscience in the deterrent state:

Why is it not possible, at least, for a member of the politically conscious part of the public to say to government leaders who are mainly responsible in military affairs for "ordering the offices": "Whatever are my policy-level disagreements with your policies, I only but definitely will conscientiously object to what you are doing on our behalf when I know that you are planning and actually intending an attack on an entire people and ordering my office so that I would be required also to intend or cooperate in a genocidal war or deterrence policy. Until then, I will and intend, not it is true what sometimes I hear you say, but that alone which should ever be willed by anyone or politically done in this matter." [24]

To return for a moment to the paradigm of Dresden's destruction, David Irving reports that the principal component in the British Command's performance before and after the event was deception, not so much deception of the enemy as deception of the aircrews chosen to execute the German populace and, later, deception of the public as to the nature and extent of the bombing done. Thus the crews were variously informed beforehand that their target was "the German Army Headquarters," "a fortress city," "one of the main supply centres for the Eastern front," "a Gestapo Headquarters," "a vital ammunition works," "a large poison gas plant," etc. As Irving notes dryly, "The local briefing officers seem to have drawn heavily on their imagination." [25]

One intelligence officer made the mistake of briefing his squadron truthfully about the nature of the target, suggesting that the object of the attack was to kill as many refugees as possible. The group's response to this murderous news would seem an example of the kind of "conscientious objection" which a military subordinate in the thick of war could draw from Ramsey's statement on where to draw the line. The bomber crews voted unanimously to show their disapproval of the mission by co-operating *only* to the letter of their orders, i.e., on their way to and from their destruction of Dresden they omitted their usual added practice of dropping bits of concrete, steel, and old bottles on enemy villages and towns as they passed over.

Most of the immediate executioners of Dresden apparently did not "know that their government leaders were planning and actually intending an attack on an entire people" and "ordering their offices so that they would be required also to intend or cooperate in" murder on a vast scale. According to the standards Ramsey would have us apply now to conscience in the deterrent

state, their leaders' deception saved the British aircrews from sin
at Dresden. But it also condemned 135,000 civilians to death.
(It is true that this toll, while twice that of Hiroshima, still falls
far, far short of 25,000,000, which in turns falls far, far short of
215,000,000—if we wish to play Pollyanna in the age of genocide.)

As for the few airmen who heard an officer say what the target
actually was, they could have compared his statement with the
descriptions of specifically military targets given most of the
crews and could therefore have disposed themselves to fulfill
Ramsey's final criterion of conscience before military authority:
"I will and intend, not it is true what sometimes I hear you say,
but that alone which should ever be willed by anyone or politically done in this matter." The scruple raised by the one officer's
briefing would then have been reduced to a low enough level of
plausibility to be satisfied in conscience by the crews' cooperating
only to the letter of their orders and performing their act of re-
nunciation regarding steel and old bottles. So might a manual
for the Nuclear Age confessional absolve an obedient military
and citizenry of its responsibility for morally "un-do-able" actions.[26]

If, however, we swallow the conscience pill that our responsibility for the preparation of such crimes can be dismissed because only our leaders know the actual intent of our policies,
then we will have submitted to the world of the Grand Inquisitor. For it is the Grand Inquisitor who lifted the possibility
of sin from the shoulders of the people and could therefore tell an
unwanted Christ:

All will be happy, all the millions of creatures except the hundred
thousand who rule over them. For only we, we who guard the mystery, shall be unhappy. There will be thousands of millions of happy
babes, and a hundred thousand sufferers who have taken upon themselves the curse of the knowledge of good and evil.[27]

In the deterrent state our government leaders have taken upon
themselves the curse of the nuclear knowledge of good and evil.
For us to draw back the curtain of propaganda and enter into
that knowledge would inevitably be to take some responsibility

for it and thus to reject our salvation. Instead of knowledge and responsibility, we must have faith: faith in our leaders, faith in our missiles, and, most of all, faith in our own good intentions. The Christ who demands a different kind of faith, and repentance for murderous irresponsibility, is as unwanted in the deterrent state as he was in Ivan Karamazov's legend.

To preserve its own integrity in the Nuclear Age, the just-war doctrine demands of the nation the cross of unilateral disarmament—and if the nation refuses, it demands of the individual the cross of conscientious objection. Unless the just-war doctrine can support a stand in conscience against all war in the Nuclear Age, whether it be the savagery of counter-revolutionary war or the global suicide of thermonuclear war, the doctrine is revealed as a de facto capitulation to total war. The just war is by definition, among other things, a limited war, as Paul Ramsey has rightly insisted in his exposition of its central condition of non-combatant immunity. But a morally limited war has already been excluded from possibility in the Nuclear Age on the level of intention by the global context of nuclear counter-threats which constitute the only (murderous) guarantee of limitation today. The justly limited war has also been excluded from possibility on the level of execution by the escalation of non-nuclear weapons technology so that any war today is necessarily an exercise in automated mass destruction.

In contrast to this reality of total war, the acceptance by Americans of the term "limited war" to describe such massive techniques of destruction as those being inflicted on Vietnam [28] is a measure of our own unconscious dehumanization and willingness to let government propagandists trade the meaning of words for symbols of self-justification. With moralists standing ready in the wings to complete the creation of a self-justifying vocabulary by seeking "the limits of nuclear war," as if these two concepts were not already mutually exclusive according to a sane use of words, we have gradually become sealed in a discourse of the absurd—where conscientious debates can take place between moral men over the most Christian way to wage thermonuclear wars. We begin with the issue of 25,000,000 dead versus 215,000,000 dead because in the age of images and technique we are dead to the word itself, whether it be "limited war" or "Christ," that word who is the Word, and thus dead to the meaning present in reality which a sane vision of the earth must first acknowledge in order to begin building real peace.

Seen critically from outside that discourse of the absurd where limited wars can be measured in "megadeaths," Ramsey's doctrine epitomizes the plight of just-war theory in the Nuclear Age. Although the inherent logic and integrity of the just-war doctrine today demand a stand in conscience against all war, it is evident that the doctrine is too weak in its theological presuppositions to be able to support the cross, either the cross of conscientious objection or the cross of unilateral disarmament. The foundations of just-war theory do not have the strength to sustain adequately the kind of witness demanded today by its own moral logic, which taken by itself compels one to relinquish all recourse to modern war.

To define more precisely this conflict within the just-war doctrine, between the cross which its contemporary application leads to and the theological premises of the doctrine which can admit no such cross, it is helpful to follow Ramsey's analysis of what we have termed "eschatological war," a total thermonuclear conflict which would extinguish life from the face of the earth. Ramsey is honest in admitting the existence of such a threat. In *War and the Christian Conscience* he devotes a chapter to the moral questions raised by it under the heading "The Politics of Fear," which is his description for a position which would deduce backward from the risk of a world-destructive war a prohibition of all modern war. Ramsey tries to counter what many Christians would consider virtually a self-evident truth—that nothing could justify our risking the destruction of mankind—by proposing a series of distinctions:

In considering this question, we must make certain further distinctions, between the great *evil* of all-out war and the *risk* of such a war, and between the *evil* of destroying mankind by human action and the *danger* that this may happen. These distinctions have not often been clearly made by those who simply affirm that there can be "no greater evil" than nuclear warfare or that there can be "no greater evil" than man's destruction of mankind. This may be true, yet there may still be greater evils than *risking* war or than risking enormously large-scale destruction; and in any case decisions have today to be made in the light of these enduring dangers without as such *choosing* all-out war or such destruction as a lesser evil to any other alternative. (Italics in original.) [29]

The procedure here corresponds to the one followed by Ramsey in his case for the deterrent: the distinctions are meant to drive a wedge between ourselves as justly warring agents who may *risk* the destruction of mankind without incurring moral guilt, and on the other hand, the actual *evil* of mankind's destruction which we would never choose as such. In short, we are once again in the process of deliberately skimming a global holocaust by our warring actions but saving ourselves by our good intentions from any moral responsibility for its threatened occurrence.

The question to be examined at this point is what conceivable factors could have driven Ramsey, a conscientious Christian and brilliant moralist, into taking a position so absurdly contradictory to the Gospel of Jesus Christ. What could have forced him into allying the faith of the cross with nuclear deterrents, counter-force nuclear wars of 25,000,000 dead, and the "necessary" risk of destroying mankind?

The answer would seem to be that the just-war theory has left him no alternative to war. Ramsey quotes Philip Toynbee's statement that he would far rather die after a Russian occupation of his country—by some deliberate act of refusal—than die uselessly by atomization. Ramsey's response to the Toynbee position indicates the just-war doctrine's own root inability to sustain a stand in conscience against national and personal self-interest, even when the existence of the human race is at stake. He asks, "Would such an act of refusal be useful?" He spells out the meaning of his question:

There has never been *justitia* imprinted in social institutions and social relationships except in the context of some *pax-ordo* preserved by

clothed or naked force. On their way to the Heavenly City the children of God make use of the *pax-ordo* of the earthly city and acknowledge their share in responsibility for its preservation. Not to repel
injury and uphold and improve *pax-ordo* means not simply to accept
the misshapen order and injustice that challenges it at the moment,
but also to start down the steep slope along which justice can find no
place whereon to stand.[30]

For Ramsey there is no moral alternative to war, even when
war risks the end of humanity, because justice, peace, and order
can be preserved only "by clothed or naked force." Not to retain
that recourse to warfare which is a nation's only final means of
preserving justice—no matter how great the risks to man involved
in retaining it—is "to start down the steep slope along which
justice can find no place whereon to stand." War is a necessary
component of justice. A warless world would be a lawless world.
But it is certain that history will see no end to war, and the
Christian must recognize his temporal responsibility to take up
the sword: "Until that day—which Christians know, or ought to
know, is an eschatological vision and not an event in time—on
which men beat their swords into plows and their spears into
pruning hooks, the nations will need some 'alternative to
peace.'"[31] Peace itself is no responsible alternative. To choose
peace exclusive of the act or threat of war is to condemn oneself
"to inaction, to non-political action in politics and non-military
action in military affairs."[32]

There is no alternative to war because a suffering resistance
to injustice, rather than a warring resistance, can have no value
in Ramsey's theological framework. Toynbee's deliberate act of
refusal would simply not be "useful." One is reminded here that
the primary argument of Franz Jagerstatter's parish priest against
the Austrian peasant's decision to refuse conscription in Hitler's
wars was also "that it would serve no useful purpose for him to
sacrifice himself."[33] The presuppositions of Ramsey, just as those
of Jagerstatter's confessor, are not strong enough to support the
personal and social consequences of a non-violent imperative, and
thus Ramsey is forced to avoid with great ingenuity the doctrine's natural logic against modern war. In terms of an under-

standing of power and order in which armed force occupies a pre-eminent position,[34] the imperative of non-violence can only mean personal futility and social chaos. When effective political power has been identified with violence, then the just-war doctrine is a necessary moral barricade against the radical demands of the Gospel by a theology incapable of meeting those demands without becoming irrelevant to history.

But even granting Paul Ramsey's eminence as a contemporary exponent of the just-war doctrine, is it true that the doctrine itself, as opposed to Ramsey's interpretation of it, must in every case lack the theological strength to support the cross of non-violence or conscientious objection? The evidence would seem clearly contrary to such an assertion, in view of the number of selective or just-war conscientious objectors, a number which has grown considerably in the United States during the Vietnam War.

What is being suggested here, however, is not that the just war cannot be used to support logically a case for conscientious objection. As has already been pointed out, the doctrine not only can but must make such a case against all modern war in order to preserve its integrity as a theory of limited war and preserver of noncombatant immunity. Moreover, in the just-war theory, war is simply the physical factor in a moral theory. The basic concern of the just-war theory is not that we should make war but that we should make justice, justice conceived in an international sense. Always implicit is the assumption that the waging of war can sometimes be consistent with the attainment of such justice. If, as the result of weapons developments which St. Augustine could hardly have foreseen, war and justice should be seen to have reached an absolute conflict, war as the physical factor in the theory must give way to justice as the ruling moral principle.

It is clear that the dynamics of the just-war theory brought into contact with the realities of the Nuclear Age demand that the theory undergo just such a self-transformation, with the ruling principle of justice providing the force of conversion. The resultant concept could be properly rechristened as a "theory of just resistance," war having been expunged from the theory as a form of resistance no longer reconcilable with justice.

But even the logical conclusion of such an argument, the doctrine's "No!" to modern war and the consequent cross of non-violence laid on the individual, is at least in tension with, if not opposed to, the doctrine's initial premise that war is a necessary moral instrument in resisting injustice. The doctrine which has always affirmed recourse to war under certain conditions as having a necessary police function in international society must now, in order to rule out the injustice of mass murder and global destruction, act as a brake against all recourse to war. That doctrine which has always upheld the value of violence as a form of justice now has the task of upholding the value of a just refusal of violence. The just-war doctrine can and must, in terms of its controlling principle of justice and its meaning of limited war, issue in such a position negatively, by rejecting modern war as a possible instrument of justice. But can a doctrine which has, after all, always been a doctrine of war support an anti-war position positively, by granting to the objector's position of non-violent or suffering (rather than warring) resistance a value of its own?

One might argue that the doctrine could grant such a value by equating the objector's refusal of national violence with a witness toward the creation of an effective international peace-keeping force. But this would presume that such an internationally constituted force is today a viable way to restore warfare to a legitimate police function, which despite liberal hopes is not self-evident in the Nuclear Age and is in any case not a conscious source of support for most just-war objectors.[35]

The conscientious objector who recognizes honestly the imperative of non-violence in which the just-war doctrine issues for himself, nevertheless does not and cannot draw from the doctrine that faith in the imperative's value which makes his witness meaningful and possible. For the just war's moral logic is basically in the service of violence as an opponent of injustice, however much it seeks to contain or limit violence, and it says

nothing in favor of the moral value of violence's opposite, suffering, as an alternative opponent of injustice. Insofar as the doctrine upholds the value of controlled violence as a defender of
justice, it presumes the ineffectiveness of non-violence or of suffering, which is in fact the immediate result on the enemy of the
just war. The doctrine cannot be expected therefore to lend any
essential support to the suffering resistance of the conscientious
objector, even though its moral logic has argued negatively to his
conclusion. In order to see a vital meaning in a non-violent and
suffering resistance to injustice, which meaning can alone make
such action a viable alternative to war, the man of conscience
must look to a doctrine not of war but of peace.[36]

To cite again the classic case of Franz Jagerstatter's refusal
to participate in Hitler's wars, although Jagerstatter's objection
was specifically to the Nazi war effort and therefore presumed
the just-war doctrine, his witness was grounded primarily not on
the just war but on the Gospel of Peace. Unlike the mass of other
Catholics in Nazi countries who in holding to the same just-war
tradition should also have been moved to dissent from Hitler's
cause, Jagerstatter was able to resist the injustice of the ruling
powers because he put his faith absolutely in a gospel which
proclaims suffering love as redemptive. In his notebook commentary "On the Question of Our Day: Catholic or Nazi?" Jagerstatter wrote: "Christ Himself, the most innocent of all, endured
the greatest suffering ever borne by man, and through His suffering and His death purchased heaven for us. And we do not
want to suffer for Him?"[37] Jagerstatter's faith in the Gospel of
Peace made possible his refusal to serve in an unjust war by con-
ferring on him the strength to bear martyrdom. It is the Gospel
which, in the Christian's actual witness against war, will always
serve as his source of guidance and strength.

Inasmuch as war's central action of *inflicting* suffering and
death is directly opposed to the example of Christ in *enduring*
these same realities, the Church has reason for repentance in
having allowed herself to become involved since the age of Constantine in an ethic which would justify what conflicts with the

essence of the Gospel. But it is clear that the Constantinian Church is giving way, however reluctantly, to the Johannine Church, or the Church of Christ militant to the believing community of Christ crucified, and today the just-war doctrine even as an argument against war is fast becoming a relic for the Christian whose sense of his time and faith demands the fullness of the Gospel.

NOTES

1. Pope Paul VI in his address to the United Nations, October 4, 1965.
2. In a talk given in Bologna, Italy, in May 1967, Cardinal Lercaro said that the notion of a war for legitimate defense "seems to be left over from cases and mental attitudes which no longer have anything to do with facts." In June 1967, Cardinal Alfrink told a meeting of chaplains of the Dutch armed forces: "The existence of nuclear weapons excludes the existence of a just war, because the means that could be used to fight injustice would cause much greater injustice." Walter Stein's writings on the subject include his essays in *Nuclear Weapons and Christian Conscience* (London: Merlin Press, 1961, edited by Stein) and *Peace, the Churches and the Bomb* (Council on Religion and International Affairs: 1965). Justus George Lawler has written *Nuclear War: The Ethic, the Rhetoric, the Reality* (Newman: 1965) as well as a number of articles on the same subject in *Commonweal* and his own quarterly, *Continuum*.
3. Paul Ramsey, *War and the Christian Conscience* (Duke University Press: 1961), p. xvii.
4. *Ibid.*, p. xix.
5. *Ibid.*, p. 32.
6. Paul Ramsey, "The Just War Theory on Trial," *Cross Currents* (Fall 1963), p. 480.
7. Ramsey, *War and the Christian Conscience*, p. 292.
8. *Ibid.*, p. 314.
9. Hans A. Bethe, a member of the President's Scientific Advisory Committee and a consultant to the Atomic Energy Commission and the Defense Department, stated in an article published in September 1962 ("Disarmament and Strategy," *Bulletin of the Atomic Scientists*, pp. 14–22) that the U.S. then had about 500 B-52's and 1,000 B-47's, each carrying 10 or 20 megatons. He observed: "It may be useful in this connection to remember that

all the bombing raids on Germany in World War II together added up to one megaton" (p. 20).

10. Paul Ramsey, *The Limits of Nuclear War: Thinking About the Do-Able and the Un-Do-Able* (The Council on Religion and International Affairs: 1963), p. 9.

11. *Ibid.*, p. 46.

12. Paul Ramsey, *Again, the Justice of Deterrence* (The Council on Religion and International Affairs: October 1965), p. 6.

13. Walter Stein, "The Limits of Nuclear War: Is a Just Deterrence Strategy Possible?" *Peace, the Churches and the Bomb*, p. 80.

14. Ramsey, *The Limits of Nuclear War*, p. 49.

15. *Ibid.*, p. 50.

16. *Ibid.*

17. Ramsey, *Again, the Justice of Deterrence*, p. 49.

18. David Irving, *The Destruction of Dresden* (Holt, Rinehart and Winston: 1963). Robert C. Batchelder, *The Irreversible Decision 1939–50* (Houghton Mifflin: 1962).

19. Ramsey, *War and the Christian Conscience*, p. 132.

20. *Ibid.*

21. Paul Ramsey, "Discretionary Armed Service," *worldview* (February 1967), p. 10. In a critique of this chapter Ramsey claims that I have misunderstood what was actually an advocacy of selective conscientious objection in *War and the Christian Conscience*. After rereading the passages in question (*War and the Christian Conscience*, pp. 128–39), I agree that he seems at an early point in his discussion (pp. 128–29) to favor the church's support of the selective objector. But the conclusion of his chapter is what I have stated here, and I still fail to see how my quotation and paraphrase of his final words is a distortion of his own emphasis. This emphasis is if anything greater in his article "Discretionary Armed Service," which questions the value of selective objection and its legal recognition in the context of an anti-Vietnam-war protest, which Ramsey characterizes as near-hysteria. I look forward to Ramsey's further treatment of this question and hopefully a clarification of his position in two books being published in 1968: *Selective Conscientious Objection*, James Finn, ed. (Pegus Books), and a volume of Ramsey's own essays, *Justifiable War: Force and Political Responsibility* (Scribner's).

22. Ramsey, *War and the Christian Conscience*, pp. 151–52.

23. Ramsey, *Again, the Justice of Deterrence*, p. 43.

24. *Ibid.*, pp. 50–51.

25. Irving, *The Destruction of Dresden*, p. 137.

26. In his critique of this chapter Ramsey has objected strongly to any association of his position with the destruction of Dresden and Hiroshima in view of his own conclusions in *War and the Christian Conscience* that these were inherently immoral acts of

war. My point, however, is not that Ramsey approves the destruction of cities as such (he clearly does not) but that his principles regarding the degree to which any military subordinate or citizen may now assent to and cooperate in the ostensible preparation of such actions (for the sake of an effective nuclear deterrent) in fact correspond closely to the vacuum of moral restraints which lay behind Dresden and Hiroshima. The only place where Ramsey's deterrent theory would exercise a definite moral restraint on nuclear decision-making is in the conscience of the President and his advisors. It is not apparent that the world's fate should be left in the hands of the President, especially when the very public opinion which Ramsey would counsel to passive obedience (for successful deterrence) is easily moved by events to a bellicose power over the Presidency in times of crisis, as in the Cuban Missile Crisis. The citizen's only effective moral restraint against the murderous machinery of the deterrent state is, on the contrary, his total opposition to every step of its preparation.

27. Fyodor Dostoyevsky, *The Brothers Karamazov* (Modern Library paperback edition), p. 308.

28. Ramsey's case for the justice of the Vietnam War can be found in his address to the American Society of Christian Ethics, "Can Counter-Insurgency War Be Conducted Justly?" (Evanston, Illinois, January 21–22, 1966) and in his article, "Is Vietnam a Just War?" *Dialog* (Winter 1967), pp. 19–29. He holds that the vastness of the destruction carried out by the United States remains "discriminate" because the size of legitimate military targets has been increased by the enemy's guerrilla tactics:

"I myself have no hesitation in saying that the counter-insurgency in South Vietnam in its chief or central design falls within the principle of discrimination. It is directed upon combatants as these have organized themselves for war, i.e., among the people like fish in water. No Christian and no moralist should assert that it violates the moral immunity of noncombatants from direct, deliberate attack to direct the violence of war upon vast Viet Cong strongholds whose destruction unavoidably involves the collateral deaths of a great many civilians." ("Is Vietnam a Just War?" p. 23.)

The substance of this argument is the same as in *The Limits of Nuclear War* where "collateral civilian damage" in enormous numbers is held to be justified in nuclear war.

29. Ramsey, *War and the Christian Conscience*, p. 195.

30. *Ibid.*, p. 205.

31. *Ibid.*, p. 153.

32. *Ibid.*, p. 202.

33. Gordon Zahn, *In Solitary Witness: The Life and Death of Franz Jagerstatter* (Holt, Rinehart and Winston: 1964), p. 57.

34. See Ramsey's article, "The Uses of Power," *The Perkins School of Theology Journal* (Fall 1964), pp. 13–24.
35. My own support of U.N. peace-keeping forces, as stated in Chapter 10, is based not on the just-war doctrine but on non-violent principles, namely on the symbolic presence of the world community and its desire for peace through forces whose response to conflict situations is itself basically non-violent.
36. This is not to say that the conscientious objector, particularly if he denies having any religious belief, must look consciously to the Gospel. It is to say that in order for his decision to take place, the prospect of his suffering resistance against war must assume for him a redemptive meaning and value from some source.

   In these paragraphs the term "conscientious objector" refers simply to any man who objects in conscience to participation in war—whether or not he chooses to apply formally for the Selective Service classification of "conscientious objector"—and thus includes the radical witness of the non-cooperator, or draft resister, whose suffering resistance constitutes today the most powerful moral force in America working against the Vietnam war.
37. Zahn, *In Solitary Witness*, p. 216.

8

Christians and the State

WHEN IT HAS become clear that the way of life revealed in Jesus Christ is contradicted by the just-war doctrine, which has traditionally dictated that the Christian's relationship to the warring state be one of obedient homicide, then the question must arise: Just what is the Christian's relationship *as Christian,* that is, in and through Christ, to the sword-wielding state?

In his deeply illuminating exegetical study, *The State in the New Testament,* Oscar Cullmann has concluded that the relationship between Christ and Caesar has been summed up once and for all in the cross of Christ. Cullmann's careful analysis of the relevant Gospel texts shows conclusively that Jesus was condemned to death as a revolutionary against the Roman state: He was held to be a dangerous leader of the extreme anti-Roman resistance movement of the Zealots. Because Jesus was nailed to the cross as a Zealot rebel against Rome, the problem of "Church and State" is at the heart of the New Testament.

It is true, of course, that as far as its formal charge went, the Roman indictment was wrong: Jesus was not a Zealot. But in a deeper sense Rome was right in its assessment of Jesus at the cross, as was to become clear in a battle between sword and faith lasting the next three hundred years: The person and teaching of Christ constituted a revolution against Caesar's authority which made insignificant even the challenge of the Zealots. But before inquiring into that non-violent revolution of Christ against Caesar, it is necessary to consider the evidence in the New Testament which links Jesus closely with the Zealots at the same time that it distinguishes him from them profoundly in a way which Rome was unable to understand.[1]

Cullmann asserts that we cannot understand Jesus' attitude toward the state by limiting ourselves to the saying about tax-paying in Mark 12:13 ff., but that we must start instead with Jesus' attitude toward the Zealot question, a question, which dominated everything in Palestine during his life and constitutes the indispensable background for those Gospel texts relating to the state, violence, and non-resistance. The Zealots stood at the far left of the Jewish religious-political spectrum. They preached a holy war against Rome for the realization of a Jewish theocracy. The Zealots undertook increasingly more provocative actions against the Roman garrison until in A.D. 60–70 open war broke out, the Temple was destroyed by the Romans, and the Jewish resistance suppressed. The Zealots revived their movement and continued their campaign against Rome until sixty-five years later a second war occurred in which the Zealot commander, Bar-kochba, had himself proclaimed Messiah and political king over Israel. Rome reacted to this second insurrection by annihilating the Jewish national existence. The Zealots were therefore a revolutionary party which meant business from the beginning and whose violent resistance to Rome led finally to the downfall of Israel.

The Apostles are compared with Zealots in Acts 5:36, 37 by Gamaliel, who places Jesus in the same category as the Zealot leaders Theudas and Judas. In Acts 21:38, the Roman tribune thinks Paul is an Egyptian Zealot leader.[2] The Galileans "whose blood Pilate had mingled with their sacrifices" (Luke 13:1) were probably also killed in a Zealot uprising. References such as these, especially the tribune's anxious question to Paul—"Are you not the Egyptian, then, who recently stirred up a revolt. . . ?"—

lead Cullmann to speak of the Roman garrison's "persecution complex" regarding the Zealots—not unlike the attitudes of Americans toward certain parties and movements. The designation given the Zealots by the tribune in Acts 21:38 is the Latin term *sicarii,* literally cutthroats or bandits.

It is certain that at least one of Jesus' Apostles—"Simon the Zealot" (Luke 6:15 and Acts 1:13)—belonged to the Zealots, and probable that others did, such as Judas Iscariot, Peter, and possibly the sons of Zebedee. "Iscariot" may be a Semitic transcription of the Latin *sicarius.* Judas' involvement with the Zealots would help to explain his betrayal. As a Zealot

he would then have had a messianic ideal quite different from Jesus'; and his entry into the circle of disciples would have rested on a misapprehension of the goal Jesus was pursuing. Like others of the disciples, he would have pictured Jesus' role as something quite different: namely, as that of a messiah-king, after the pattern of Judas of Gamala and the later Barkochba: a king who would bring the Roman rule to an end and thus establish the kingdom of God on earth. On this view, Judas' betrayal would stem from a disillusionment which the other disciples also experienced when they saw that Jesus conceived his messianic role quite differently, defining as satanic that political messianic hope which was the highest ideal of the Zealots.[3]

For similar reasons we may ask if Peter was not a Zealot. It was Peter whose denial of Christ's messianic role of suffering drew from him the rebuke, "Get behind me, Satan!" (Mark 8:33), and Peter again who drew the sword in the garden only to hear Jesus say, "Put your sword into its sheath; shall I not drink the cup which the Father has given me?" (John 18:11). Cullmann adds a philological detail, that, according to an old Hebrew lexicon, *baryona* (applied by Jesus to Peter in Matt. 16:17) is a word borrowed from Acadian meaning "terrorist"—which would also designate the Zealot.

James and John exhibit Zealot tendencies in their request to sit on the right and left hand of Jesus when he is enthroned in glory as king of the world (Mark 10:37) and in their desire to call down fire from heaven on the Samaritans who refused to receive Jesus (Luke 9:54). The nickname Jesus gave James and John, "sons of thunder," points toward Zealotism.

Yet although Jesus' most inner circle of disciples included at least one named Zealot, and probably several others in fact, including Peter, Jesus himself regarded the Zealot ideal as satanic. It is this ideal of temporal dominion which Satan offered him after his baptism, which recurs in Peter's words, and which is finally banished once and for all by Jesus' reacceptance of his suffering servanthood in Gethsemane. The mysterious saying of Jesus, "From the days of John the Baptist until now the kingdom of heaven has suffered violence, and men of violence take it by force" (Matt. 11:12), may indicate the tension in Jesus' attitude toward the Zealots, and particularly his own Zealot followers: between approval of their desire for the Kingdom and rejection of their violent efforts to attain it. Even the Zealots' violence was a struggle for the Kingdom, whose redemptive aspect Jesus perceived and redirected, but in itself such a struggle was futile and had to be rejected: ". . . for all who take the sword will perish by the sword" (Matt. 26:52), as the Zealots were to do repeatedly up to the eventual extinction of their party and nation.

Given the the dual claims by Jesus and the Zealots to kingship, and the prolonged inability of even his closest followers to appreciate the radical difference between the two ideals, we can understand the confusion of the Roman state in condemning Jesus as a Zealot leader. As to this being in fact the case, we can point to the following factors: first, the accusation which the elders brought against Jesus before Pilate was that of "perverting our nation, and forbidding us to give tribute to Caesar, and saying that he himself is Christ a king" (Luke 23:2). In short, Jesus was accused before Pilate of being a leader of the Zealots. Secondly, the form of capital punishment inflicted on Jesus, that of crucifixion, indicates that the death sentence was in fact passed by the Romans, not the Jews, for an alleged offense against the Roman state. Crucifixion was a Roman punishment. "If Jesus had been convicted of blasphemy by the Jews, and if Pilate had merely to ratify this verdict, Jesus would have been stoned to death."[4] Thirdly, the inscription over the cross, "King of the Jews" (John 19:19), was not just Pilate's fancy but rather a carrying out of the standard Roman legal procedure for a death sentence: the grounds of the verdict had to be posted on the cross. The *titulus* placed above Jesus shows that he was executed as a Zealot revolutionary, as a pretender to the royal throne of Israel. Fourth, the prisoner Barabbas, whom Pilate set alongside Jesus for the crowd to choose between, is described as having been one of "the rebels in prison, who had committed murder in the insurrection" (Mark 15:7). Barabbas is clearly a Zealot who was involved in a violent uprising. His being set beside Jesus in this way by Pilate shows that the two of them were condemned by the Romans for the same kind of crime.

Finally, one of Jesus' last sayings, to the weeping women on the way to his execution, confirms the nature of that execution: "Daughters of Jerusalem, do not weep for me, but weep for yourselves and for your children. . . . For if they do this to the green wood, what will be done to the dry?" (Luke 23:28–31). Cullmann's exegesis of this saying summarizes the relationship of Jesus to Zealotism:

All exegetes agree that Jesus refers to himself as the green wood. But who are intended by "they"? And why does Jesus refer to himself as the green wood? I believe there can be no doubt in this situation, where Jesus is being led to the place of execution by the Romans, that only the Romans can be the subject of the sentence. Then the saying of Jesus can have only the following meaning: If the Romans execute *me* as a Zealot, who am no Zealot and who have always warned against Zealotism, what will they do then to the true Zealots! For the Romans Jesus was in reality green wood, for he had indeed renounced Zealotism. Then this saying of Jesus expresses exactly what I have endeavored to show here: 1) Throughout his entire ministry Jesus had to come to terms with Zealotism; 2) He renounced Zealotism, although he also assumed a critical attitude toward the Roman state; 3) He was condemned to death as a Zealot by the Romans.[5]

Even if Jesus had Zealot revolutionaries among his closest followers, was repeatedly confused with the Zealots, and was finally executed as just such a revolutionary by the Roman state, the fact remains that Jesus himself was emphatically not a Zealot—that he regarded the Zealot ideal instead as his greatest temptation, one to be rejected as satanic, and that the meaning of his death transcends its particular legal cause. What significance, then, does this backdrop of revolution have for the Gospel of Jesus Christ?

It first of all makes clear the fact that Jesus, while not a Zealot himself, was nevertheless a man easily identified with the dominant revolutionary movement of his time. Jesus attracted revolutionaries. They formed a significant part of his following and were eager to identify the revolution as they understood it with the strength of the man, Jesus. When that strength of Jesus took the outward form of weakness at the cross, his Zealot followers deserted him. The power of their kind of revolution was dead. Jesus had died an apparently helpless victim of the Roman state they had hoped he would overthrow.

But to jump ahead in history, beyond that darkness and unbelief which filled Jesus' followers at the sight of the cross, it was not the Zealot sword which finally overcame Rome, but the Christian cross. Zealotism perished by the sword it took up against Rome. The Christian Gospel lived and thrived under the sword Rome raised against it, until finally, after three centuries of persecution, Rome confessed that it could not defeat the cross. It is at that point, and in the perspective of the suffering history leading up to it, that we should raise again the question of Christ and revolution. Because whether we choose to designate Christ or the Zealot as the revolutionary in the proper sense, it was Christ who endured the sword and overcame the oppressive empire. The disillusioned revolutionaries who had retreated at the sight of the cross were revived through the strength of an open tomb, and, armed with a new vision of revolution, went on to initiate thousands in the Christian revolution with the sign of a cross. If revolution is identical with armed rebellion, Jesus was not a revolutionary. But if revolution means simply a radical resistance, whether violent or non-violent in form, to injustice practiced by the state, then perhaps the cross which overcame Rome can be so designated. If the Christians had thought to sing "We Shall Overcome" under Nero, as we can presume they did in some form or other, they would have had a long wait ahead of them. But they would have been right.

It is no exaggeration to say that the Christ of the Gospel, and of a suffering but overcoming community centered on his cross, bears a much greater likeness to the fiercely revolutionary Jesus of the Italian film, *The Gospel According to Matthew,* as directed by the Communist Pier Pasolini, than he does to the harmless plaster savior of most Christian churches. Our wonder at the strength of a Communist's portrayal of the Christ indicates how far modern Christianity has drifted from its source. Pasolini's choice of unknown Communists for the main roles in his filming of Matthew's Gospel was no strange twist but simply a modern duplication of the original setting in which Christ lived and died, as a revolutionary among other, more common-minded revolutionaries. Pasolini is the Zealot Peter once again confronting the power and attraction of the man of the cross, this time rediscovered in Assisi—according to Pasolini's account of how he came to make the film—on a day when Pope John came to visit the home of St. Francis.[6]

At the same time as we affirm the revolutionary character of the Gospel with regard to the state, as shown by Christianity's prolonged struggle and victory over the Roman Empire, we must affirm also a sense in which Jesus—and the Christian living in him—is indifferent to the state. On the one hand, Christ transcended the state with his authority, thereby inserting a revolutionary principle into the relationship between Christian and state so that at any moment the Christian may be called on to say "No!" with his life to the Beast of the Apocalypse—to the state in its totalitarian pretensions. But on the other hand, despite (or perhaps because of) Christ's absolute freedom from the dictates of the totalitarian state, there is no evidence that he was particularly concerned with the fact that he was living under one. Jesus was free but he was no "freedom-fighter." He left the liberating tactics of Jewish nationalism to the Zealots. This side of Jesus' attitude toward the Roman state, his toleration of it, can be discerned in his answer to the question about paying tribute.

Although Jesus was condemned to death as a revolutionary, the charge initiated by the elders that he "forbade us to give tribute to Caesar" (Luke 23:2) was false. Jesus' answer to the question about the tribute cannot honestly be interpreted as a counsel to refuse tax-paying: "Render to Caesar the things that are Caesar's, and to God the things that are God's" (Mark 12:17). Neither is it the counsel to servile submission to the state which Christian nationalists have claimed to see in it. The question itself as posed by several Pharisees and Herodians was a trap, designed to identify Jesus as either a collaborationist with the Romans so as to disillusion his followers or as a Zealot revolutionary so as to convict him in the eyes of the Romans. Jesus' answer is in one sense a refusal to be so categorized. He does *not* divide the world into two equal kingdoms, Caesar's and God's, asking man to render to each in turn the claims of his particular sphere. Such an answer would have placed him in the camp of the collaborationists, who maintained that Caesar was God's counterpart, and would have contradicted everything else Jesus taught about man's total allegiance to God. To the question as posed between the poles of collaborationist and Zealot, Jesus gives no answer. He does not say what things are Caesar's and what things are God's, although it is clear from Jesus' teaching that God claims all—anything given to Caesar is given provisionally, subject to the contingency which may force the Christian to choose between the relative and the absolute claim, and thus "to obey God rather than men" (Acts 5:29).

But Jesus' answer here is ironical rather than evasive. Ethelbert Stauffer, whose twofold knowledge of New Testament exegesis and numismatics makes his *Christ and the Caesars* a fascinating work, has pointed out the significance of Jesus' asking his questioners to bring him a *denarius* (Mark 12:15).[7] There were many Roman coins then used as legal currency in Palestine but the *denarius* which Jesus asked them specifically to produce had a special significance: It was the coin prescribed for taxation purposes throughout the Empire. Moreover, this tax coin carried not only the image of the reigning emperor, Tiberius, which Jesus asked his questioners pointedly to identify, but also the legend *"Tiberius Caesar Divi Augusti Filius Augustus"* ("Emperor Tiberius August Son of the August God") and an image of the emperor's mother sitting on the throne of the gods. Besides being the coin of taxation, "this *denarius* of Tiberius is the most official and universal sign of the apotheosis of power and the worship of the *homo imperiosus* in the time of Christ." [8] Jesus, in asking his questioners to produce from their own pockets this coin of taxation and symbol of the imperial cult, forces them to acknowledge that they have already rendered homage to Caesar— in their use of the coin which bears his image—and that they have likely given him a good deal more that is God's alone in the cult symbolized by the coin. Jesus answered the question of the tribute money at its root: in terms of the hypocrisy of his questioners. If we wish to generalize the significance of his answer with respect to ourselves, it might take the form of a searching look into our reasons for often asking moral and theological questions in a form which leads away from a critical conclusion. Do we really want the answers to the ultimate questions we claim to be concerned about—in this case, the Christian's witness to the state? Or is our theologizing an exercise in self-justification?

Nevertheless, although the edge of Jesus' answer cuts at the motives of his questioners, it is true that he accepts here a relative legitimacy of Caesar. Something is to be rendered to Caesar in the form of the coin he has struck. In view also of the lack of references to the Roman state in Jesus' teaching, his relative acceptance of Caesar seems to have come from an indifference both to the state as such and to the particular form of government under which he lived. This indifference to national authority is explained in his response to Pilate's question about his kingship: "My kingship is not of this world" (John 18:36). Thus Father John L. McKenzie has interpreted Jesus' attitude toward the state in terms of Rome's "triviality" viewed in the light of the Gospels.[9]

Jesus expected nothing of the state and lived in it as he lived in a climate. Its particular form made no difference to him, just as whether the Christian today is living under a Communist or capitalist state should make little final difference to him. Faith lives and acts where it is awakened by the Father. The regime over the man of faith has no say in the matter.

Taking these two aspects of Christ's relationship to Rome, on the one hand his death under its authority and his non-violent revolution through the Church against its suppression of the Gospel, and on the other hand his apparent indifference to the state as such during his life, one can begin to construct a Christian attitude toward the state in terms of a revolution of con-
, science—the Christian conscience always transcending in Christ the state's authority and normal level of conduct, and in this sense always revolting against Caesar's constant tendency toward absolutism, but undergoing this revolution of conscience without ever seeking the state's violent overthrow. For "my kingship is not of this world; if my kingship were of this world, my servants would fight . . ." (John 18:36).

The commandment of non-violence is given explicitly by Jesus to his followers in Matthew 5:39, "Do no resist one who is evil. But if any one strikes you on the right cheek, turn to him the other also." This commandment is again framed by the historical context of Zealotism, that overriding issue of Jesus' time in terms of which "resistance" had only one meaning: lethal violence. For this reason the Mennonite concept of "non-resistance" is a little short of Jesus' meaning in his own context and by its literal reading of the text produces today too passive an understanding of the ethic being laid down.[10] "Do not resist" means here "Do not resist violently in the manner of the Zealots." That a *non-violent resistance* to evil is not only permissible but called for by the love on which Jesus based everything is evident in his own sharp responses to hypocrisy and injustice. His resistance to certain attitudes of the Pharisees shocks one with its intensity (Matthew 23), and his reaction to the officer who struck him before the high priest was not a turning of the cheek but a direct questioning of his action (John 18:23). As for the routing of the money-changers from the Temple, while there is reasonable doubt from an exegetical standpoint that Jesus hit any of them with a whip,[11] the passage as a whole serves to reinforce the intensity and activity involved in a truly Christian response to evil, expressed in our own time by "non-violent resistance" rather than "non-resistance." It is just as false to read into the Gospel a withdrawal from the world's conflicts as it is to equate a whip of cords with a hydrogen bomb. Jesus resisted evil with an intensity which revealed the uselessness and irrelevance of violence, and this resistance of love constitutes the Christian Revolution.

In the Pauline epistles, the Christian revolution of conscience toward the state is carried a step further by Paul's interpretation of the state as one of the "powers." Throughout the epistles Paul makes frequent allusions to certain cosmic powers (*exousiae*) which he also designates as principalities, thrones, and dominions: "For in Him are all things created, which are in heaven and on earth, the visible and the invisible, whether thrones, dominions, principalities, powers; all things are created through Him and for Him" (Colossians 1:16). The powers arise from the background of Jewish apocalyptic writings, but Paul's use of the terms differs from his sources in his lack of interest in their possibly personal nature. Professor H. Berkhof, who has made the best critical study of the powers, claims that we can even speak of a certain "demythologizing" in the transition from the apocalypticists to Paul: "The apocalypses think primarily of the principalities and powers as heavenly angels, Paul as structures of earthly existence." [12] For Paul the powers condition earthly life. They are to be found in every realm of life, and everywhere in a paradoxical relation to man. Because of the Fall the powers both unify men and separate them from God:

The state, politics, class, social struggle, national interest, public opinion, accepted morality, the ideas of decency, humanity, democracy—these give unity and direction to thousands of lives. Yet precisely by giving unity and direction they separate these many lives from the true God; they let us believe that we have found the meaning of existence, whereas they really estrange us from true meaning.[13]

The powers rule life. Apart from Christ man is at the mercy of them. Although under God's creative will the powers were to have mediated and expressed his love for man, sin has resulted in the powers themselves becoming as gods (Galatians 4:8) and thereby enslaving man. The powers continue to have a positive function by structuring man's fallen existence and preserving him from the utter chaos of his sin. But while thus ordering man's life, the powers at the same time block him from the freedom for which he is destined with Christ. Man is freed from the powers only in Christ: "He disarmed the principalities and powers and made a public example of them, triumphing over them thereby" (Colossians 2:15). By the Christian's living in Christ, the powers are disarmed for him and become what God meant them to be: instruments helping to shape and direct his return to God.

In his classic text on the state, Romans 13:1 ff., Paul uses this same term, *exousiae*, for the "governing authorities" and thus sets his passage urging subjection to rulers within the context of his theology of the powers. The even more immediate context here is Paul's statement (Romans 12:19–21) of Christ's nonviolent imperative, a formulation which draws on passages in Deuteronomy and Proverbs:

Beloved, never avenge yourselves, but leave it to the wrath of God; for it is written, "Vengeance is mine, I will repay, says the Lord." No, "if your enemy is hungry, feed him; if he is thirsty, give him drink; for by so doing you will heap burning coals upon his head." Do not be overcome by evil but overcome evil with good.

Paul then launches immediately into his text on the state: "Let every person be subject to the governing authorities [*exousiae*]. For there is no authority except from God, and those that exist have been instituted by God" (Romans 13:1). The passage goes on to say that the ruling authority "does not bear the sword in vain; he is the servant of God to execute his wrath on the wrongdoer" (13:4). The Christian is to be subject to the authorities by paying "taxes to whom taxes are due, revenue to whom revenue is due, respect to whom respect is due, honor to whom honor is due" (13:7). Paul then reiterates the commandment of love (13:8–9) and underlines love's non-violent expression: "Love does no wrong to a neighbor; therefore love is the fulfilling of the law" (13:10).

In terms of its immediate context in Romans, Paul's passage on the state can only mean that *even though* the state does exactly the opposite of what the Christian is to do, by taking vengeance on him who does evil, *nevertheless* the Christian is to be subject to the governing authorities. The Christians are told by Paul, "never avenge yourselves," in stark contrast to the state which with its sword is said to be "the servant of God to execute his wrath on the wrongdoer." But while the Christian is subject to the sword-wielding state's authority, he must himself remember that "love does no wrong to a neighbor; therefore love is the fulfilling of the law."

If there is any contradiction here, it is one created by imposing our modern mind-set and categories on Paul's counsel to Christians living in Rome a few years after Christ's death. In the first place, while Paul states Jesus' ethic of non-violent love in absolute terms to his fellow Christians, both before and after his words on the state, he does not make any effort to apply it to the state. He is concerned only with the Christian's observance of it. The state comes into consideration here only insofar as the Christian is related to it by being a citizen under its authority. The passage is addressed to the non-violent Christian *under the state*, with no thought given to the prospect of the Christian's ever having authority over the administration of the state. The "governing authorities" are those to whom Christians are to be subject. What Paul says therefore about these authorities "not bearing the sword in vain" is said about a body apart from the community of faith, a foreign body to which the faithful have to subject themselves, yet without in any way contradicting the commandment of love which always retained its primary authority in Christ.

Secondly, Paul does not justify the state's use of the sword any more than he would justify the Christian's suspending Jesus' imperative of non-violent love with the excuse of serving the state. He simply says that "the ruler is the servant of God to execute his wrath on the wrongdoer." It must be recalled that Paul is writing in a tradition which had always affirmed God's, and now affirmed Christ's, lordship over all of history so that even sin, without being justified, was chaneled into the movement of the divine will through history. In this context wars are the judgment of God, a chastisement upon us for our infidelity to his word, but without thereby justifying the sin of those who bear down upon us with the sword. Thus the prophet Isaiah had identified Israel's enemy, Assyria, as the instrument by which God chose to punish the Israelites for their sins—yet without justifying the Assyrians for their sins in so doing. In the same vein Jeremiah said the enemy Babylonians were the agents of God's judgment on Israel. These "treasonous" prophets recommended that the Israelites not resist their invaders with force but meet them instead with faith alone. Jeremiah first recommended surrender, and when that counsel was refused by the government, he encouraged individuals to desert.

The point here is that in the prophetic tradition which Paul inherited, governing authorities of even the most warlike and threatening enemies of Israel had long been considered "servants of God to execute his wrath on the wrongdoer." But no approval of the violent retaliatory code by which they so acted was thereby implied. In fact, that same prophetic tradition in Isaiah and Jeremiah asserted that the Israelites on their part should not only recognize the divine justice of the invader's sword—in retribution for their sins—but should respond to it by faith alone.

In the case of Christians, who unlike the Israelites did not identify their faith with a particular political society and governing body, the "wrath of God" over against the wrongdoer would have particular reference not so much to any threatening foreign government as to the Roman government over them. The governing sword-bearer of Rome was not thereby vindicated in his retaliatory action, but as in the case of the Assyrians and Babylonians, only the *effect* of that action upon the guilty citizen was justified. Thus Paul's sequence in Romans: Beloved, never avenge yourselves; overcome evil with good. . . . But you must nevertheless be subject to the governing authorities who do (unwittingly) execute God's wrath. . . . Still, remember that the love which you Christians live by does no wrong to a neighbor.

Paul's theology of the principalities and powers transforms the prophetic tradition of God's general lordship over history into Christ's personal triumph over its specific, rebellious structures, "the powers," at the cross. The state is one such power. In Romans 13, hedged in by the Christian imperative of non-violent love, one side of the consequences of Christ's triumph over the power of the state is drawn for the Christian: He is to be subject to the governing authorities insofar as they have been directed by Christ into an unwitting fulfillment of the Father's will. But Paul also recognizes the other side of the ambiguous power vested in governing authorities, resistant to God's wisdom, as shown by the cross itself: "We impart a secret and hidden wisdom of God, which God decreed before the ages for our glorification. None of the rulers of this age understood this; for if they had, they would not have crucified the Lord of glory" (I Corinthians 2:7–8). The application of this side of Paul's vision of the state is made in I Corinthians 6:1–8, where he urges Christians to avoid any resort in legal disputes to government courts and judges—"before those who are least esteemed by the church" (6:4). Although Paul affirms that the rulers of the age have been disarmed through Christ for the Christian, his two-sided vision of them is consistent with the Apocalypse's theme that they will rise up in the period before the Second Coming in an increasingly desperate, final attempt to defeat through the deified state the cross which has in effect already overcome them.

In the Apocalypse, the cosmic powers converge in the single power of the totalitarian state, the Beast (Apoc. 13) and the Great Whore of Babylon (Apoc. 17). This concentration and apotheosis of brute power is paradoxically the final sign of

Christ's victory as Lord of History over the powers and his trans-formation of history into "a new heaven and a new earth" (Apoc. 21:1). It is a repetition in the Church, as the center of history, of what occurred to Jesus at the cross. The Beast "was allowed to make war on the saints and to conquer them" (Apoc. 13:7), just as the Roman state was allowed to execute the Son of God at Golgotha. The non-violent imperative for the Church in its gathering crisis is precisely the same as it was for Jesus:

If anyone has an ear, let him hear: if anyone is to be taken captive, to captivity he goes; if anyone slays with the sword, with the sword must he be slain. Here is a call for the endurance and faith of the saints. (Apoc. 13:9–10)

The saints in their endurance and faith constitute the only re-sistance to the Beast, and that by reason of their life through "the Lamb that was slain": "All who dwell on earth will worship it [the Beast], everyone whose name has not been written before the foundation of the world in the book of life of the Lamb that was slain." (Apoc. 13:8)

The theme of the saints' non-violent resistance to the Beast—and to the second figure of the deified state, the Great Whore—is carried through the Apocalypse as the continuing expression of Christ's victory at the cross and therefore the key to history's culmination. The saints in their suffering love are the leaven of the entire historical process: "These are they who have come out of the great tribulation; they have washed their robes and made them white in the blood of the Lamb . . . and God will wipe away every tear from their eyes." (Apoc. 7:14, 17)

"And they have conquered him [the great dragon who is called the Devil and Satan] by the blood of the Lamb and by the word of their testimony, for they loved not their lives even unto death." (Apoc. 12:11)

" 'Blessed are the dead who die in the Lord henceforth.' 'Blessed indeed,' says the Spirit, 'that they may rest from their labors, for their deeds follow them!' " (Apoc. 14:13)

"And I saw the woman, drunk with the blood of the saints and the blood of the martyrs of Jesus." (Apoc. 17:6)

"And in her [the fallen Babylon] was found the blood of prophets and of saints, and of all who have been slain on earth." (Apoc. 18:24)

The military symbolism of Christ's return on a white horse leading "the armies of heaven" (Apoc. 19:14) is combined with the sign of the Lamb's victory of suffering love: "He is clad in a robe dipped in blood" (Apoc. 19:13). The vision of triumph "by the sword of him who sits upon the horse, the sword that issues from his mouth" (Apoc. 19:21) signifies that victory of the spirit gained through the word of God, "the sharp two-edged sword" (Apoc. 2:12). This violent symbolism of a non-violent victory expresses the final paradox of a cross which has always dismayed man in his demand for tangible power: The symbols of Christ's finally victorious power are drawn from the world of power which he overcame by dying to it. Even the suffering saints for whom the Apocalypse was written as a call for perseverance, during the persecutions of the first century, needed symbols derived from the kind of power they were resisting to express the then-hidden power of the cross. In the experience of crucifixion, even the deepest faith lives in darkness and clings to the world as a sign of resurrection during the moment which cries out against love's apparent ineffectiveness: "My God, my God, why hast thou forsaken me?" (Mark 15:34). The apocalyptic imagery of God's victorious armies, plagues, and fire and brimstone testifies to man's need for the old earth to symbolize his transition into the new. But with the vision of "the holy city, the new Jerusalem, coming down out of heaven from God" (Apoc. 21:2), the peace of that new earth foreshadowed by the suffering love of the saints has transcended any reliance upon the old. The revolution of peace has been fulfilled at the tree of life, "and the leaves of the tree were for the healing of the nations" (Apoc. 22:2).

The testimony of the New Testament to a basic and irreducible tension between the non-violent Christian whose ethic transcends national loyalties and state absolutism, and the sword-wielding state, is confirmed by that struggle between Church and empire which lasted three hundred years. It ended only when the empire in the person of Constantine gave in and made peace with the Christians. Constantine surrendered not because of any personal attraction to the Gospel, nor because Christians had become a majority (in the time of Constantine they were still a tiny minority without power or influence in the empire), but simply because non-violent Christianity could not be exterminated. The struggle ended because Constantine was enough of a politician to recognize from history that the sword was incapable of destroying the cross in any direct conflict.

But as a politician Constantine also initiated a process which from a critical perspective today raises the question of whether the victory of the cross was not also simultaneously the beginning of its defeat. For Constantine was wise enough not simply to grant the Christian Revolution the right to exist in the empire, which would have merely brought the tension of the cross closer to his throne, but instead by apparently surrendering his throne to the cross before the Milvian Bridge he enlisted Christianity in the service of the empire and killed the revolution by making it the Established Church (a process which was completed by Theodosius). The imperial edict of Constantine, which in January 313 made Christianity a legal religion in the Roman Empire, read: "Let this be so in order that the divine grace which we have experienced in such manifold ways, may always remain loyal to us, and continue to bless us in all that we undertake, for the welfare of the empire." [14] Grace had become a loyal subject of the emperor.

When Constantine raised the cross above his troops, he raised before the Christian Church the same temptation which Satan had set before Christ on the mountain with the sight of all the kingdoms of the world. And the Christian Church—for understandable reasons and without the critical perspective of 1600 more years—accepted Constantine's offer. From our standpoint today we can only surmise that the elation of a long-suffering Church at the sight of the emperor's cessation of the struggle, and of his acceptance of its symbol of strength, overcame all other considerations. Within the suffering history of the line of martyrs who had struggled against the sword, the sword's sudden capitulation to the cross, and its further enlistment of the cross over the emperor's own battles, could only have seemed a miracle. Yet "the miracle at the Milvian Bridge," by which Constantine is said to have conquered through the sign of the cross, had reversed the meaning of the cross:

Constantine tacitly ranged himself in the succession of the martyrs in that he was the first emperor to bestow upon himself the title Victor. This designation, which the pagans gave only to the gods and the Christians only to the martyrs, was assumed by the Christian emperor on the ground that what the martyrs had commenced with their blood, he had completed with his sword.[15]

The cross had won its victory by forcing Constantine to accept its existence, but Constantine had quickly nullified the victory by joining the cross to his sword.

There is no point in trying to revise the visions of the Christian community in the fourth century or in wishing its members had had the wisdom which they could not have had without the centuries of experience since then, so as to have seen the consequences of Christianity's deepening involvement in violence and persecution. It is certain they were a good deal less clearheaded in their choice than when Christ faced Satan on the mountain. It is also certain that the Christian Empire, which endured for a thousand years, came under Christ's lordship over history in a way which resulted in countless benefits to European man. But without questioning the providence of the Lord operating through Christendom, we are faced today, long after Christendom's dissolution, with the fact that it was founded in the first place on a fiction—on the supposition that Christians could take up the state's sword without compromising the Savior's cross.

It was a short step from the reconciliation between Church and state under Constantine to St. Augustine's formulation of the just-war doctrine a century later. Augustine ratified theologically an existential fact: that Christians were serving in Roman armies, particularly to turn back the barbarian invasions and thus "defend the cross" from desecration. The just-war doctrine, especially as elaborated by the scholastics, was in certain respects an effort to restrain the sword of the state, and should not be confused with the concept of the crusade, with which it is in fundamental conflict. Nevertheless the just-war doctrine, by introducing war into the meaning of the cross, did make less jarring Christianity's transition from the non-violence of the New Testament to the holy violence of the Crusades. With the spectacle of crusading Christians riding down to slaughter "unbelieving" men, women, and children by the thousands in order to "liberate" the land of a man who had said, "My kingship is not of this world; if my kingship were of this world, my servants would fight . . .", any trace of a distinction between cross and sword vanished. The cross had been transformed and sharpened to the point where it could spill blood faster than any heathen weapon. To say this is admittedly to overlook the complexity of the Crusades, the first of which can even be described as a means of peace, by uniting warring Westerners not in an attack on Jerusalem but in defense of Byzantium (thus helping reunite the two Churches then breaking apart).[16] But the central significance of the Crusades lay in their reinterpretation of the cross in terms of holy warfare. After the Crusades established the cross in many men's minds as a symbol of violence, the cross' further history in pogroms and inquisitions only served to deepen the unbeliever's reaction of terror to any appearance of a symbol whose original meaning had been a non-violent love for all mankind.

For a modern Christian to respond to the disparity between the New Testament's strong witness to the state, and the Church's historical capitulation to it, he must not only recognize the original testimony of the Gospel and the centuries of history which have so distorted modern Christianity's outlook on the question, he must also meet the theological issues which have arisen as a direct result of that distortion. Not all of these are so crude as the anti-Communist crusade which controls so much of Western Christianity's approach to war and peace or as the fundamentalist use of peripheral texts in the New Testament to prove that Jesus was a soldier at heart. Certain theological issues which can be traced to the Constantinian synthesis are serious and deserve careful consideration. We have already treated the question of the just war as it is raised for us today in a serious way by Paul Ramsey. Another such Constantinian issue which merits consideration is the question raised by Ernst Troeltsch in *The Social Teachings of the Christian Churches* and by H. Richard Niebuhr in his revision of Troeltsch's categories in *Christ and Culture*, the question of the Christian community's relationship to the world (and the state in particular) in the context of its presumed responsibility for the world's behavior.

Troeltsch's response to the question is given in his distinction between the two main types of Christian social organization, the Church and the sect. The contrasting types of Church and sect represent the social consequences of the most significant Christian attitudes toward the world, a universalism which would embrace mankind as a whole through the Church but at the expense of failing to confront men with the fullness of Jesus' ethic, and on the other hand, an intensely evangelical outlook which would aspire to a fully Christocentric life in the community of the sect but at the expense of withdrawing from the life of the world. Since Troeltsch first formulated these two categories some fifty years ago, the question of the Christian's relationship to the world has been posed in the form of an insoluble dilemma: either to meet the world in a socially responsible way (in the Church) or to live the full life of Christ in withdrawal (in the sect). Troeltsch chose the Church response as the more significant alternative:

> The main stream of Christian development flows along the channel prepared by the Church-type. The reason for this is clear: the Church-type represents the longing for a universal all-embracing ideal, the desire to control great masses of men, and therefore the urge to dominate the world and civilization in general.[17]

Given the social responsibility vs. personal purity formulation, it is not hard to see why Troeltsch and the great majority of Christian thinkers following him have wished to consider themselves churchmen rather than sectarians. "The sect," says Troeltsch, "does not educate nations in the mass, but it gathers a select group of the elect, and places it in sharp opposition to the world." [18] What the sect gains on the side of intensity in Christian life, it loses in the spirit of universalism. In its concern for inward perfection, the sect withdraws from mankind as a whole. In its emphasis on the New Testament as the Law of God to be realized in personal fellowship, the sect tends toward legalism and an emphasis on "good works." The sect may seem to be more Christlike in its own limited sphere of concern, but to the world at large it is withdrawn, self-righteous, and irrelevant. It can be safely ignored.

Less frequently noted but equally significant as Troeltsch's characterization of the sect in terms of withdrawal is his characterization of the Church by its domination over the world. The Church represents "the desire to control great masses of men" and "the urge to dominate the world and civilization in general." The universal vision which any churchman would see in Christ's apostolic mandate, "Go therefore and make disciples of all nations" (Matthew 28:19), is identified by Troeltsch with a triumphal control over the world which derives more from the age of Constantine than it does from the Gospel of Christ. Despite his Protestantism, the "Church" of Troeltsch's formulation is the established Church and can make disciples of all nations because its cultural status gives it a natural prerogative over all men. The churchmen who have rightly rejected the social irresponsibility of Troeltsch's "sect" have been less critical in their acceptance of the Constantinianism implicit in his "Church." From the critical perspective of the New Testament, the horns of the Church-sect dilemma are equally unacceptable.

In *Christ and Culture*, H. Richard Niebuhr has expanded Troeltsch's typology but without departing from his general framework. Niebuhr's solution to the problem posed by his title is in a commitment to "Christ the Transformer of Culture," a conversionist solution which recognizes the fallen state of human nature, but rather than withdrawing from the world as a consequence brings the transforming power of Christ into the world: "Christ is seen as the converter of man in his culture and society, not apart from these, for there is no nature without culture and no turning of men from self and idols to God save in society." [19] Niebuhr has thus laid down what has since been assumed to be the definitive approach to Christian social ethics. One must indeed agree with the theme of transformation, as opposed to the withdrawal of a "Christ against culture." But Niebuhr, too, has drawn his conclusion from a Constantinian formulation of the problem, so that "Christ the Transformer of Culture," although less domineering than Troeltsch's "Church," is still a category implying too early a triumph over those powers which in the New Testament are seen as crucifying both Christ and his followers until the end of time. The solution of *Christ and Culture* is essentially a treatise on the resurrection which has detoured around the cross.

Truer to the New Testament than any of the categories of Ernst Troeltsch, or even of H. Richard Niebuhr, is the thesis of Karl Rahner that the Church today is a "Church of the diaspora," a Church which exists everywhere in the world (the Church as catholic) and everywhere as a minority (the Church as diaspora). Today's Church of the diaspora corresponds to the vision Christ set before his followers. The founder of Christianity promised not that the Church would convert the world but that it would endure until the end of time precisely as a sign of contradiction. Rather than a triumph in time, Christ promised his disciples

that love would grow cold; that he, in his disciples, would be persecuted in the name of God; that the struggle would narrow down to an ever more critical point; that the victory of Christianity would not be the fruit of immanent development and widening and a steady, progressive leavening of the world but would come as the act of God coming in judgment to gather up world history into its wholly unpredictable and unexpected end.[20]

The community of belief foreseen by Christ is neither triumphant by converting and dominating the world nor sectarian by withdrawing from it. It is a Christian community living at the very center of the world in the form of Christ's decisive confrontation with that world—a cross of suffering, redemptive love.

From an historical standpoint, what Rahner has drawn the attention of Christians to are the conclusions for them implicit in the long-established fact of the Church's post-Constantine form. The Church of the diaspora is the Church in a post-Christendom age. The Church of the diaspora cannot possibly dominate the secular world as would Troeltsch's "Church," nor can she even hope to "transform it" as Richard Niebuhr wished, except insofar as she commits herself far more profoundly than she has to the cross which has itself made necessary her diaspora status. The Church's diaspora can be traced to the heart of the New Testament at Golgotha (an event corresponding to the Jews' suffering diaspora), but Christians have only begun to draw for themselves the social and ethical consequences of their permanent minority status. The illusion and permanent temptation offered by Constantine continues to obscure the Christian's witness to the world and to the modern state in particular.

The only commitment which makes Christological sense for the Church today in her response to the world is her commitment to a *catholicism* not of domination, not of equivocation and compromise, but a catholicism of the cross, whereby the universality of the Church is understood in terms of a global service and unflinching love of the God who is present in all men. The Church of the diaspora has far greater possibilities of realizing existentially the meaning of catholicism than did the Church which held spiritual and cultural power over all of medieval Europe. The identification of catholicity with a church whose ethic can direct the interests of a Holy Roman Empire shrinks the meaning of catholicism in the very act of seeming to give it imperial power. There is no withdrawal more corruptive of the Church than that withdrawal of the cross which masks itself as involvement, as Christ and Caesar become interchangeable commitments. The Church of the diaspora is not and cannot be an imperial Church, and for that very reason the possibilities of her attaining a Christocentric catholicity are limitless.

To define more closely the radical ethic toward the state of a catholicism of the cross, we can return to the sharp distinction made by Paul in Romans 13 between the sword-wielding conduct of "the governing authorities" and the non-violent love of the Christian. It is clear that there are two realms of conduct distinguishable in Paul's words here, but it is equally clear that they are not the two realms of Luther's exposition. Paul is not compartmentalizing the Christian's role in the world into a personal ethic on the one hand and a political ethic on the other, so that he who must turn the cheek for Christ's sake when he suffers personal injustices may in the service of the state feel it "a Christian act and an act of love confidently to kill, rob, and pillage the enemy, and to do everything that can injure him until he has conquered him according to the methods of war" (Luther's treatise "On Secular Authority").[21] As we have seen, the point of Paul's exhortation, which in keeping with the theological and historical context of his letter simply presumed that the Christians he was addressing would have no authority in the state, was: "You Christians, alienated as you are from that Roman state over you which bears the sword, and distinguished as you are from it by your life in Christ, should *nevertheless* be subject to it. But in being subject to it, remember that *love does no wrong to a neighbor.*"

The two realms of conduct distinguished by Paul are not two equally justified realms between which the Christian is to divide his life in a contradictory way, but they are rather the realm of conduct to be expected of the state over him, and second, the realm of conduct always obligatory on the Christian, whether he is acting personally or as a subject of the state. The state is obviously not living in Christ, nor does Paul even conceive of such a possibility. The state cannot be expected therefore to forego vengeance and to overcome evil with good, as the Christian is always obliged to do (Romans 12:19–21). But the state *can* be expected to act according to a relative justice with that sword which the Christian must never bear. And in a total view of things, the state as a historical reality acts "as the servant of God to execute his wrath on the wrongdoer." For Christ's lordship over history does not exclude the actions of the bearers of the sword, even though the bearers of his life are the crucified and the non-violent.

In the last analysis, there can be *no ethical* justification even for the governing authorities bearing the sword, because the only valid ethic is that revealed by Christ in the Gospel, a love which does no wrong to a neighbor. But nowhere in the Gospel does Christ envision such a transformation of the world in his name that it would eliminate the tension between that ethic as lived by his band of followers and the world at large. Christ envisioned no Christendom, nor the possibility of there ever being "Christian rulers," except in the form of the satanic temptation which he rejected and overcame. Rather than a triumphal, state-endowed Church, the "Church of the diaspora" is a reality fundamental to his vision: "For many are called, but few are chosen" (Matthew 22:14). In its relation to the state, it is a suffering, not an established Church, which Christ foresees: "For my sake you will be dragged before princes and kings, to bear witness before them and the Gentiles" (Matthew 10:18). In Paul's terms the state is one of the powers of the world, in effect overcome by Christ at the cross but still alien to him and waging a last-ditch resistance to his power in its sporadic persecution of his followers. The state can have no valid ethic apart from Christ, but as a power still resistant to him the state will act as if Christian ethics had no authority over it. The state's particular realm of conduct is therefore not justified; it is simply inevitable given its own assumption of independence from Christ, and is a constant factor to be reckoned with by the Christian as he forms his attitude toward the state. In Paul's context, the governing authorities and the Christian recognize different authorities as ultimate. For that reason, it was necessary for him to remind the Christians in Rome to be subject nevertheless to those who made a pretense at absolute authority. Even the bearers of the sword were instruments of God's power, and not to be feared by Christ's followers.

The fundamental difference between the Pauline context for understanding Romans 13 and the context imposed on it by most of its interpreters is that Paul assumes no direct Christian responsibility for the conduct of the state. The basic assumption of such writers as Troeltsch, H. Richard Niebuhr, Reinhold Niebuhr, and for that matter the mainstream of Christian theology following Augustine, is founded not on Paul but on their own Constantinianized attitudes: that the Christian must assume moral responsibility for the conduct of a power which, in Paul's context, it was simply assumed would always act as if it recognized no authority in Christ. One could hardly expect a continuity between the Christian imperative to overcome evil with good and the methods of the Roman leviathan which loomed over the Christians of the first century. Nor is it likely that Christ's followers would have forgotten so soon that it was under Caesar's authority that the Lord of glory was crucified. Christ and Caesar were set in such tension that Paul had to insist on Christians' proper subjection to state authority. But he would have been astounded at any interpretation of his words which saw in them an ethical sanction for the state's conduct and for the Christian's taking up the sword in its defense. The "responsibility ethic" of Paul proclaimed the Christian's responsibility for the Christ in all men, but not as mediated by a power which could always be expected to assert its own independence from Christ. Christian ethics were for the Christian. They commanded the governing authorities as well, but the Christian could not expect the powers as such to abide by Christ's ethic, and for the Christian to act as if the state's self-defined and self-protective ethic were in harmony with Christ's unbounded love and could therefore be absorbed into his own commitment would be an absurd contradiction. The Christian's responsibility was directly to the Christ of mankind, beaten and crucified, not to the particular state, which if it didn't always crucify Christ itself could be expected as often as not to leave him to die.

A final theological issue which is closely related to the Constantinian phase of church history is the question of a natural-law ethics, a morality of reason and nature, as it applies to the state in particular. Some Catholics, notably Father John L. McKenzie, have recently joined Protestant exegetes in suggesting that in fidelity to the New Testament the Church should purge itself of the natural law in order to concentrate on that Christian morality which alone has weight in the teaching of Jesus and in the writings of his disciples. From an exegetical standpoint, the argument of such a position is difficult to counter. McKenzie has taken what are generally held to be the classic texts in the New Testament for the doctrine of natural law, Romans 1:19–21 and 2:14–15, and has shown that the only *nomos*, or law, with which Paul is concerned is the Law of Moses.[22] In Romans 2:14–15, the Gentiles "who exhibit the work of the Law" (of Moses) have had that work "written on their hearts" not as some kind of natural revelation but in the direct form of actions which conform to the precepts and prohibitions of Moses' Law. The works of the Law done by the Gentiles must have been communicated by God, for otherwise the Gentiles would have been incapable of them, but their conformity to the Law is merely material, not formal: They know not what they do, neither the true nature of their actions nor their ultimate source. Within Paul's understanding of the Law of Moses as a revelation of sin's reality and of man's powerlessness to overcome it without Christ, there would seem to be little room for a natural law having any greater efficacy. McKenzie summarizes Paul's thought on a morality of reason and nature by saying that Paul could only have regarded it as a morality that fails: "I think that Paul would say that Jesus did not live and die in order that men might live by a morality of reason and nature. This they had already." [23]

The cogency of such an argument derives not only from the biblical scholarship of McKenzie but even more from the inadequacies of natural-law ethics as it has been taught by the Catholic Church. The just-war doctrine is only an outstanding example of a traditional Catholic tenet of natural law which is contradicted by the Gospel. Other examples would include Catholic natural-law teachings on wealth, slavery, politics, sex, and segregation—views now either thoroughly revised or in the process of revision but once central enough in Catholic thought to lay open to question the very idea of the natural law on which they were based. In view of the failures of the natural law as taught by the institution which has most championed the validity of natural law, today it is easy to reject even the possibility of a valid morality of reason, whether one does so by way of St. Paul or simply through a rational rejection of an ethics of reason. But such a rejection might be too quick.

One must agree with the biblically based critics of natural law that it cannot be used as a substitute among Christians for a Christocentric ethic, nor as a compromise Christian doctrine more palatable to the world, both of which uses continue to dominate much natural-law thinking and thus drive back even further the possibility of a biblically grounded appreciation of the concept. But from a theological standpoint, the rejection of a Christ who would make himself known to men beyond the New Testament creates as many problems as it solves in what has been called a "Post-Christian Age." With respect to the obvious presence of Christ today in men who know not his name, or who refuse to give it any honor, what is needed more than a rejection of the natural law is its transformation into a principle corresponding *in its moral demands* to *the ethical possibilities made real* through the grace and teaching of Jesus Christ. The natural law need not and should not be an ethic of calculative and vindictive justice. As Father Josef Fuchs, one of the foremost Catholic theorists of natural law, has written:

The meaning of the natural law is love.

Nevertheless this love is not any human love of God (*amor*) but the love that God himself 'infuses' into the heart of man, and through which man is now able to love God (*caritas*). It is the same love that burns in the Holy Trinity, in which the Father and the Son breathe the Holy Spirit. The love of the justified therefore participates in the internal love of the Holy Trinity. A life in accordance with the natural law signifies, then, not only a representation of the Glory of the Father resplendent in the *Logos*. It signifies a continuation of this love of the Father and the Son in the Holy Ghost. The natural law indicates to the justified the inadequate human way of true and gracious imitation of the intimate life of the Holy Trinity.[24]

It is from such a trinitarian perspective on natural law that we have interpreted the non-violent doctrine of Pope John XXIII in *Pacem in Terris* as a natural-law imperative. A true insight into the nature of man as we confront it in our fellow men demands always a response of non-violent love. The extent to which this humanly demanded response can be given apart from the support of Scripture returns one to the need for a Christocentric ethic. Anthropology and Christology are ultimately one: The reality in every man which constitutes the foundation of his existence is the presence of Christ. Non-violence is humanly demanded because it is Christically demanded. The New Testament reveals the basis for this human demand and the way of life which can respond to it fully. But there is no reason to believe *a priori* that man's nature and reason cannot be exalted by the growth of Christ's presence in suffering love completely apart from the writings and institutions of Christianity. If the natural-law doctrine can be understood as a reaffirmation of the truth that Christ is greater than his Church, then it is too soon to reject it.

It should be recognized that a Christically based doctrine of natural law, in its affirmation of non-violence as an imperative of reason, does not ignore man's dependence on God nor his fallen state. Non-violence is an imperative of reason, but it can be fulfilled only through grace. As Father McKenzie interpreted Paul, a morality of reason and nature is a morality that fails. But it is a morality which fails not because it asks too little of man, but because it demands of man that he travel a high road of peace on which reason is finally blocked and turned back on itself by self-interest and lack of faith. As in Paul, the law convicts man of his need for a redemptive faith.

Moreover, the existence of sin and violence is a permanent reality within such a doctrine. Sin is the reality, or lack of it, which blocks a normal realization of the non-violent imperative and makes it necessary for a redemptive love to attain the communion of reconciliation through an incarnation of suffering.

Traditional natural-law theorists have seen violence and war in the support of human rights as an imperative ordained by sin. But violence and war turned around are suffering, which is equally a consequence of sin, and it is this non-violent reality in a sinful world which Christ infused with love to make the principle of redemption. Human rights must be achieved and defended through a suffering, non-violent resistance. Non-violence is a natural-law imperative, which in a fallen world demands man's Christic response of suffering love.

With the recognition of non-violence as a natural-law imperative, it is clear that the relationship between the Church which must uphold this imperative for all men, and the state which for reasons of self-definition and self-preservation will almost always reject it, is one of permanent tension. But as Pope Benedict XV wrote, "The Gospel has not one law of charity for individuals and another for states and nations, for these are but collections of individuals." [25] Pope Benedict did not give this principle the specific meaning it has taken on here, by extending the imperative of non-violence across both Church and state. Still we must insist that the meaning of a universally compelling law of charity can only be such a catholic cross, which in its deeply human demands and in its living fulfillment of suffering love knows no confinement to a monastery but confronts man wherever he lives and undergoes conflict. The Church must always recognize the source of violence in the historically permanent fact of sin, and the deep roots of sin in the often brutal movements of national power, but the Church can never agree simply to live with sin or its divisions. The human family was meant to live in community, and the Church must resist every effort of the state to place a sword between brothers under one Father.

Thus the Christian lives his permanent revolution toward the state, demanding always that its authorities take a step further toward the cross which constitutes their, as well as his, center of existence. Every disarmament agreement and every reduction of international tensions requires of its participants an act of faith in man which is just such a step toward the cross; the Christian will always ask one more step. He will never expect the governing authorities to embrace the cross, just as Paul did not expect them to, and he will remain subject to them in all that is just. But to render unto Caesar the things that are Caesar's is to bear in mind always that it was Caesar's cross on which the Lord of glory died, so that the Christian, too, may finally have to render to Caesar a cross rather than a denarius.

NOTES

1. The following account of the scriptural evidence concerning Jesus and the Zealots summarizes Cullmann's *The State in the New Testament* (London: SCM Press, 1963), pp. 12–42.
2. Josephus records the insurrections led by Judas and the Egyptian. See *Jerusalem and Rome: The Writings of Josephus*, ed. Nahum N. Glatzer (Meridian Books: 1960), pp. 142–43, 160.
3. Cullmann, *The State in the New Testament*, p. 19.
4. *Ibid.*, p. 37.
5. *Ibid.*, p. 41.
6. "Pasolini said he first got the idea of the film, and of using the Gospel of Matthew particularly, through an accident. He was in Assisi, the place of St. Francis, and just about to leave when Pope John arrived in the town. The crowds brought all traffic to a standstill, forcing him to wait a half day in his hotel room where the only handy reading material happened to be a Bible. He began with the Gospel of Matthew, found it extraordinarily beautiful, and decided on the spot to make a movie of it. The film is dedicated to 'the dear memory of Pope John.'" Gunnar D. Kumlein; "A Marxist's Christ," *Commonweal* (July 2, 1965).
7. Ethelbert Stauffer, "The Story of the Tribute Money," *Christ and the Caesars* (London: SCM Press, 1955), pp. 112–37.
8. *Ibid.*, p. 127.
9. See McKenzie's article, "The State in Christian Perspective," *The Critic* (June–July 1964), pp. 15–21.
10. I am particularly indebted in this work to one Mennonite theologian, John Yoder, and to Mennonite sociologist Paul Peachey. As a Catholic Christian, I have a great deal to learn from the Mennonites' faithfulness to the Gospel. But even the Mennonite witness is not altogether free from some distortion of Christ's words, as I have tried to indicate here. On this point Reinhold Niebuhr agrees with the Mennonites because he can dismiss non-resistance more easily than non-violent resistance as being politi-

cally irrelevant. See his *Why the Christian Church Is Not Pacifist*.

11. G. H. C. Macgregor among other exegetes has questioned the whole basis for the violent images regularly deduced from this passage: "It is the Fourth Gospel alone which mentions the 'scourge.' Jewish tradition held that the Messiah at his coming would bear a lash for the chastisement of evil-doers (cf. the 'fan' in Matt. iii. 12). Scholars are agreed that the whole significance of the scene in this Gospel is Messianic, and the Evangelist's well-known love of symbolism suggests that the 'sourge' is to be regarded as an emblem of authority rather than as a weapon of offence. But even if the word is to be taken literally, a correct rendering of the Greek makes it clear that the whip was used only on the animals." *The New Testament Basis of Pacifism* (Fellowship Publications: 1960), p. 17.

12. H. Berkhof, *Christ and the Powers* (Herald Press: 1962), p. 18.

13. *Ibid.*, pp. 25–26.

14. Stauffer, *Christ and the Caesars*, p. 263.

15. Roland H. Bainton, *Christian Attitudes toward War and Peace* (Abingdon Press: 1960), p. 86.

16. I am grateful to Thomas Merton for reminding me of the complexity of this history, which makes the Church's deepening involvement in "Christendom" both more mysterious and more real than can be shown in our paradigmatic treatment here.

17. Ernst Troeltsch, *The Social Teaching of the Christian Churches* (Harper Torchbooks: 1960), I, 334.

18. *Ibid.*, p. 339.

19. H. Richard Niebuhr, *Christ and Culture* (Harper Torchbooks: 1956), p. 43.

20. Karl Rahner, "The Present Situation of Christians: A Theological Interpretation of the Position of Christians in the Modern World," *The Christian Commitment* (Sheed & Ward: 1963).

21. *Works of Martin Luther* (Muhlenberg: 1930), III, 269–70. Quoted by Thomas G. Sanders, *Protestant Concepts of Church and State* (Holt, Rinehart, & Winston: 1964), p. 38.

22. See John L. McKenzie, "Natural Law in the New Testament," *Biblical Research*, IX (1964), 3–13.

23. *Ibid.*, p. 13.

24. Josef Fuchs, *Natural Law: A Theological Investigation* (Sheed & Ward: 1965), p. 175.

25. Pope Benedict XV, Encyclical Letter *Pacem Dei Munus Pulcherrimum* on Peace and Reconciliation, May 23, 1920, in *Pattern for Peace: Catholic Statements on International Order*, ed. Harry W. Flannery (Newman: 1962), p. 17.

THREE

Cross and History

9

Cain and the Cross

THE ROOTS OF violence in man go far deeper than the just-war doctrine and baptized nationalism characteristic of the Constantinian phase of Church history. In the history of man, the Church's involvement in violence has been merely a religious justification and extension of a prior human reality, the pervasive violence in mankind as a whole and its raging presence in each human heart. No man alive to history and to himself can deny the universal reality of man in combat, of humanity apparently driven by a destructive instinct traceable to the very sources of human life; struggling and fighting its way upward from the slime of the earth into the emerging light of rational self-consciousness, and in that dawn of conscious being man's probable articulation of himself as not only knowing and communing but also, in order to achieve and maintain his precarious hold on existence, man the aggressor.

It is indicative of just how profoundly rooted aggression is in man that the world's most significant fossil, *Homo habilis*, the two-million-year-old tool-making ancestor of man discovered in Tanganyika's Olduvai Gorge in 1961, was probably murdered. *Homo habilis* died at about twelve years of age of a radiating fracture of the skull, an injury whose only likely explanation is a blow inflicted by another of man's ancestors.[1] If a tool-making Cain stalked his brother a million and a half years before the demonstrated presence of what science has been accustomed to call true man, then we have little reason to be surprised at the evident depths of the Cain instinct in ourselves and our civilization. Rap Brown has told us correctly that violence is as American as cherry pie. To push the slogan back two million years, we can say with self-justification for all of us that murder is as human as *Homo habilis.* The question which will remain after the slogans have departed is: How human in fact—from the standpoint not of paleontology but of moral science—was the *Homo habilis* who crushed the skull of a child? And to bring the question back to the star-spangled arena where cherry pie and homicide are interchangeable: How human is the white or black man whose only power toward his brother is the threat of destruction? If humanity is defined by more than the bones of its own victims or the color of the flesh which in an American jungle gives them the look of life, then the question is worth repeating until the Cain who is all of us has been seen sharply and understood at the moment when he stands with weapon poised against his brother. Is Cain at that moment human? If he is not, how can all of us who know him intimately, in action and intention, lay claim to humanity? What, after all, is man?

A recent approach to man which has increased our understanding of his violence is that of ethology, the modern study of animal behavior. Konrad Lorenz, the Austrian naturalist who is the father of ethology, has, in his book *On Aggression,* drawn on his knowledge of animal behavior to consider the nature of aggression in an ascending scale of life culminating in man. Lorenz defines aggression as "the fighting instinct in beast and man which is directed *against* members of the same species." (Italics in original.) [2] The significance of Lorenz's careful study of aggression up the evolutionary ladder is that it indicates at every level of animal life the existence of definite values in intraspecific aggression. Aggression within a particular species, whether it be the conflicts of coral fish off the Florida Keys or of baboons in Uganda, has important survival values, the first of these being the even distribution of the animals of the species over an inhabitable area. Starving is obviated by a mutual repulsion acting on the animals and effecting their regular spacing over an area capable of nourishing them. The fighting and mutual threats at the borders define this territorial distribution.

Aggression is therefore closely related to territory, as another, more popular writer of the "new biology," Robert Ardrey, has emphasized in his brilliant and provocative work *The Territorial Imperative*. Ardrey's thesis is that "the continuity of human evolution from the world of the animal to the world of man ensures that a human group in possession of a social territory will behave according to the universal laws of the territorial principle." [3] The first of these laws is an innate compulsion to defend one's territory over and above all other values. The supplement to this law is the recognition of the territorial rights of the next animal or man, as urged and enforced by the superior belligerence of each territory's holder when challenged on his own property. Just as animals become progressively more hostile as an alien member of the species challenges their particular domain, so will a Vietnamese or an Israeli fight with ferocity to retain control of the land beneath his feet.

Both Ardrey and Lorenz subscribe to the view of the new biology that there is no qualitative break between the moral nature of the animal and the moral nature of man. The conclusions they draw regarding man are therefore grounded on the aggressive and territorial instincts manifested by fish, wolves, dogs, rats, deer, birds, farmyard animals, monkeys, Americans, Japanese, South Africans, and Israelis. Prescinding for a moment from a judgment on the moral continuum which the new biology sees between the rat and the human being, we might do well to consider first in a specifically human context the central thesis of Lorenz and Ardrey: that aggression is natural and valuable.

The value of the aggressive or fighting instinct in man corresponds to the first half of this book's theme: revolution. To distinguish first between aggression and violence, we can suggest that to fight is not necessarily to be violent. Violence is an action contrary to the nature of man.[4] It is the action which violates man in his being, that unique union of spirit and matter for whom an injury is that which affects the whole person. The concept of violence and war encouraged by a number of earlier moralists, of an action involving only material evils (destruction, death) for the sake of spiritual goods (freedom, justice) was the expression of an easy dualism which few would wish to subscribe to today. Man is one. Violence can be primarily physical or primarily spiritual, a blow on the head or a look of hatred, but violence as such wounds the whole man. In his whole person man as man demands a response of reason and respect, cooperation and friendship, love and communion. Humanity's defining characteristic is its natural movement in these directions and its fulfillment in community. Humanity's opposite, violence, is characterized and can be quickly recognized in action, by its inherent tendency toward complete destruction.

Aggression, on the other hand, is the fighting instinct in man whose *usual* expression has been violence. But aggression need not and should not take the way of violence and destruction. Any man moved to transform the human spirit in his particular sphere of God's creation will have to fight tenaciously with the prejudices and powers of resistance in both himself and unsympathetic men. The revolutionary of the human spirit is a gentle man, but it would be sentimental to describe as "gentle" the impact on society of his demands for justice. The non-violent revolutionary's unswerving program for a human, global justice will be recognized as an act of aggression by the privileged and indifferent. His challenge to their complacence is a laying of hands on their eyes and a sharp pressure on closed lids, after the manner of Jesus who in healing the blind first made contact with their unseeing organs. The spiritually blind who refuse this healing contact will react to it as to a sword: "Do not think I have come to bring peace on earth; I have not come to bring peace, but a sword. For I have come to set a man against his father . . ." (Matthew 10:34–35).

Martin Luther King referred to this aggressive aspect of non-violence as "creative tension." It is the prophetic demand for justice, the confrontation which forces submerged evils to surface in the lives of men so that their inhumanity, once ignored, must now either be recognized by them as such and overcome or in its exposure left to ripen into impotent hatred. It is in this sense that the cross of Jesus is aggressive, because his apparently passive acceptance of Golgotha, *when seen by us,* challenges deeply at every point in our lives our self-resistance to the personal opening and eventual self-surrender which would provide an entry for the communal life of the Trinity. The aggression of "creative tension" is a non-violent confrontation with our own evil—and in the aggressor's invitation of brotherhood, with the possibilities of grace.

This non-violent aggression of the cross is far removed from the instinct which compels coral fish confined in a small aquarium to attack one another as intruders. But the aggression of the coral fish is not so distant from the aggressive instincts rooted in each human psyche, which is in turn the nature which when perfected by the cross is transformed into the saint's passionate plea that justice be extended to all his brothers. This is not a smooth, evolutionary continuum, because at critical points an ongoing creation and grace transform the matter of life which lay before them; but there are definite links up the scale which serve to re-emphasize at its height the genuine humanity of Christ and his fulfillment of the entire flow of life.

To return back down that scale, we must recognize that aggression in man prior to the transforming influence of the cross is the Cain instinct which left to itself will kill relentlessly. Oscar Wilde was describing the Cain instinct when he wrote that "all men kill the things they love." The modern novel has become almost a hymn to the Cain instinct, for a civilization as violent as ours has little else to celebrate.

In order to understand in action, however, the kind of violence most expressive of the Cain instinct, one can find no better example than the behavior of the Los Angeles Police Department when it broke up a large peace march on June 23, 1967, in front of the hotel where President Johnson was staying. The following account of the end of the march by one of its participants, whose story is corroborated by dozens of other eyewitness reports, illustrates all too vividly both the reality of the Cain instinct and the extent to which it can be aroused by non-violence:

Shortly after 7 P.M., the rally broke and the crowd began forming the parade. Most seemed to be in good spirits. A complete cross-section of America. All ages, all types. Many small children and toddlers.

Armies of cops strung along the westbound lane of Motor Avenue. More arriving and all looking grim. . . .

Turning onto the Avenue of the Stars. More and more cops, stationed every few feet. About 500 feet up the Avenue, a whistle blast. Cops started running towards the hotel. Returned at a run, trying to look dignified, a minute later.

Rumbles of a sitdown at head of march. Rumbles also of trouble. Nothing concrete. Cops moving across island. A girl offered a fuzz a flower. He knocked her hand away.

About 8:30. My part of parade, roughly the center, came to a halt. Rumors that police were narrowing the march to two abreast ahead. Someone said cops had ordered march dispersed. No one sure what was happening.

The monitors were doing a hell of a job maintaining order; the cops, on the other hand, were looking more and more uptight, and more and more of them were showing up from somewhere.

A man who identified himself as a physician kept saying they can't stop us from exercising our rights of free speech.

The police began to put on pressure, and we were aware of something going on up ahead. Apparently the cops were trying, and succeeding, in breaking the parade into two vulnerable parts.

One of them came running down the line, whispering out some order. Suddenly they were massed waves deep, jackboots and helmets gleaming in the fitful glare of television kleig lights. People found themselves packed tighter as the minutes passed. There were warnings to be careful of children.

About 9 P.M., perhaps a few minutes earlier. Suddenly the cop in front of me swung his truncheon against the face of a man. Blood spurts. Others join in. The first cop started hitting a girl, about 20, with a baby in her arms. When she fell down trying to protect the child, the same cop kicked her in the back. The doctor tried to go to her aid and was beaten down by several cops.

A general melee ensued at this time. The shout of "Sieg heil" got started. Other cries of protest. Screams. Shouts.

At this point, some joined arms for a sitdown, but they were too disorganized. Most didn't know what to do. They tried to push back, but couldn't. A solid mass of people was backed up against the railing of the Olympic Avenue overpass.

A wall of cops moved forward against an immovable mass, with much jabbing and swinging of clubs. More and more fall. Screams and shouts of anger. Swearing back out of impotence. Someone started singing "We Shall Overcome" and "God Bless America."

Sudden movement; we were stumbling down a landscaped embankment towards Olympic. The ground was full of wires and sprinklers, so that many fell and were beaten senseless by the pursuing cops.

There seemed to be any number of police phalanxes by now. We were being steadily moved towards Olympic and against other cops who were pushing in the opposite direction.

As the crowd broke for the opposite side of Olympic, police cars and motorcycle cops roared in very fast. Motorcycle cops rushed along the curb, stopping every ten feet or so and striking out blindly with clubs.

Several people, apparently innocent bystanders, were pulled out of cars and beaten. A number of people, including several young girls, lay bleeding on the edge of the pavement.

At this point, maybe 9:15, one witness claimed later to have watched a young girl run over the chest by a police motorcycle. She was reportedly thrown into a squad car and was not seen as of Saturday night.

I heard a young cop scream, "Get close, damn you. Gimme a chance. I'll kill you all."

Someone appealed for people to go back to the park. Bedraggled remnants of the march still being sometimes herded, move in confused lumps back down the Avenue of the Stars. Some fell off at Pico, to find their cars and split. Now about 9:45.

Most people were splitting. Others milled around. There were constant comments of "It can't happen here. This is America. . . ." [5]

The instinct in man demonstrated by the Los Angeles Police Department against peace marchers has been given its classic expression by Sigmund Freud: the death instinct. We have rephrased the death instinct here as the "Cain instinct" because Freud's concept requires a biblico-theological context both to explain it and to replace its implication of autonomy in man by the possibility of its transformation through grace into a properly human power.

Freud formulated the death instinct in *Beyond the Pleasure Principle* (1922) but gave it its most pointed expression in 1933 in his public reply to Albert Einstein's query to him, why does mankind wage war? Freud felt that the underlying reason for war was an instinct in all living beings impelling them toward aggression and destruction. This instinct was too deeply rooted in man to afford any hope that it could ever be eliminated. In fact even the effort to suppress it would have disastrous consequences, inasmuch as the death instinct if thwarted in its action outward against external objects would turn and work its destruction within.[6] Freud thought therefore that

the diversion of the destructive impulse toward the external world must have beneficial effects. Here is then the biological justification for all those vile, pernicious propensities which we are now combating. We can but own that they are really more akin to nature than this our stand against them, which, in fact, remains to be accounted for.[7]

With regard to the question of why the death instinct exists in man, Freud attempted no answer. He merely reported his observation that "the living being defends its own existence by destroying foreign bodies."[8] For some reason the processes of human life seemed to demand the destructive tendencies of the death instinct up to and including the carnage of modern war.

The only hope of avoiding war was, in Freud's view as in the new biology, not the suppression of man's aggressive tendencies but their diversion into a channel other than that of warfare. Supporting this work of diversion was a second instinct in man acting as a counteragent to the death instinct: Eros, the instinct to conserve and unify. Because of this second drive in man, everything which produced ties of sentiment between men would serve as war's antidote.

To transpose Freud's perception of the death instinct into a context which offers an explanation for it is to encounter it anew as the Cain instinct. In itself the story in Genesis 4 of Cain's murder of his brother Abel does not tell us the reason for the Cain instinct in man any more than Freud or the new biology does. All we are told is that the Lord preferred Abel's offering over Cain's and that Cain grew angry. Then "Cain said to Abel his brother, 'Let us go out to the field.' And when they were in the field, Cain rose up against his brother Abel, and killed him" (Genesis 4:8). Anger and jealousy seem to account for Cain's motives, but what is the ultimate root of the anger and jealousy themselves and of their expression in death?

Genesis 3 suggests that the answer is to be found in the sin of Adam—or as modern exegetes translate the Hebrew term *ha'ādām*, which is not a proper name—in the sin of "the man." Because "the man"—a symbolic figure for mankind as a whole—has sinned, the Cain instinct is born in the human family. The first consequence of sin described after "the man" and his wife have been driven from the garden is fratricide, Cain's murder of his brother Abel. Genesis 4 defines every killing of one man by another as fratricide. Sin destroys community and makes one member of the human family unrecognizable to the next in his true character as brother. Only when brothers in this family of man have become distant and unrecognizable through sin can their murder of one another begin. Thus the Cain instinct, which denies the truth of human brotherhood, is born. By its denial of that which is basic to man, his brotherhood with all other men in one family, the Cain instinct is by definition inhuman. Its seed is sin. But to push the question back further, where does the seed of the Cain instinct, sin itself, begin?

Father Piet Schoonenberg, the Dutch Jesuit theologian, has suggested that sin begins not in a Garden of Eden but at the cross of Christ.[9] Schoonenberg describes original sin as a being-in-situation common to all men whereby they are dead to grace and love. This universal situation of sin he attributes to man's rejection of Christ at the cross. The Incarnation made the Son

humanly present on the earth, thereby opening his divine life
fully to man's human response. But at the cross mankind responded to this presence by doing violence to Christ and rejecting him from the framework of earthly existence. The consequence, from the standpoint of man's action at Golgotha, is a
disaster: that absence of Christ or sinful situation into which each
man is born. But equally the consequence of the cross, from the
standpoint of God's action, is the renewed life of Christ realized
in the Resurrection and offered again to man in a different form.

Our search for the roots of the Cain instinct in man brings us
finally to the murder of the man-God, whose loving acceptance of
his murderers, on the other hand, is the power capable of redeeming the Cain instinct. The cross is at once both death and life to
mankind. After man's rejection of the Incarnation, God has re-
saved him by his transformation, in and through the Resurrection,
of the most awful crime in history. From man's standpoint, that
transformation of guilt was made possible through Christ's acceptance as man of what man had done to him. Moving this insight to the center of our discussion here, we can say that the
form of man's rejection of Christ—the cross—has made necessary
each man's reacceptance of Christ in terms of an existential commitment to that same cross *from the other side;* from the new
standpoint of the active, redeeming one crucified rather than as
before, the passive, killing executioner. The cross has two sides,
violent and suffering, and to accept Christ each man must pass
over from the first to the second, thus entering into Christ's
suffering acceptance of man in his violence to him. Man can be
freed from his own violent guilt for the cross only through his
Christic acceptance of the essential humanity of those men involved in *his own* crucifixion. Reconciliation between men and a
revitalized human family occurs through this same crucial process. The Cain instinct can be redeemed from the side of man
only through a reversal of the cross which is its source.

The Cain instinct is aggression distorted by sin and unredeemed, as expressed in man's violence to man. As an instinct
traceable in its inhumanity to mankind's sin at the cross (whose

immediate locus is every man's repeated crucifixion of the Christic humanity which he meets in himself and every neighbor), the Cain instinct is present in varying degrees in all of us, making us aware of the threat of violence from within. But although we must begin by admitting this deep-rooted source of violence, which is equivalent to an admission of one's sinfulness and inhumanity, we should not try to explain violence purely in terms of the Cain instinct. Violence is complex and usually expresses much more than the inhuman drive toward destruction, as Freud was quick to acknowledge. War in particular, as the height of violence, is an enormous complex of competing drives and values. From a theological and existential standpoint, it should be acknowledged that the concrete act of violence occurs for many reasons and is often a confused expression of higher values and even of love.

One reason for a spontaneous violence which no affluent American has the right to judge, much less the right to retaliate against with overwhelming power, is the poverty bearing down on most of the people of the world and the countless frustrations involved in it. The theory which explains violence as a response to frustration, proposed by the psychologist John Dollard and his co-workers in 1939,[10] has perhaps its primary exemplification in the slums of the world's great cities, where life itself strikes men as so futile that brutality seems their only way to surmount it, if only momentarily.

The kind of environment which makes violence inevitable, but a violence for which the primary moral responsibility must be sought outside the environment, is revealed in moving terms in Oscar Lewis' classic study of a poor Mexican family, *The Children of Sanchez*. Through Lewis' tape-recorded interviews the four grown children of Jesús Sánchez, raised in a one-room home in a slum tenement at the heart of Mexico City, tell a story of unbearable poverty, chaos, wrath, and violence—but a story redeemed again and again by a warmth and humanity which endure under the almost incessant violence. Roberto, the younger brother, sums up the only society he has known:

The law of the strongest operates here. No one helps the ones who fall; on the contrary, if they can injure them more, they will. If one is drowning, they push him under. And if one is winning out, they will pull him down. . . .

Could it be for the lack of education? There are so many people who cannot even sign their names! They talk about constitutionalism . . . it is a pretty, resounding word, but I don't even know what it means. For me, we live by violence . . . homicide, theft, assault. We live quickly and must be constantly on guard.[11]

Roberto lives by stealth and violence, the law of the Casa Grande *vecindad,* his large one-story slum tenement, but he is also a man who bursts with affection for the members of his family and experiences a wondering pain at the fate overcoming all of them. At one point he confesses shortly, "If there is anything good in me, it's because at least I have a blind faith in Christ, Our Lord." [12] If he is violent, he acknowledges it and places himself last among men:

When I enter a church, I feel I'm carrying a heavy load, especially on my conscience. I always stay in the last row, just inside the door, and although it is crowded with worshipers, I feel alone with my thoughts and prayers. As far as I am concerned, only God and I are in the church. And when I leave, I feel relieved. Even my clothes weigh less. That's why if I don't go to Mass every week, I don't feel right.[13]

The violence of men such as this, in streets dark with filth and despair, is fundamentally the violence of the privileged who have chosen not to see them.

Linked closely with the violence of the privileged revealed in the frustrations of the poor is the violence of race. Its most enduring symbol and victim is the late Malcolm X, who was himself more a victim than an instigator of race violence. There is no greater American tragedy than *The Autobiography of Malcolm X,* for it is the story of an uncompromising man of truth who died misunderstood on the verge of the truth he needed to liberate black America from white oppression, and, equally, white America from black slavery.

Because of his years in the depths of black northern ghettos, Malcolm felt profoundly the anguish of his people and the racial explosives beneath American life everywhere. His whole life after his conversion to the Muslim faith was an effort to speak the truth with absolute honesty about white and black and thus bring these explosives to light. It is true that as a follower of Elijah Muhammad, Malcolm preached racist doctrines, but the core of his own emphasis was true: He told the white man that collectively he was a devil because Malcolm knew this to be a social fact—or to translate his perception into Pauline terms, Malcolm in effect recognized white racism as one of the principalities and powers enslaving man, and he spoke directly to its sources. Malcolm spoke just as hard a truth to black as to white, telling the respectable members of the black middle class that they had abandoned their brothers in the slums to live as comfortable parasites on the belly of white racism, and telling the Negroes in the slums that they had been brainwashed into becoming comic imitations of a corrupt white society, surrendering their own heritage and character.

Malcolm's great strength in a Negro community which had accepted and cooperated with the lies of white racist mores lay in his incorruptible commitment to speaking the truth. He says in his autobiography:

I'm telling it like it *is!* You *never* have to worry about me biting my tongue if something I know as truth is on my mind. Raw, naked truth exchanged between the black man and the white man is what a whole lot more of is needed in this country—to clear the air of the racial mirages, clichés, and lies that this country's very atmosphere has been filled with for four hundred years. (Italics in original.) [14]

The irony of Malcolm's life is that the violence for which he became known, and died a victim to, was more the reactive violence of his stunned targets than the violence of his own words and actions. The blunt truth he spoke had the intended effect of raising America's hidden explosives to the surface, but they rose too quickly and killed him abruptly, in his very act of realizing a vision of man potentially strong enough in truth to guide the imminent explosions into a purposeful, non-violent direction.

For Malcolm's greatest power—and now after his death his least appreciated one—was not simply his courage in speaking the truth, but his ability to grow in it. In this respect Malcolm and Gandhi were of one mind: in their absolute openness to the growth of truth in themselves, regardless of whatever personal or doctrinal adjustments such openness demanded. Because of this power to grow in truth Malcolm was able to renounce all traces of racism in a public letter to his friends and followers at the conclusion of his pilgrimage to Mecca:

For the past week, I have been utterly speechless and spellbound by the graciousness I see displayed all around me by people *of all colors*. . . .

There were tens of thousands of pilgrims, from all over the world. They were of all colors, from blue-eyed blonds to black-skinned Africans. But we were all participating in the same ritual, displaying a spirit of unity and brotherhood that my experiences in America had led me to believe never could exist between the white and the non-white. . . .

You may be shocked by these words coming from me. But on this pilgrimage, what I have seen, and experienced, has forced me to *re-arrange* much of my thought-patterns previously held, and to *toss aside* some of my previous conclusions. This was not too difficult for me. Despite my firm convictions, I have been always a man who tries to face facts, and to accept the reality of life as new experience and new knowledge unfolds it. I have always kept an open mind, which is necessary to the flexibility that must go hand in hand with every form of intelligent search for truth. (Italics in original.)[15]

This pilgrimage to Mecca shortly before Malcolm was murdered overwhelmed him with a sudden new vision of the unity of mankind and of the global significance of the black man's struggle for justice. At this point he had unquestionably passed from the racist doctrines and gathering violence of Elijah Muhammad into a pure Muslim faith open to the world. He struggled to put his new vision into words for his friends:

I've had enough of someone else's propaganda. I'm for truth, no matter who tells it. I'm for justice, no matter who it is for or against. I'm a human being first and foremost, and as such I'm for whoever and whatever benefits humanity *as a whole*. (Italics in original.)[16]

The man who symbolized black racism and violence to most of America had reached this conviction:

Mankind's history has proved from one era to another that the true criterion of leadership is spiritual. Men are attracted by spirit. By power, men are *forced*. Love is engendered by spirit. By power, anxieties are created. (Italics in original.)[17]

Malcolm had not yet been converted to non-violence, despite his grudging admiration for Martin Luther King, but his new belief in the possibilities of brotherhood had brought him to the verge of a faith in redemptive suffering. Two days before he was shot to death Malcolm told a *Life* photographer: "It's a time for martyrs now. And if I'm to be one, it will be in the cause of brotherhood. That's the only thing that can save this country. I've learned it the hard way—but I've learned it. . . ."[18]

But Malcolm was killed before he could rethink his prophetic role in terms of global brotherhood, and his dominant legacy today in the black community is that of the earlier, more violent follower of Elijah Muhammad. Now the man whose power of non-violence Malcolm had begun to respect, Martin King, has also been murdered by an America whose values seem to have established it as the Pontius Pilate of our age. What might have been a redemptive movement joining the powers of Malcolm's truth and Martin King's non-violence has with the killing of both given way to the threat of enormous violence. The question before Americans today is: How far from complete self-destruction is a society which continues to respond to its prophets with a rifle?

When violence is embraced by men suffocating under poverty and racism, their violence is derived from their oppressors and cannot be reduced simply to the Cain instinct. When it appears as the only alternative to a capitulation to massive injustice, violence itself remains inhuman and an invitation to fratricide; but these evils will be obscured in men of good will by immediate values calling for defense. It was a deep concern for human dignity and justice which moved the early Malcolm to preach a disciplined, defensive violence to the black man, and it is this same concern, running wild under the indifference and hostility of white America, which is behind the explosions from Watts to Detroit. Gandhi would have sympathized with Malcolm even at his early stage, for Gandhi recognized this relative value in discriminate violence for that man who can see no other alternative to a cooperation with injustice; but he saw it as a value only in the context of a man's lack of vision or strength. As Arnold Toynbee has written, "If we have really lost the power or the will to practice the virtues of Gethsemane, then it is certainly better to practice those of Sparta or Valhalla than to practice none at all." [19]

Violence is preferable only to cowardice, when no other resistance to injustice is conceivable to a man. Non-violence is for the strong, not the weak. But in itself non-violence is a human imperative *to be strong*.

If one were to single out a supreme test case in history for the principle of non-violent resistance, as critics are inclined to do in order to dismiss its value anywhere, it would be the case of the Jews under the Nazis. Or to reverse the approach, as we have been doing in this chapter in order to focus on the opposite pole, violence—if one were to single out a supreme case in history which would seem to *legitimize* the use of violence and grant it the *right* to bear a higher value, it would be violence used by the Jews against the Nazis. It is not necessary to theorize on this second possibility, for history had been witness to the Wall and to the sons of Abraham who resisted it.

The Jews' resistance to the Nazis behind the wall of the Warsaw Ghetto is a historical reality of such continuing vividness and even sacredness on the one hand, and of such clear inhumanity on the other, that any effort to view it with scientific objectivity is doomed to take on the face of death itself. The "objectivity" of the rational mind categorizing the values of a still-living history suggests at this point nothing so much as the swagger stick of the S.S. officer dispatching the people of Israel to one or the other side of the holocaust. Our approach here will be no effort to see in their historical totality the last days of the Warsaw Ghetto, even if that were possible, or to extract a definitive hierarchy of values from the anguish there. The question raised has to do with the value of violence as the Jews' form of resistance. Our approach, subjective and tentative, is through the eyes of the man who has created the greatest monument to those days; through John Hersey's novel, *The Wall*.

In a certain respect *The Wall* is like *Doctor Zhivago*; in the midst of death it is a celebration of life. In the "Editor's Prologue" it is said that Noach Levinson, the archivist of the Ghetto and narrator of the book, "was much interested in survival—and not merely his own." [20] Levinson was one of the few survivors of the Ghetto, although he died less than a year after its destruction as a result of the attrition he suffered there. But the survival in which he was interested, of the archives which detail the life of the Ghetto, is a more enduring one. And the survival of Jewish life recorded in his pages is the endurance of life itself under the most determined blows of the forces of annihilation. Life endures, even beyond the chasm of evil which reduced Polish Jewry to a handful, and Rachel Apt's closing words of the book, spoken hours after the remnant's escape from the Ghetto—"*Nu*, what is the plan for tomorrow?"—lift one to a simple but at that point supreme affirmation of life: There is a tomorrow, for the Jews and for humanity as a whole.

But from the depths of the chasm, during those months behind the Ghetto wall, the question of survival overwhelmed the Jews, whose numbers dipped rapidly with each day's selection by the Nazis for the constantly departing freight trains. The decision reached finally to fight the Germans with a pitifully few arms was founded not on the hope that the fighters' lives would thereby be saved or even lengthened—the prospect was for even more immediate death—but on the belief that some vestige of life and human dignity would be affirmed for all through that final, futile resistance. As Levinson puts it in his journal entry shortly before the decision was made, "Now, there is but one question. In what manner will we go? Proudly? Or cravenly?" [21] The survival at stake here is the survival of human dignity.

Resistance to injustice is as much an imperative of human nature as a non-violent love is. The two values behind man are love and truth. Love means suffering and non-violence. Truth means resistance and revolution.

If a man loves in a torn world, he will suffer for the sake of that love. Suffering love is supported by a faith in God's love. When love reaches its apex on the cross of human existence, man's eyes are forced to turn upward. At that moment there is no vision left on earth to console them, and there is only anguish in the voice which cries out for God's reasons. Love on the cross is the man-God himself suffering in the darkness of those reasons. Yet because love dies in the darkness of faith, it is raised to a vision of truth.

Love plus truth means a suffering resistance: again the cross of love but at that other moment of crucifixion when the truth of love is definable with respect to man; his need and his injustice. The Son is crucified. He resists the murder of mankind in himself through a love directed at his murderers: "Father, forgive them. . . ." The resistance is again love, but a love directed at man for the sake of his unrealized Truth: ". . . for they know not what they do." Suffering love by itself agonizes over man and loses itself in God. Truth directs that love back to the world of man, resists man's evil non-violently and heals him in ways that can be seen, in terms of human values that must be defended for man to go on living. "They know not what they do" affirms the possibility of the redemptive truth still hidden—that they *will know* what they *have done* and in that knowing renounce their blind rejection of the Truth.

Love and truth are inseparable, yet love is existentially the higher. Truth gives reasons to love's suffering but love reaches its greatest height in a suffering whose truth is darkness; only God's truth. Truth is *why* love is, but love doesn't always know *what* truth is. Yet when love knows the truth and sees it denied

by man's actions, as it will continually, love's suffering takes on
direction and becomes a suffering resistance. Love then suffers
for truth, the truth of the situation and the truth of man himself,
by resisting man's injustice and brutality.

In the Warsaw Ghetto the issue was the truth of man himself,
whatever it is that distinguishes him—even the strongest were
tempted to add, just barely—from brute creation. The formation
of the Jewish Fighter Organization took place through a sudden
resolution of the long-standing issues which had kept the various
Jewish parties and organizations contending among themselves
even within the Ghetto. The most divisive differences among the
Ghetto factions suddenly dropped away beneath the weight of
an appalling denial: the Nazis' incredible denial, total and syste-
matic, of man himself.

Levinson observed:

The Communist is my comrade. The once-contemptible smuggler now
smuggles for me. The Zionist dreams of freedom for me, it matters
not where:—either in Jerusalem or on the Aleje Jerozolimskie, Warsaw. For we have reduced all our various politics to a single maxim:
  The fact that a man is a man is more important than the fact that
he believes what he believes.[22]

After noting this discovery by them all of the maxim to counter
the denial, Levinson adds his reservation as an intellectual, and
the *but* which would signify the maxim's immediate implementa-
tion:

Nothing is quite that simple: I know it. But when circumstances
grow unbearably complex, it is natural that we should grope about
for a very simple credo. And so, after all, we tell ourselves, man's real
quiddity is that he is a human being, not that he is a Zionist, a Communist, a Socialist, a Jew, a Pole, or, for that matter, a Nazi. *But*
(and here is why we prepare to kill) any man who cannot recognize
this basic maxim is an agent of Anti-Humanity, and his purpose,
whether conscious or not, is the wiping out of mankind. We must kill
him first, for the sake of all the others.[23]

Man's real quiddity is that he is a human being. The truth of
man is not party, race, or nation. His truth is humanity itself. But

the maxim does not apply to him who cannot recognize it, who is an agent of anti-humanity by taking part in the great denial.

This is the philosophy which Levinson says he has learned really from Rachel Apt, conveyed to him in far simpler words than his own. "I look at her unprofitable, soft-skinned face and her sparkling eyes—and I believe in the simple, one-sentence politics of Humanity." [24] It must be recalled that Rachel Apt is that homely girl—Levinson seems almost incapable of referring to her without stressing her odd face—whom no reader can think of without beauty at *The Wall's* conclusion. Rachel and Berson, she in her natural strength and responsiveness and he in his unexpected growth into greatness, *are* the humanity of *The Wall*. When Levinson attributes to Rachel also his integration of the killing corollary into the politics of humanity, it is a paradox worth taking seriously: "She takes apart and analyzes a revolver before my eyes, fondling the weapon—and I believe paradoxically in the sanctity of man's life." [25]

In the face of the most enormous denial in history of the truth of humanity, was the only affirmation of life remaining to the victims the fondling of a revolver? Had the resistance-imperative of truth for once become so immediate and demanding as to conflict with the non-violent imperative of love?

There is no question that the stand made by the Warsaw Ghetto fighter groups for almost a month against overwhelmingly superior German forces in the spring of 1943 is one of the great stories of the human spirit. It is a story which not only compels our admiration and gratitude—for that affirmation of humanity—but also harmonizes with a popular understanding of the kind of resistance which, it is said, Jews should have offered if possible everywhere to the Nazis. But it is no detraction from Rachel Apt and the Ghetto fighters to say that in the perspective of a history larger than their own, Anne Frank and Ernie Levy may have offered an even more enduring, more redemptive resistance to the anti-humanity they all faced. If there are sacred values in both legacies, there is less danger that the second will ever be exploited by a nationalistic spirit. To try to do so by saying in

the name of a militant Israel that "there must be no more Anne
Franks" is too obviously to reverse the mandate: There must be
no more Nazis. But if that is to occur, there must be many more
Anne Franks, from Israel and from elsewhere, reaffirming and
carrying forward the values of the first. In fact the final beauty
of Rachel Apt places her much more in this tradition than in the
line of freedom fighters.

The Wall's concluding comments on resistance and violence
come in a reflective denouement after the weeks of street fighters
challenging tanks and whole battalions. The scene is the incredibly calming spectacle of several dozen Jews crouching for
thirty hours in a sewer pipe beneath the streets of Warsaw,
having just escaped from the Germans' final razing of the Ghetto.
While they await their deliverance by long-overdue trucks sched-
uled to arrive at the manhole above, Noach Levinson takes the
opportunity to question closely each member of the group about
the more obscure points in his history. His most significant dialogue is with Rachel:

> Rachel:—I didn't have much chance to learn about God; I am rather
> unclear as to God. But so far as the rest of our religion is concerned,
> I think there is only one thing: not to hurt anybody. For me the
> whole of the Torah is in one sentence in Leviticus: Thou shalt love
> thy neighbor as thyself.
> N.L.:—Even if thy neighbor is a Nazi?
> Rachel:—How else cure him of being a Nazi?
> N.L.:—Maybe there is no cure. Maybe you have to kill him.
> Rachel:—I've tried that, and where did it get me? Where am I now?
> N.L.:—In a sewer.[26]

The revelation is a partial one and not definitive of the issues
raised in *The Wall*. Had Rachel not tried to kill the Nazi, the
sewer would likely have been the train to Treblinka. The possibility of resisting with one's humanity a summons to the death
camp had seemed to lie only in the direction of the fighter
groups. But Rachel is aware of the ambiguity present in even
that resistance and admits another, unrealized possibility
(whether it is realizable only in the eschaton or not is left open
by her question): "How else cure him of being a Nazi?" In other

respects Rachel did cure through love, so the truth is less a conviction of herself than an axiom of human nature. It is the truth
that to kill rather than cure with love draws one into the enemy's
sewer. The sign of this truth is not Rachel but Yitzhok, the young
group commander and fearless killer of the Germans who finally
kills a newborn Jewish baby as well, in order to silence his crying and keep secret the location of the Jews' bunker. In this act
and in the name of the murdered child, Israel, there is a suggestion that the Jewish freedom fighter may be forced by force
into killing the religious meaning of Israel.

The greatest resistance to the Nazis shown in *The Wall* is not
the courageous violence of the fighter groups but the non-violent
resistance of Berson. Again the truth is present in complexity:
Berson is himself a member of a fighter group, has no hesitation
in using a gun (though he seldom does), and is in fact the
Ghetto's principal supplier of arms through his smuggling activities from outside the wall. But it was Berson who reflected earlier
on another Jew's determination to kill every German he could,
and who had concluded: "No, there is only one resistance: it is
inward. It is living one's Jewishness as well as possible, meeting
things as they come." [27] And the final power and symbol of
Berson is found in something altogether different from his traffic
in arms: It lies in his "guerrilla concerts" to the Nazis.

One night at the height of the resistance and with the Ghetto
streets occupied by the Germans, Berson picked up his concertina
and walked out of his bunker. Several minutes later the Jews in
the bunker heard somewhere outside the proud strains of
"Hatikva"—"Hope," the Jewish national anthem—being played on
the concertina. It continued for six or seven bars, then stopped
abruptly. Minutes later the concertina could be heard again, this
time at a great distance, now playing the "Horst Wessel" song;
with a slightly Jewish accent, it seemed. Berson's concert continued through that night and other nights, his selections always
chosen according to their appropriateness for German ears and
jumping rapidly through the Ghetto, whose tunnels and alleys

he knew from having designed its communications system, keeping just ahead of the shots and shouts of the Nazis.

Apart from Rachel's expression of hope, Berson's concertina raises the last sound heard in *The Wall*. When the trucks arrive finally at the manhole cover, it is broad daylight on the Warsaw street, and before all the Jews have climbed into the trucks a military whistle is heard. The drivers panic and the trucks pull out, leaving a few Jews to face the Germans after all, including Berson, who had remained in the sewer to help everyone else up the ladder. But as the trucks gain speed, the passengers hear behind them, above the whistling and shooting, the bold notes of a concertina playing the "Hatikva." We are not wrong to conclude that even in the face of the Nazis, man's resistance to inhumanity and the hope of Israel are given their most powerful expression in a concertina.

Is there a general truth about the largest and most complex manifestation of violence, war, which will permit us to evaluate war as a possible or impossible expression of genuine values? Up to this point in our analysis we have been concerned with the value structures of particular forms of violence—the Cain instinct manifested in its radical brutality, the violence of poverty and race, the violence of the Warsaw Ghetto—which could be isolated sufficiently in each case to expose a pattern of action. The phenomenon of war arches over all such reasons for war and is least of all reducible to any single factor or value. As a group of American psychiatrists stated in an analysis of war:

The theory that wars, particularly contemporary wars, are the sum total of countless individual human aggressions is not a tenable one. . . . Modern warfare is a complicated institution, the result of the intermeshing of many factors—social, economic, political, and psychological.[28]

In our treatment of the just war, we have already rejected the possibility of any genuine doctrinal synthesis between war and Christianity. But this was done by beginning at the cross and demanding that war justify itself doctrinally in that light. If we here reverse the procedure, beginning instead phenomenologically with war, and ask what values war is capable of bearing, the results of our analysis will prove to be more revealing of the normative role of war in history. Beginning from the historical character of war, we might also be able to discern the cross' partial existence in war itself.

In *A Study of History* Arnold Toynbee has shown that war has been the proximate cause of the breakdown of every civilization which is known for certain to have broken down.

> Though Slavery, Caste, the Conflict of Classes, Economic Injustice, and many other social symptoms of the nemesis of Original Sin have played their part as instruments of Man's self-torment, War stands out among the rest as Man's principal engine of social and spiritual self-defeat during a period of his history which he is now beginning to be able to see in perspective.[29]

War strangles the men and civilizations which wage it before they can realize in time the power that war has assumed over them. The confirmation of this truth in our own time can be seen in the breakdown of Western man from the immediate and gathering effects of World War I. George Kennan has based his classic analysis, *Russia and the West under Lenin and Stalin,* directly on the effects of World War I: "The Russian Revolution and the alienation of the Russian people from the Western community for decades to come were only a part of the staggering price paid by the Western people for their insistence on completing a military victory over Germany in 1917 and 1918."[30] Another part of the staggering price of World War I and the humbling of Germany was, of course, World War II, whose conclusion at Hiroshima and Nagasaki inaugurated the nuclear arms race. But at this point war has extended its self-annihilative power from particular civilizations to a power over the entire world. Whether one views nuclear war pragmatically or theologically, its face is the same: War has become eschatological, the proximate cause and sign of mankind's end. But this is perhaps to say that with nuclear weapons war has ceased to

be war, by having its destructive power multiplied almost infi-
nitely, and has simply become eschatological destruction.

From the standpoint of those who have been involved in the
non-nuclear phenomenon of *war*, war has a million faces—each
face dependent on the war experience of the individual man. To
see the phenomenon of war in its concreteness would be to see
simultaneously these million faces of war as it confronts all its
participants. Or, since this is impossible, to see the phenomenon
of war is to see the most common aspects of this million-sided
experience. As found concretely in man's experience, war is therefore not so much the war of the politician and general, who in
terms of their numbers and the intensity of their experience see
relatively little of the war they conduct, but rather war as known
by the warrior, as he carries forward into battle the politician's
and general's commands. The observation that there would probably be fewer wars if those who conducted wars had to fight
them personally indicates the distance between war as a concrete
phenomenon and war as a political instrument. Once it is decided
to understand war primarily as a political and strategic instrument, its proper use being dependent on attendant causes and
circumstances, then war as a phenomenon—as it impresses its
existence on the fighting man at its center, engaged in its concrete reality—becomes irrelevant.[31] Only the politician's and
strategist's war, a deceptively small aspect of the total experience,
is then considered in defining the essential character of war and
the values it can bear.

In short, one can view war at a distance, politically and ideo-
logically; or close up, phenomenologically and personally. One
can see war in terms of ends and policies or in terms of corpses
and gutted cities. As a rule it is simply assumed that war is a
legitimate instrument of politics under certain conditions, thus
making its political character morally independent of the phenomenon except for a few general principles. We will seek to
determine through the actual phenomenon of war the values war
in its concrete character is capable of bearing, and thus evaluate
its possible use as a means for a political end.

At the center of war is killing and being killed. Few men, however, go to war in order to be killed, and it is even doubtful if very many go with their eyes open to the killing they will be called on to do. The central phenomenon of war, the killing confrontation with the enemy, is a cold shock to the warrior suddenly immersed in the reality of his new purpose in life: to inflict death, and secondarily to face death in the fire of the enemy's guns. To the warrior before this moment of truth war will have meant a number of things: the movement of his nation sucking him into its collective fear and enthusiasm, his obedience to the command of a draft board, an abstract hatred of the enemy, travel, comradeship, a release from the boredom of his own life. Through this process the secondary aspect of war, that of *being killed*—secondary because it is the soldier's risk, not his purpose—will have occurred to him and may even have stricken him with fear. But war's primary aspect, killing, will have remained unknown, its radical inhumanity concealed beneath layers of socially assumed indifference toward the life of the enemy. At the moment when war finally reveals its character as the killing of men, the warrior is shocked, as if he were never actually meant to become involved in what was war's concrete purpose for him from the beginning.

The relation between the Cain instinct and war is therefore no facile one. War is not "the sum total of countless individual human aggressions." War is not only collective violence. It is first of all *organized* violence, involving massive planning and preparation. The soldier's Cain instinct needs to be subsidized by the state before it can kill in war. Furthermore, as the psychologist Gordon Allport has pointed out:

Studies of soldiers in combat show that hate and aggression are less commonly felt than fear, homesickness, and boredom. Few citizens, in an aggressive nation, actually *feel* aggressive. Thus their warlike activity cannot be due solely to their personal motivations.[32]

From the warrior's point of view modern war is less the result of personal aggression than it is of passivity. In the age of conscription, the soldier's decision to participate in war is initially the decision of his government, to which he simply adds his consent. The structure of most modern states is from a military standpoint totalitarian. The citizen prepares to fight in war because the state tells him to fight, and because personal, social, and national pressures combine effectively for the state to make the drafted citizen fear to disobey this order or even to question it in his own mind. Hatred of the enemy may also be a factor in his going to war, but if it were a decisive factor in the raising of modern armies there would be no conscription. Men seem to kill in war less because of any overwhelming drive to kill than because they have been told to do so and did not realize the inhuman nature of the act which their consent put before them.

The confrontation involved in war's central act of killing has nowhere been revealed more starkly than in Ernest Hemingway's novel *For Whom the Bell Tolls*. In a sense Hemingway's presentation does not correspond to our previous analysis because his protagonist, an American member of the resistance in the Spanish Civil War who is preparing to blow up a bridge, is both a volunteer to a cause he believes in, and when we encounter him a man already experienced by war in killing. But these factors, the genuine commitment in war and the past knowledge of death, would if anything disguise or dull the shock of a killing confrontation and in fact they seem to change it very little. The novel itself indicates that killing, if done by a man who has not forgotten his own humanity, can never be experienced as anything other than an inhuman act. An early exchange between Robert Jordan and Anselmo, the old peasant who is to help him with the bridge, defines the issue:

"You have killed?" Robert Jordan asked in the intimacy of the dark and of their day together.

"Yes. Several times. But not with pleasure. To me it is a sin to kill a man. Even Fascists whom we must kill. To me there is a great difference between the bear and the man and I do not believe the wizardry of the gypsies about the brotherhood with animals. No. I am against all killing of men."

"Yet you have killed."

"Yes. And will again. But if I live later, I will try to live in such a way, doing no harm to any one, that it will be forgiven." [33]

Anselmo believes in no God but still regards killing as a sin, albeit a tragic necessity. It contradicts his own humanity.

"Then it is thyself who will forgive thee for killing."

"I believe so," Anselmo said. "Since you put it clearly in that way I believe that must be it. But with or without God, I think it is a sin to kill. To take the life of another is to me very grave." [34]

Reflecting later over the body of a young loyalist soldier he has killed and whose letters from home he has just read, Robert Jordan agrees with Anselmo's view:

I believe in the people and their right to govern themselves as they wish. But you mustn't believe in killing, he told himself. You must do it as a necessity but you must not believe in it. If you believe in it the whole thing is wrong.[35]

The epiphany of killing as sin occurs at the blowing up of the bridge at the novel's conclusion. Robert Jordan must kill a sentry posted by the bridge. From his hiding place on a mountain Jordan studies his target through binoculars prior to shooting him to death:

Robert Jordan took his glasses from his shirt pocket and turned the eyepieces until the end of the bridge showed sharp and gray-painted-metal clear. Then he moved them onto the sentry box.

The sentry sat leaning against the wall. His helmet hung on a peg and his face showed clearly. Robert Jordan saw he was the same man who had been there on guard two days before in the afternoon watch. He was wearing the same knitted stocking-cap. And he had not shaved. His cheeks were sunken and his cheekbones prominent. He had bushy eyebrows that grew together in the center. He looked sleepy and as Robert Jordan watched him he yawned. Then he took out a tobacco pouch and a packet of papers and rolled himself a cigarette. He tried to make a lighter work and finally put it in his pocket and went over to the brazier, leaned over, reached inside, brought up a piece of charcoal, juggled it in one hand while he blew on it, then lit the cigarette and tossed the lump of charcoal back into the brazier.

Robert Jordan, looking through the Zeiss 8-power glasses, watched his face as he leaned against the wall of the sentry box drawing on the cigarette. Then he took the glasses down, folded them together and put them in his pocket.

I won't look at him again, he told himself.[36]

Here Jordan's vision is the one sight which an effective soldier cannot afford to have in war, a vision of the enemy as human, relaxing in terms of the same weaknesses and characteristics as are possessed by the man about to kill him. The enemy is human. But in the circumstances of war, where the mountain pass has become a scene for sabotage and death, the man clearly delineated in the eyepieces is the body to be objectified moments later at the end of a rifle sight and killed. Jordan has been granted the fullness of what most other soldiers, in the smoke of battle, experience in a less vivid way or not at all—an immediate recognition of the target as brother and a quiet moment before firing in which to feel the impact of this insight. The effect is shattering: "I won't look at him again, he told himself."

Another killing confrontation is the final scene of the novel. But in this case we know that Robert Jordan will kill only to be killed, as he lies alone with his leg broken, sighting his machine gun on a loyalist officer leading a group of men up the slope. The officer who is Jordan's target is already known to the reader, so that with both sides fully humanized the double killing foreseen at the conclusion is a revelation once again of the fratricidal character of war, as emphasized by the John Donne lines behind Hemingway's title: "Any man's *death* diminishes *me*, because I am involved in *Mankinde*; and therefore never send to know for whom the *bell* tolls; it tolls for *thee*." In war the bell tolls for you the warrior, always the target at the end of your gun.

In modern war, however, it is by no means certain that the warrior will ever experience that moment of truth when war reveals its killing nature through a sudden insight into the enemy's humanity. What is even more inhuman in war than the killing confrontation, and what is becoming more and more common with the perfection of military technology, is the warrior's failure to have any confrontation whatsoever with the enemy. The warrior has become a technician, confined beneath the earth in a missile silo thousands of miles from his victims or in a plane high above a target whose only face is the foliage of a jungle. Without a powerful effort of imagination, contrary to his self-interest and the effective performance of his task, the warrior in such a situation remains unaware of the humanity of his target and is thus unaware of the inhumanity of his own act. Even in the midst of ground fighting, today there is seldom the kind of glimpse of the enemy as human which forced Robert Jordan to look away from his target. On the ground the enemy now lies faceless behind an almost solid wall of firepower, although in the case of American troops occupying Vietnam the enemy is also more visible, inasmuch as he lurks behind every villager's smile or sullen glance. But the wall there between warrior and the enemy's humanity may be more difficult to breach than the firepower.

This progressive dehumanization of the enemy through the very mechanics of war is to be expected. It is in the nature of war and its development to establish through the use of ever more powerful weapons a killing distance between the individual warrior and his enemy, so that the normal inhibition to killing— a mutually recognizable humanity—is no longer present. Only then are normally gentle men able to kill in war without feeling. The enemy is known only in terms of the immediate danger he represents or as an object which propaganda has drained of humanity and refashioned as diabolic. Because war is a massive and highly organized use of violence, it is largely dependent for its execution on the concerted killing efforts of large numbers of men who would never kill under normal conditions. Yet they will kill without hesitation in war because of the effective killing distance placed between themselves and the enemy as man. When this killing distance has been filled with the fury of mutual violence, then the Cain instinct provoked by the enemy will take full command in the warrior with a deliberately murderous violence. But even in war hatred is not a permanent attitude and violence's more enduring support is the Cain instinct in a less heightened form: a simple indifference to the enemy's humanity as kept distant enough for effective killing. As the weapons of war become more powerful, this killing distance increases. Thus the inhumanity of war fostered by the weapons themselves increases at the very time when the weapons' threat to mankind has made it most imperative that enemies become present to one another as men.

Killing distance is not merely spatial. Even at that time in war's development when the warrior could still see the enemy's form, he failed to see his claim on life profoundly enough to affirm it by his own actions. Robert Jordan looked away, but when the time came he shot the sentry. Killing distance is the consequence of man's fear and self-confinement, his inability to make an act of faith in man as such, or in some power beyond power. It is the Cain instinct expressed in a more subtle form than hatred and aggression. There is more killing distance between ourselves and the rest of humanity than any of us would like to admit. But murder is not usually a norm. Outside war, killing distance is constantly being overcome by some form of community. When killing distance is extended and made normative by the weapons of war, its murderous potential is realized.

The warrior's concrete purpose is to kill the enemy, but he must also face the enemy's efforts to kill him. At the center of war is not simply the effort to inflict injury and death on other men, but also the risk of having injury and death inflicted on oneself. War is primarily killing but war is also suffering, and suffering is the matter of redemption. The existence of suffering as war's secondary aspect is what makes possible in war the presence of the cross.

Mankind's confusion and self-deception regarding the meaning of war can be seen in the fact that we send men to war to kill for us but praise them afterward for having suffered or died for us. This is to respect and honor the soldier for the right reason but to sentimentalize the reality in which he took part. We wish to have the protection of the Roman soldiers but in the image of Christ crucified. The truth is that the soldier in war is both executioner and victim, both Pilate and Christ.

Some of the most beautiful descriptions of the Christ at the center of war's agony are found in Teilhard's letters to his cousin Marguerite during his service as a stretcher-bearer in World War I. Teilhard was not altogether free from an idealization of war. In his letters he says much of war's suffering and dying, little of its injuring and killing. But although he understood war primarily in terms of its secondary aspect, Teilhard's perception of the suffering side of war is profound in its recognition of the human redemption being wrought out of horror. He wrote of the scene of one battle:

I don't know what sort of monument the country will later put up on Froideterre hill to commemorate the great battle. There's only one that would be appropriate: a great figure of Christ. Only the image of the crucified can sum up, express and relieve all the horror, and beauty, all the hope and deep mystery in such an avalanche of conflict and sorrows. As I looked at this scene of bitter toil, I felt completely overcome by the thought that I had the honour of standing at one of the two or three spots on which, at this very moment, the whole life of the universe surges and ebbs—places of pain but it is there that a great future (this I *believe* more and more) is taking shape.[37]

Teilhard's Christocentric vision of war as a crisis of evolution which had to be gone through lacks only a perception of the upward step which might take man beyond it. If we distinguish in war, as he did not, between the Christ who suffers war's agonies and the Pilate who inflicts them, then man's final redemption from war would have to take the form of a deeply global commitment to the suffering love which has been war's redemptive significance from the beginning—and a corresponding resistance, in and through that love, to Pilate's continuing act of execution in war. The creators and wagers of war must be resisted, but resisted in and through that suffering love which has been the very means of man's redemption, *while waging war*, from the killing inhumanity which is its essence. Mankind can be redeemed totally from war by the same Christic reality which has redeemed individual warriors from slavery to war's inhumanity. The paradox of war is that the warrior who does its inhuman work of taking life cannot live without love. Love can take deep root in the suffering side of the warrior's task, thus working against and perhaps saving him from the inhumanity of his killing.

To the question, then, of whether or not war can bear the value of love, our answer is yes—but yes only for war as suffering. For war as killing, which is, of course, war's immediate purpose and primary aspect, we must answer no by recognizing the absolute conflict between its inhumanity and love's drive for communion. War can bear the value of love not as waged but as suffered, so that it is not the warrior's action but his victim's which provides the possibility of a partial redemption of war's reality. The fact that the warrior himself is victim as well as executioner is what makes possible his own redemption. The warrior is victim to the suffering consequences of both the enemy's and his own violence. That unintended aspect of his waging war returns him to the life which he lost by killing it in his neighbor-enemy. Suffering returns him from killing to life, for to live is to suffer. But to become human through life is to find meaning in its suffering, and the meaning of suffering is love.[38] The suffering which his war-making draws down on the warrior can therefore serve as the occasion for his redemption in love from that same war-making.

Suffering is the matter of redemption and can rescue the warrior from his killing. But suffering is impotent without love's energizing form, and to experience suffering in war from the enemy's inhumanity is in itself an experience of hatred which calls forth not love, but a return hatred and violence. Luther's view, taken up later by Paul Tillich,[39] that it is the strange work of love to destroy by violence what is against love, is a theological abstraction which ignores the existential truth that such a violent "love" normally has the effect of heightening what is against love. A "love" which expresses itself in violence is for the victim indistinguishable from hatred and naturally arouses a counter-hatred and violence.[40] When love tries to do its strange work of destroying, it destroys love itself and creates an honest hatred in return. Violence in action is no work of love but rather the natural expression of hatred. But what can we mean then by saying that suffering in war, which insofar as it comes from the enemy's violence will be experienced as hatred, can be—and often has been—the occasion of a redemptive love?

We could not mean that this suffering received from the enemy will give rise to a spontaneous love in return. But besides the enemy, there is also the warrior's own fighting group, in which the sufferings of war will be experienced in common. Suffering in war takes on the meaning of love in service to that community. The warrior in battle belongs to a limited community whose outward purpose is a deadly violence, but whose internal relationships may be marked by an extraordinary care and sacrifice. What many men rightly treasure from the horrors of war is the intense communion which they experienced with their comrades in the sharing of enormous burdens and suffering. The fact that this community of sharing is in war a necessity for survival does not make it inauthentic. More than a few men have given their lives for it. No man conscious of a higher purpose than the warrior's cause has the right to despise his sacrifice or the community on which it was founded. As J. Glenn Gray has written in his beautifully perceptive book, *The Warriors*:

> Are we not right in honoring the fighter's impulse to sacrifice himself for a comrade, even though it be done, as it so frequently is, in an evil cause? I think so. It is some kind of world historical pathos that the striving for union and for immortality must again and again be consummated while men are in the service of destruction.[41]

What makes war especially intolerable is the contradiction it presents between the presence of a genuinely redemptive suffering love *within a fighting group* and the murderous violence which that same group directs outside itself at another, similarly constituted group of the enemy. The killing distance enforced by war makes possible the infliction of mutual agony between

enemies whose redemptive power of suffering love is expended
totally within their own groups. In most cases the fact that these
men are sacrificing themselves and murdering their neighbor-
enemies nominally for the sake of opposing causes is irrelevant,
even when these warring causes can be defined precisely enough
to show a genuine value at issue in the conflict. Warriors
sacrifice themselves in battle much less for national causes than
they do for their besieged comrades. The commitment felt most
deeply by the warrior is always to the community of his own
fighting group. If the same group were fighting for a different
cause, it would often make little difference to the soldiers within
it, as has been shown by the continuing loyalty of armies beneath the conflicting power alliances of their nations. This is
not simply the warrior's blind obedience or his despairing skepticism concerning the existence of a greater truth for which men
fight, but at least in part an implicit affirmation of the truth,
reached through war's chaos and suffering, that truth itself is to
be understood personally—with respect to his comrades—more
than in the ideological phrases of national leaders. The tragedy
of the warrior is that his painfully won insight into the existential
character of truth, a truth known in and for a living community,
is only a partial one in its context, inasmuch as this insight will
have been realized and forged into a commitment only in terms
of a group of persons whose outward purpose is to kill other,
more distant persons. As such, his commitment is both profoundly
personal and profoundly depersonalized, depending on whether
one views it from within the group or from an opposite enemy
group. Yet it is subjectively an honest commitment which has
simply been put to the service of murderous powers in the
world. But from an objective standpoint, the only proper, non-
contradictory locus for the warrior's commitment of suffering
love to the truth of the person is in a totally non-violent community at the service of global peace.

Even at the most selfless height of war, which few warriors
reach, above the hatred which strangles many men in war, the
warrior's love is a limited love expended in a murderous effort.

Within the perspective of an ongoing Christogenesis of the universe his love is not lost and takes its place in the upward unification constituting a cosmic Christ. But in terms of its total redemptive possibilities in that Christogenesis, the warrior's love within a killing community is tragic, abortive, contradicted by the killing purpose within which it finds life. Mankind's sin at the cross of every man's personal rejection of his neighbor is the source of war, and confines the warrior's love to a closed community incapable of opening itself to a hostile world. The warrior's love is restricted by sin to a group obedient to the "territorial imperative" which man has in common with the beast. Mankind's love on the cross of some men's non-violent acceptance of their persecuting neighbors (while resisting their injustice) is the source of peace, and opens the love of these men to a world redeemed by love. Human love is opened to the world by divine love. The warrior's love is therefore a love which can find its fulfillment only in the total openness to the world expressed through non-violence.

What can be said of saints who have been at the service of war? First of all, that their sanctity was not due to their participation in war's central act but in spite of it. They were saints not because they killed but because they did its opposite, suffered with love. Their holiness survived in war only through war's secondary aspect, suffering, and their profound commitment to it in love.

Secondly, such saints have lived in the Constantinian milieu from which Christians are only now beginning to emerge. It is difficult even today to understand the overwhelming influence this milieu has had on the development and self-understanding of Christianity. God did not abandon man in history during this period of achievement and distortion. Christianity itself is a radical commitment to God at the center of history. As such, it is the most difficult as well as the most vital of faiths, one which has had to work out its inevitable tensions with a world whose redemptive center of love is the man whom it crucified.

Christianity in its love affair with a world which is both Christ and crucifier has undergone a growth of self-understanding in and through the Constantinian milieu, and the saints have been the most forward branch of that growth. Their sanctity was of their time, a carrying out in a particular history of God's progressively unfolding will. The divine will was revealed fully in Christ, but it is only through its interaction with man's progressive understanding of himself in history that the given fullness of Christ in the Gospel can be realized by man in time. The saints have led in the growth toward a Christically balanced view of the world—a world which is neither victim nor executioner but a synthesis of the two. But to identify Christ through every action of his saints with the militant aspect of the milieu they were leaving behind would be an idolatry of the past. The Christ of history is always the Christ up ahead who is simultaneously the fullness of the Christ given in the Gospel. His presence today is the revolution of peace whose center is the same suffering love which Joan of Arc and Louis of France committed themselves to in the heart of battle, and in so doing looked beyond battle to a vision whose fuller presence now—for the sake of their love—we dare not ignore.

In a famous essay published in 1910, William James expressed the need for mankind to develop a moral equivalent of war, inasmuch as war was deeply rooted in man's instincts and had served in history as the source of many virtues but had become on the other hand so self-destructive as to make imperative the discovery of a peaceful substitute. In the perspective of what we have already seen about war, we can say that the moral equivalent of war is the revolution of peace. For the phenomenon of war is a moral contradiction between man's murderous instincts and the suffering love to which he will rise in battle to aid his comrades in arms. To trace war's evil to its source, we can describe the violence of war as a complex manifestation of the Cain instinct rooted in the sinful side of the cross. The moral equivalent of war, Cain instinct, and cross as murder, is the constant struggle of peace, moral revolution, and cross as suffering love. War can be redeemed finally by the cross which exists unfulfilled but as a flame of hope even in the trenches of war itself.

NOTES

1. When Dr. Louis S. B. Leakey announced the discovery of the fossil in 1961, he told a Washington press conference that the child had been murdered. Leakey's colleagues frowned on the sensational conjecture. But Robert Ardrey writes in *The Territorial Imperative:* "I have examined the fossil, and the once-living being died of a radiating fracture of the skull. Did the youngster run into a tree on a dark night? The fracture is centered on top of his head, an awkward situation for such an injury. Did a stone roll down the steep slopes of the gorge to score a direct, unlucky hit on his crown? There was no gorge two million years ago; the site was then a flat plain beside a lake." *The Territorial Imperative* (Atheneum: 1966), pp. 261–62.

2. Konrad Lorenz, *On Aggression* (Harcourt, Brace & World: 1966), p. ix.

3. Ardrey, *The Territorial Imperative*, p. 232.

4. See G. S. Windass, "Reflections on Violence," *Cross Currents* (Winter 1964), pp. 4–5.

5. James Shafikh, "Police Riot Mars Peace March," *Los Angeles Free Press* (Monday, June 26, 1967), pp. 1–2. This special edition of the *Free Press* contains 8 pages of photos and accounts of the March.

6. This point has been documented by Dr. Karl Menninger in his book *Man against Himself* (Harcourt, Brace & World: 1956), where he shows with numerous case histories how the inversion of aggression can result in the act of suicide.

7. Sigmund Freud, "Letter to Albert Einstein: Why War?" *The Pacifist Conscience,* ed. Peter Mayer (Holt, Rinehart & Winston: 1966), p. 245.

8. *Ibid.*

9. Piet Schoonenberg, S.J., *Man and Sin* (Notre Dame: 1965), pp. 193–98.

10. John Dollard *et al., Frustration and Aggression* (Yale University Press: 1939).

11. Oscar Lewis, *The Children of Sanchez* (Vintage: 1961), pp. 232–33.

12. *Ibid.*, p. 223.

13. *Ibid.*, p. 212.
14. *The Autobiography of Malcolm X* (Grove Press: 1966), p. 273.
15. *Ibid.*, pp. 339–40.
16. *Ibid.*, p. 366.
17. *Ibid.*, p. 368.
18. *Ibid.*, Alex Haley, "Epilogue," p. 429.
19. Arnold J. Toynbee, "Militarism and the Military Virtues," *War and Civilization*, selected by Albert V. Fowler from *A Study of History* (Oxford University Press: 1950), p. 20.
20. John Hersey, *The Wall* (Cardinal: 1953), p. 9.
21. *Ibid.*, p. 367.
22. *Ibid.*, p. 476.
23. *Ibid.*, pp. 476–77.
24. *Ibid.*
25. *Ibid.*
26. *Ibid.*, p. 701.
27. *Ibid.*, p. 16.
28. *Psychiatric Aspects of the Prevention of Nuclear War* (Group for the Advancement of Psychiatry, Report No. 57: 1964), p. 229.
29. Toynbee, *War and Civilization*, p. viii.
30. George F. Kennan, *Russia and the West under Lenin and Stalin* (Hutchinson: 1961), p. 32.
31. I am aware that the phenomenon of modern war affects the civilian at least as much as it does the soldier with its suffering and death. This was the primary reason for rejecting earlier under the canons of the just-war doctrine any waging of modern war. But even so, the soldier's eyes are closer than the civilian's to the total phenomenon of war, which is killing as much as it is being killed. To see war from the soldier's standpoint is also to come nearer to the permanent characteristics of war, which has not always enveloped the civilian as much as it does today.
32. Gordon W. Allport, "The Role of Expectancy," *War: Studies from Psychology, Sociology, Anthropology*, edited by Leon Bramson and George W. Goethals (Basic Books: 1964), p. 178.
33. Ernest Hemingway, *For Whom the Bell Tolls* (Scribners: 1943), p. 41.
34. *Ibid.*
35. *Ibid.*, p. 304.
36. *Ibid.*, pp. 432–33.
37. Pierre Teilhard de Chardin, *The Making of a Mind* (Harper & Row: 1965), pp. 119–20.
38. See Viktor E. Frankl, *Man's Search for Meaning* (Washington Square Press: 1963).
39. In *Love, Power, and Justice* (Oxford University Press: 1960), pp. 49–51, 113–15.

40. See "Peace Is the Will of God," a statement presented by the Historic Peace Churches to the World Council of Churches in 1953. Published with a rebuttal by Reinhold Niebuhr and Angus Dun by the Historic Peace Churches and the Fellowship of Reconciliation.

41. J. Glenn Gray, *The Warriors* (Harper Torchbooks: 1967), p. 50.

10

Is There a Politics Without Violence?

In a book titled *The Christian in Politics,* a British political analyst observed in early 1962, "It is at least possible, as things stand today, that the hand which formally and technically releases large-scale nuclear war on the world will be Christian." [1]

During the week of October 21, 1962, this observation came close to being realized. The Cuban missile crisis brought the world to the edge of nuclear war, and one of the two national leaders involved in the confrontation over the abyss was a Christian. The other was a Communist. In the end the Communist backed away so that the Christian was not compelled to initiate Armageddon. Since then few Westerners have suggested that the Christian should have backed away before the Communist did. Indeed the Christian's tenacity at the nuclear trigger has been heralded as his "finest hour."

Yet it is no disservice to the memory of John F. Kennedy to suggest that he had finer hours than when a combination of circumstances, his fellow Americans' nationalism, and centuries of Christians' distortion of the Gospel in public life put him in the position of threatening the ultimate blasphemy against the cross to which he was personally committed. In fact the world can be thankful that this contradiction occurred in Kennedy rather than in one of the scripture-quoting demagogues who might have occupied his office then and whose self-righteousness would have made impossible Khrushchev's retreat. From the standpoint of political tact, Kennedy's handling of the Cuban missile crisis was masterful. But from the standpoint of life, the Catholic President's risk of global death stands condemned by his own reverence for everything the world sustained. Moreover, it is possible that the missile crisis needs to be demythologized. For the Communist may have been right.

Nikita Khrushchev's recent claim on NBC television that he placed missiles in Cuba to prevent another American invasion against the Castro regime does not have to stand on the credibility of Khrushchev. In December 1963, less than a month after President Kennedy's assassination, Jean Daniel, one of France's most eminent correspondents, reported Premier Castro's interpretation then of the missile crisis as given to Daniel in an interview.[2] Daniel's questions on this point had been prompted by Kennedy himself, who in one of his last actions as President had seen the French correspondent in Washington before his trip to interview Castro and had asked him to find out Castro's view of what had happened to bring on the crisis.

Castro told Daniel that the Cubans had learned that the CIA was planning another invasion of Cuba, "but we had our doubts as to the attitude of the President." Only when Alexei Adzhubei, Khrushchev's son-in-law, reported that the President had reminded him that the United States had refrained from intervening in Hungary did Castro conclude that an American attack was certain. He interpreted this to mean that Kennedy was asking the Soviet Union not to interfere with a United States invasion of Cuba. Castro then asked the Soviet Union to "do whatever is needed" to help and the two countries agreed on the installation of missiles.

It has been said in reply to Khrushchev's claim to be defending Cuba, supported by the details given by Castro four years earlier, that it does not do justice to the strategic effrontery of the Soviet operation. But the strategic justification brought forward for

American actions was criticized severely during the crisis itself by neutral observers, particularly in India, who saw no strategic difference between the United States missile bases in Turkey, on the frontier of the Soviet Union, and Soviet missile bases in Cuba. Kennedy was acutely aware of this parallel and even conceded privately that the Turkish bases were obsolete enough to represent no military sacrifice were they to be dismantled in an exchange with Khrushchev. Yet when Khrushchev asked Kennedy on October 27, 1962, for just such a reciprocal removal of bases, Turkey and Cuba together, Kennedy refused—at a point less than two days before the time he said the United States would begin bombing the Cuban missile sites. According to Elie Abel, who has written the definitive work on the American side of the crisis, "There was general agreement among the President and his advisors that no matter how little the Turkish missiles might be worth, in the military sense, to trade them off now would be to undermine the faith of the whole North Atlantic alliance in America's pledged word." [3]

To avoid disaster Khrushchev was therefore forced to dismantle his missiles alone in return simply for Kennedy's pledge not to invade Cuba. For Castro the President's word, lacking a reciprocal action, did not seem sufficient, especially after the Bay of Pigs, so Khrushchev's willingness to back down on this crucial point meant for the Soviet Premier an "undermining of the faith" of Cuba in Russia's pledged word. When posters in Havana proclaiming Cuba's eternal friendship for the Soviet Union were ripped down, and street urchins sang:

> "Nikita, Nikita,
> Lo que se da
> No se quita."

> (Nikita, Nikita
> That which is given
> Is not taken back.)

the evident loser of the duel was Khrushchev. But in terms not of prestige and the faith supporting military alliances but of man's right to continue his life in history, there is something to be said for the Soviet Premier's willingness to give his adversary more than he was given.

President Kennedy remarked later that had he as an American President withdrawn missiles as Khrushchev had, he would have been impeached.[4] Since then Khrushchev has in fact been removed from office, perhaps partly as a result of his retreat over Cuba. Perhaps, too, we should be grateful to him, or should at least acknowledge the possibility of an element of sacrifice having come from a position where we would not have expected it.

Even if the facts of the missile crisis were no different than the American myth would have them, the events of the week of October 21, 1962, would still have signed the death of Christian political theory. To hold as this theory did that the Christian in politics could conscientiously release nuclear war on the world is to reduce the cross of suffering love from which the Church began to a myth of self-destruction. Yet Christian political theory —whether it be the Christian realism of the Niebuhrians or the modern scholasticism of Catholic theorists—has not simply recovered from its *reductio ad absurdum* in the nuclear confrontation. It has not even noticed it. Which is to say that Christian political theory was so dead even before nuclear history reduced it to absurdity that no mourning was necessary after the full revelation of the corpse. The death of a politically relevant Christ had occurred in the Constantinian era which eventually made possible John F. Kennedy's tenacity behind the nuclear trigger and which made necessary, for the world's sake, his Communist opponent's folly in retreat. Today it is taken for granted by Christian political theory that Christ may swing the now-nuclear sword when necessary. If out of perversity a Communist should at the last moment withdraw the world from the swing of destruction, the explanation to be supplied is, as Dean Rusk succinctly put it, that the opponents were eyeball to eyeball and "the other fellow just blinked." [5] Thus does Christian realism receive its final summary in *High Noon*.

If there is to be a new politics of belief following the death of Christian politics, it will first of all have to meet critically, and subdue, the issue which has disrupted Christian theory from

Augustine to Niebuhr and has finally destroyed any possibility of its further growth: the issue of violence, now raised to a nuclear power. Christian theory absorbed violence as a premise of the state so as to limit morally a permanent factor in the human condition. At certain points this strategy had its positive effects but the over-all significance has been contradiction; between the cross and the sword, between catholicity and national self-interest. Christianity has in the long run limited violence far less than violence has limited Christianity. The distortion is most evident in the descending meaning of the cross, beginning with Christ as a symbol of non-violent love for all men and touching bottom in the Christian's righteous destruction of the "infidel," whether Jew, Moslem, or Communist. Christian theory has not always mirrored the progressive barbarism of Christian practice. In the late sixties, for example, Reinhold Niebuhr has shown the cross' capacity to resist the Christ-washed militarism being offered in his name by the Vice-President and other officials. But even at its best Christian political theory has posed no critical alternative to man's progressive dehumanization through a mushrooming violence. Realism has precluded moral revolution. At its worst such theory has sacramentalized violence in the holy wars which made cross and sword indistinguishable. In the Nuclear Age, Christian theory by its age-old distortion of the cross has all but forfeited any right to reinterpret its source.

But the cross as source remains, and with it the continuing possibility of resurrection. We have already indicated that such a resurrection lies in the direction of a catholicism of the cross, hence in the freeing of the cross from the Christianity which has forged its identity with the sword. A new politics of belief will of necessity find its roots not so much in institutional Christianity, still living largely in the Constantinian era, as in those men of peace who have explored the political meaning of the cross apart from the Church. A politics of belief for the Nuclear Age must find its point of departure therefore in the experiments in truth of a Gandhi or a Hammarskjöld in order to have any hope of finally reaffirming, at a point transcending its Christian reduction, the cross which belongs to mankind as a whole.

Our basic question for a new politics of belief can be stated simply: Is there a politics without violence? Its fuller formulation can be drawn from Max Weber's classic statement of the relationship between politics and violence in his essay "Politics as a Vocation."

Weber established the link between politics and violence through the state. "Politics" is "only the leadership, or the influencing of the leadership, of a *political* association, hence today, of a *state*." [6] (Italics in original.) And the state is violent:

Ultimately, one can define the modern state sociologically only in terms of the specific *means* peculiar to it, as to every political association, namely, the use of physical force . . . the state is a relation of men dominating men, a relation supported by means of legitimate (i.e., considered to be legitimate) violence.[7]

From his understanding of the nature of the state on one hand and of Christian morality on the other, Weber made his well-known distinction between an "ethic of ultimate ends" and an "ethic of responsibility." The ethic of ultimate ends corresponds to the Gospel. It comprises Jesus' mandates in the Sermon on the Mount and can be understood in the maxim "The Christian does rightly and leaves the results with the Lord." The ethic of ultimate ends is concerned only with a pure intention and pure means. If these means carried out in a political context should result, however predictably, in an evil end opposed to the intention, then in the actor's eyes the world is to blame. His responsibility ended with the moral means he chose. The title of such an ethic is paradoxical: An "ethic of ultimate ends" is concerned with moral *means* precisely because its ends *are ultimate*, that is, they are whatever historical ends God grants the means he has made imperative for man's salvation.

The ethic of responsibility is concerned with the politically foreseeable results of one's action. The actor here takes responsibility for his actions' consequences in the context of a political order where imperfection and evil are presupposed. He will therefore adjust his action toward the desirable end from the standpoint of the means' effectiveness on sinful men rather than their purity for the actor. The political realist, by following an ethic of responsibility, is committed to achieving his end even at the expense of morally dubious means and will shoulder the blame if he does not. The end he is intent on will presumably be good but his means, because political, are necessarily violent.

Because the decisive means for politics is violence, Weber saw a chasm between the ethics of the Gospel as summed up in the Sermon on the Mount and the ethics of the politician:

He who seeks the salvation of the soul, of his own and of others, should not seek it along the avenue of politics, for the quite different tasks of politics can only be solved by violence. The genius or demon of politics lives in an inner tension with the god of love, as well as with the Christian God as expressed by the church. This tension can at any time lead to an irreconcilable conflict.[8]

If we pose the question then in Weber's context—Is there a politics without violence?—the answer is clearly No. Politics is state politics dependent on violent means. The politician must act responsibly in a national context, impervious to the moral perfection demanded by the Gospel, and thus he will act with the violent means necessary to attain a good social end. In evidence here are the seeds of Reinhold Niebuhr's thesis of "moral man and immoral society." For Weber, who identifies the Gospel with its moral demands, there is no salvation in politics. For Niebuhr, despite his agreement with the Weber framework, the Christian can remain in it as politician because the Gospel signifies primarily the justification by faith of sinful man. As Niebuhr's anthologist, Robert C. Good, has remarked: "We cannot be responsible without guilt. . . . Niebuhr's ethic rests squarely upon the doctrine of justification by faith." [9]

Gandhi, however, was scandalized by the suggestion that a man of faith could continue to sin in his own efforts and then rely on Jesus to save him from the consequences of his actions. When a Christian friend suggested early in Gandhi's life that such a doctrine of justification was the simple answer to the Hindu's exhaustive efforts at self-purification, Gandhi replied that he was seeking redemption not from the consequences of his sin but from sin itself, or rather from the very thought of sin.[10] Gandhi felt no need to rely on such a doctrine to sneak the man of belief back into a political commitment presumably in contradiction to the moral demands of faith. He believed that it was precisely an ethic of ultimate ends which was properly political. In his account of his first, twenty-year-long campaign for Indian rights in South Africa, Gandhi summarized thus the political ethic created through Satyagraha's baptism in fire:

We are merely the instruments of the Almighty Will and are therefore often ignorant of what helps us forward and what acts as an impediment. We must thus rest satisfied with a knowledge only of the means, and if these are pure, we can fearlessly leave the end to take care of itself.[11]

Gandhi's position was that the only responsible political ethic was an ethic of ultimate ends. For Gandhi identified the politician's response to man's need with his response to God's will.

One of America's most brilliant diplomats and political historians, George F. Kennan, has indirectly supported Gandhi's position in his address at Princeton Theological Seminary, "Foreign Policy and Christian Conscience." Kennan believes that Christians should be more concerned with questions of method in foreign policy than with committing themselves to the realization of specific ends. Kennan's diplomatic experience taught him that principled means are a much more formative influence toward good ends than are the politician's efforts at farsightedness and calculation at the expense of moral means: "I can testify from personal experience that not only can one never know, when one takes a far-reaching decision in foreign policy, precisely what the consequences are going to be, but almost never do these consequences fully coincide with what one intended or expected." [12]

Perhaps this insight illuminates the problem of Lyndon Johnson and Vietnam more than any devil-view of the President. The claim to be seeking peace is not simple hypocrisy. But to reduce the politics of peace to a calculation based on technology but overlooking morally the brutal means of modern weaponry is to live in a hopeless illusion of political power. Least of all does the politician have the power to forecast desirable results when these are calculated from a murderous technology which he employs unconsciously. The widening effects of such terrible means are never fully in sight and can be sensed only by those who experience the technology at the point of destruction. American foreign policy is increasingly the product of the computer, and the computer is blind to tragedy.

Gandhi's political ethic made the end of peace realizable by the end's presence in the means themselves. Nevertheless, although Gandhi prosecuted these non-violent means relentlessly, he left the precise character of their end up to God. His constant readiness to compromise with his adversary on everything short of principle was an aspect of his non-violence which often brought his campaigns to an end short of the victory desired by his followers at the same time as it made possible a reconciliation between opponents transcending any preconceived goals. Gandhi knew that far more could be built politically at a future time on such a coming together of opponents than could be drawn out of a more impressive series of concessions granted reluctantly. His constant aim therefore was to appeal by suffering love to the humanity of the opponent and to gain not a particular end but the fullness of humanity. Even India's independence was incidental to Gandhi's goal of heightened brotherhood —which is the reason why Britain and India were able to have such good relations after the prolonged—and for the Indians, bloody—struggle for independence. Gandhi's ethic of ultimate ends kept him ever open in the midst of the struggle to his opponent's feelings and claims for a counter-justice. He made himself responsible for the growth of humanity, in both victims and executioners, rather than any ideological end whose realization might require dehumanization.

From what we have said of Gandhi, however, it is evident that his political ethic transcends Max Weber's categories at least partly because Gandhi's was a politics of protest rather than a politics of rule. Weber's link between politics and violence through the state is inapplicable to Gandhi because the latter waged his struggles from within the state and against its power. The Gandhian community stood fast against the state's violence and eventually overcame it, in both South Africa and India, but when the victory meant the resisters' assumption of state power, as it did in the latter case, it also resulted in their disowning of Gandhi's non-violence. While it is apparent that Weber's definition of "politics" is too narrow because its meaning is confined to a politics of rule, the question remains whether the ruling aspect of politics can ever be non-violent.

At this stage of the question it is first of all necessary to recognize that there is no absolute dichotomy between a politics of protest or dissent and a politics of rule. The two exist interdependently—indeed the life of a democracy is dependent on their interaction and a consequent non-violent social reform. When dissent or protest receives no response from a presumably democratic government, then we are simply witnessing a dictatorship between elections. Under normal conditions a politics of protest will create a response in the government to human distress which would otherwise go ignored. Howard Zinn has pointed out that what the civil rights movement revealed was the need for a people concerned with liberty to create a political power which resides outside the regular political establishment.[13] The practitioner of such a politics of protest, whose effectiveness is dependent on its non-violent character, is no less a politician for having forsworn actual rule over a violent political order. From the standpoint of social change in the kind of political order where control means the acceptance of corruption and violence, a politics of protest is the only politics worth practicing. And in the context of a global status quo which is murderous in its distribution of wealth at the same time as it is supported by genocidal armaments, a non-violent politics of protest, and eventual revolution, is essential to human hope.

To transfer the question of violence then from protest to rule is not to fall back into Weber's assumption that the only politics worth discussing is a politics of rule. It is rather to consider the possibility of non-violence on that side of politics where its own violence has so often reduced a ruling power to impotence.

Gandhi, in responding to the question of the non-violent state, always quoted John Henry Newman: "I do not ask to see the distant scene: one step enough for me." Gandhi visualized the goal of a non-violent state but he refused to fall into the utopian trap of worrying about the details of so distant a possibility when there was a wealth of immediate issues demanding resolution. He did, however, respond to the question sufficiently to make the outlines of his vision clear.

By a "non-violent state" Gandhi did not mean a state free of coercion, which would pass beyond the definition of a state (depending as it does more or less on coercion) to that of a stateless society, which is unattainable in reality. The "non-violent state" of Gandhi's conception was the state that is predominantly non-violent. The determinant of such a state was not its institutional structure but the non-violence of its citizens. The institutional form of the non-violent state would simply be the concrete expression of the moral level of the people.

The non-violent state would come into being through non-violent revolution. One cannot imagine such a state being established except through an enormous spiritual transformation won through the prolonged suffering love of thousands of satyagrahi revolutionaries. The resulting state would be the realization of democracy, because a genuine democracy must be the form for the weakest members of society and must respond by its programs to their needs. This can occur only through a non-violent revolution, which would succeed in minimizing exploitation and coercion. The democracy thus created would be, in Gandhi's words, "the rule of unadulterated non-violence." [14]

The non-violent or democratic state therefore presumes the self-purification of the individual citizen. This was the starting point of all Gandhi's campaigns, which were first of all moral

revolutions: in the heart and mind of the individual. Gandhi dis-
trusted mass movements as much as he did the existing structures
of the state. He identified power not with millions of marching
feet but with the moral regeneration of a single person. If
enough persons could undergo such regeneration, combining to
form a non-violent political movement, their power would create
the non-violent state.

The mark of the non-violent state's citizens will be service,
equality, and sacrifice. Its central power will be based on "universal suffrage exercised by a disciplined and politically intelligent electorate." [15] The non-violent state's police force will make
a minimum use of coercion, corresponding to the moral level of
the citizenry. Foreign aggression will also be minimized by the
non-exploitative and peaceful character of the state, but if
aggression came it would be met by a non-violent army supported
by the moral resistance to oppression of all the state's citizens. In
this regard, Gandhi wrote, "Even if Hitler was so minded, he
could not devastate seven hundred thousand non-violent villages.
He would himself become non-violent in the process." [16] Or
before such a massacre of a non-violently resisting population
could be carried out, the dictator's troops would have refused
to execute his orders.

As we have said, Gandhi did not expect to see this vision
realized in his lifetime and elaborated it only at the insistence of
followers intent on sharing his final vision of how men might
live in peace on earth. The significance of the vision for Gandhi,
and for those of his followers committed to living rather than
dreaming, lay in its power as a standard and a direction arrow
for the free society. As Gopinath Dhawan, the author of the best
study of this aspect of Gandhi's thought, has put it:

The establishment of peace and the fulfillment of democracy are
synonymous with the cultivation of non-violence. Non-violence alone
can reconcile national existence with international cooperation, even
as it alone can harmonize individual liberty and social life. [17]

If one were to begin a study of Gandhi's thought with this
ultimate vision of the non-violent state, the resemblance to Marx-

ism would be striking. In fact Gandhi did not hesitate to declare as the ruling principle in his Ashrams and the other institutions under his guidance the Marxist dictum, "To each according to to his need, from each according to his capacity."

Gandhi's Ashrams were experiments in a realized Communism, following Marx's source, the Christian community described in the Acts of the Apostles. Gandhi's agreement with Marx's end (and the Church's beginning) was as complete as was his rejection of the means Marx saw as necessary for realizing that end.

Gandhi assented to the description of himself as "a Communist minus violence." His successor, Vinoba Bhave, whose walking revolution of Bhoodan (land for the landless) is the most vital socialism India has today, has said he would be the first to join the Communists were they to give up class hatred and violence. But if Gandhi was "a Communist minus violence," given as we are today the Communism which has identified itself with totalitarianism and every form of weaponry up to the nuclear rockets which periodically grace Red Square in celebration of the Revolution, the "minus" is a more significant measure of Gandhi than the "Communist." To be, as Gandhi was, a Communist *with non-violence*, is to have Marx's eschatological vision together with the only means capable of incarnating it in living men. It is also to temper the passion of that vision with the patient realism of a Newman, whose industry in life achieved its greatest revolutions after his death: "One step enough for me." For the Christian observer of Gandhi, to be a Communist without violence is to be a revolutionary with Christ—or more exactly, it is to be the continuing presence of the Revolutionary Christ in the age of a murderous status quo.

The question of a non-violent politics of rule is inseparable from the question of global exploitation. The point from which we must begin in the present world is the existence already of a ruling politics whose violence through exploitation practically precludes any possibility of a non-violent defense of that rule. "Exploitation is the essence of violence," said Gandhi.[18] A politics without violence is first of all a politics without exploitation, and the imperialism which rules the world today thrives on the exploitation of the growing global population that Frantz Fanon has called "the wretched of the earth." At this point in history non-violence is consistent only with the politics of protest rising from the wretched of the earth, in their struggle for a global political order whose justice might finally affirm their humanity. Only after such a revolution of values and of corresponding structures might a non-violent politics of rule become possible. For the present, an accurate indication of how unfeasible is a non-violent defense of the United States can be found, ironically, in a pamphlet which argues for just such a defense, *In Place of War* (prepared by a working party of The American Friends Service Committee). In noting the hopeful sign that the Pentagon has been carrying on small-scale research into non-violent techniques, the American pacifist authors admit, "One gets the impression that the aim is to prepare to counter the use of non-violent methods by opponents, rather than to anticipate that the United States might someday employ them." [19] The image of Dr. Strangelove worrying over the non-violent threat of a Brazilian peasant is perhaps a hopeful sign after all, but it holds little promise of a situation where they would exchange roles.

If one way to break the nationalistic nexus between politics and violence is to dissent from within the nation-state, working against its twofold violence of exploitation and warfare, another way is to transcend the state by allying oneself with a global institution, notably the United Nations. Ultimately the two ways are one, for the purpose of a politics of dissent is to move the nation-state toward global values, whereas the purpose of a global politics is to recognize and support the rights of that major part of humanity being ground into the earth by the rich nations and their competing ideologies.

The United Nations provides the institutional base for a non-violent politics which is daily strengthening the reality of global man. To say this is to bring down on one all the skepticism built up by two decades of verbal violence in the United Nations halls.

But it is not so much the presence of verbal violence as it is the over-all decline of military violence which is most noteworthy about the U.N. era. The point is a fragile one, particularly at a time when the Vietnam War threatens to reduce both a nation and the world to ashes. But it is still true, as Adlai Stevenson pointed out in a Dag Hammarskjöld Memorial Lecture, that the central trend of the U.N. era has been the emergence of a policy of cease-fire and peaceful change: "It is precisely the fact that so much violence and so many quarrels *have not led to war* that puts a special mark on our time." [20]

Those nations which have departed from this general trend toward the peaceful resolution of conflicts have usually had to confront a world resistant to their war policies, as shown by the United States' isolation over Vietnam. The point is again complicated by a constantly accelerating armaments industry which has already stockpiled enough weapons in opposing countries to make man obsolete. To affirm the emergence of global man, fully in a few remarkable individuals and partially in humanity as a whole, is not to deny these facts underlining the threat of mankind's suicide. It is to affirm that other side of the struggle within man between life and death, the side which finds its expression in a growing community of peace in the midst of the threat of overwhelming violence.

Yet can it be said that even the most positive aspects of the United Nations represent a politics without violence? After all, even the United Nations emergency forces which have safeguarded the peace in the Congo and on the Egypt-Israel border have carried weapons and have sometimes used them lethally.

If one is constrained to define non-violence in a legalistic fashion, as a literal abstention from all violence, then it is true that the United Nations has no right to the term. Nor does Mohandas Gandhi, who could conceive of cases where the killing of a human being would be necessary, relative to one's own sinful impotence to prevent otherwise the slaughter threatened by a madman or a murderer. Even a saint in his total commitment to non-violence cannot honestly avoid facing the sinful weakness of his own and others' humanity which could compel a deed contradicting his commitment. To confess this truth of the human situation is not to create a base for the ethical justification of one's inhumanity. It is simply to recognize this constant threat of impotence in one's being for what it is, sin, and then to get on with man's proper work of enlarging his non-violent power and the community of peace which is Christ's presence in the world.

The United Nations peace forces have in fact served as non-violent armies. No one believes that the effectiveness of these peace-keeping forces in the special situations in which they were used was due to their meager numbers and armaments. In most cases they could have been overrun in hours by the forces they were restraining. The effective restraint U.N. forces provided was a matter not of arms but of presence, actually a dual presence— the symbolic presence, in and through the soldiers' essentially non-violent presence, of the global community of nations and its desire for peace. The armies facing these forces have had to recognize that to kill a U.N. soldier would be to kill something of humanity's hope for peace, a truth which applies to all killing in war but which has become especially vivid for us in the soldier in the blue beret. Adlai Stevenson has put it well: "A United Nations soldier in his blue beret is like no other soldier in the world —he has no mission but peace and no enemy but war." [21]

There have been suggestions made in the past for the transformation of the U.N. forces into a totally non-violent presence, devoid even of their now largely symbolic arms. The possible value of such a step can be seen with respect to the forced withdrawal of U.N. forces from the Egyptian frontier in May 1967 preceding the Arab-Israeli War. Secretary-General U Thant insisted that he was compelled to follow President Nasser's request that these troops be withdrawn because they had remained there after the Suez war of 1956 only through the consent of the Egyptian government. The Secretary-General pointed out rightly that if he had refused Nasser's request and had kept the troops on the frontier by force the entire concept and future of U.N.

peace-keeping would have been endangered. Those critics who have dismissed the Secretary-General's action as a provocative act, precipitating the war, seem not to have understood the nature of such U.N. operations in the first place. Thant has said in his defense:

> We must remember that UN peace-keeping is a highly novel and sophisticated concept. It relies on reason, local co-operation, skillful diplomacy, restraint and good faith.
> It does not, and cannot, rely on military force or threats, on power politics or on physical domination. It is a voluntary operation, and any suggestion that it should . . . cease to be so could be fatal to the whole idea.[22]

If the peace-keeping operation on the Egyptian frontier had been carried out, however, by a force without weapons and explicitly committed to non-violent methods in response to any attack, their maintenance there during the crisis would have carried much less belligerent overtones to Egypt and might have held off the war. The threats to the concept of peace-keeping which would have arisen from a refusal of Nasser's request in the actual situation derive mainly from the implication that armed force would have been the final ground for such a refusal. The U.N. forces' ambiguity in retaining the possession of some weapons, and their record of having used these, sometimes rather clumsily as in the Congo during the days preceding Dag Hammarskjöld's death, made it imperative that the forces' presence on the border cease rather than issue in an armed occupation of Egyptian territory and a shooting conflict with their host Nasser's forces. A wholly non-violent force would have offered less ground both for Nasser's request and for U Thant's valid fears in responding to it.

It may be that such a further step into non-violence by the U.N forces is not feasible. The reason for raising the point here is that sooner or later the U.N. peace-keeping forces will have to stand against attack (as they were forced to do in the Congo), and it is better that they do so as much as possible through their symbolic power as mankind's conscience, and with as little risk as possible of generating the ultimate war they are meant to prevent.

Another extension of non-violence by the U.N. could occur through the internationalization of the Peace Corps. If the existing U.N. development programs were strengthened by Peace Corps volunteers from around the globe, but particularly from the major industrial powers, the peaceful influence of the world body would be substantially increased at the same time as the promise of President Kennedy's program would be saved through the only organ now capable of executing it. It is evident that if the Peace Corps is not internationalized soon, it will become simply another pawn of U.S. interests. The original vision of Kennedy has been profaned by the Vietnam War and its ramifications in all United States foreign and domestic programs. The basic fact is that the nature of the Peace Corps is opposed to what the United States represents in the world today and will represent for the foreseeable future. Given the more and more global (and profoundly anti-war) mood of many United States students, the transference of the Peace Corps to U.N. supervision would increase its American volunteers severalfold. If some such step is not undertaken, initiated either by the United States as a laudable sign of a renewed commitment to global community or by the U.N. independently of the American program, the Peace Corps as it exists now will become on the government's side another heavy arm of the affluent state abroad and on the volunteers' side no more than a haven for draft evasion.[23]

A politics of protest and a global politics are therefore one in their responses to the wretched of the earth and to the entire human family's desire for peace. Yet the emphasis of each is necessary. A politics of protest rises to counter particular evils of one's own nation and to work for peace at one's doorstep. It is joined by a global politics which testifies to the hopes and aspirations of mankind as a whole, as these are embodied especially in an institution which transcends national self-interest. A politics of protest will become frustrated by its own apparent impotence at home unless it can effectively identify itself with the world community. A global politics will become vapid without constant attention to the particular demands being raised by men in revolution against the injustices of the regimes and economic systems they live under. Together these two politics constitute the revolution of peace which is man's hope for life and his strength against death. A Stevenson phrase has again caught the vision—"a dynamic system of order": "What the world needs is a dynamic system of order—a system capable of bringing about not just a precarious halt to hostilities but a curative resolution of the roots of hostility." [24]

It is not easy to sustain such a politics, either institutionally in the United Nations or personally in the men committed to the vision behind the U.N. Self-interest, whether national or personal, is foreign to a politics of peace, and if indulged in at length will be fatal to one's own commitment and in a lesser way to the aspirations of humanity. Those who work in the U.N. to implement its vision are in any case members of particular nations and will find it difficult to transcend the backgrounds of more selfish loyalties. This was the point of Nikita Khrushchev's remark that "there is not a single neutral person on this globe." But the response to this remark by the man whom it was meant to slight, Dag Hammarskjöld, that "there is no neutral man, but there is, if you have integrity, neutral action by the right kind of man," [25] has its proof—and a sign of the U.N.'s endurance—in the life and death of Hammarskjöld himself.

From the standpoint of a new politics of belief, Dag Hammarskjöld is Gandhi's successor. Gandhi explored an ethic of ultimate ends in terms of a politics of protest and urged its extension to a global level. Hammarskjöld actually made that extension, and thus offers the final key to a new politics of belief following the death of the various Christian politics which tolerated nationalism and violence up to the threat of global self-destruction.

Hammarskjöld, like Gandhi, paid homage first of all to Truth.

It was the source of his extraordinary power of reconciliation. His colleague, Henrik Klackenburg, has said that Hammarskjöld brought about reconciliations by his sheer integrity, by the force of his rectitude which placed a moral obligation upon parties in dispute to reach an agreement. [26] Hammarskjöld said it was always necessary to see the parties and their claims objectively, while imagining himself in their position. His enormous respect for Truth and for each man's share of it impressed itself naturally on the disputants, and they accepted him willingly as a mediator. He wrote of truth in his diary, *Markings*: "Respect for the word —to employ it with scrupulous care and an incorruptible heart-felt love of truth—is essential if there is to be any growth in a society or in the human race." [27]

Whereas Gandhi united Satyagraha, or truth-force, with "Ahimsa" and "Sarvodaya," a reverence for all living beings and a life of service directed toward revolutionary social changes, Hammarskjöld's commitment to Truth was joined to Albert Schweitzer's ethics, combining a reverence for life with the ideal of service. Although Gandhi was not a Christian and Hammarskjöld not a church member, both of them identified their commitments with the man of the cross, and in a remarkably similar fashion, as shown by a meditation each made on the significance of Christmas:

"We dare not think of birth without death on the Cross. Living Christ means a living Cross, without it life is a living death." (Gandhi, December 25, 1931.)

"For him who looks towards the future, the Manger is situated on Golgotha, and the Cross has already been raised in Bethlehem. 'Strive, the pains of death endure, peace eternal to secure.' " (Hammarskjöld, December 24, 1960.)

The parallel between Gandhi and Hammarskjöld can be developed further in terms of their understanding of the role of trust in political affairs. For Gandhi the notion of trust was basic to his definition of the Satyagrahi (the man committed to achieving peace through a non-violent "truth-force"):

A Satyagrahi bids good-bye to fear. He is therefore never afraid of trusting the opponent. Even if the opponent plays him false twenty times, the Satyagrahi is ready to trust him for the twenty-first time, for an implicit trust in human nature is the very essence of his creed.[28]

Hammarskjöld as Secretary-General of the United Nations thought a constant effort to embody such trust in himself was not naïve but deeply realistic in the struggle for peace. In an address at Cambridge University in 1950, he quoted Martin Buber at length to show how the opposite tendency toward an existential mistrust has become increasingly characteristic of our time and the major source of war:

There have always been countless situations in which a man believes his life-interest demands that he suspect the other of making it his object to appear otherwise than he is. . . . In our time something basically different has been added. . . . One no longer merely fears that the other will voluntarily dissemble, but one takes it for granted that he cannot do otherwise. . . . The other communicates to me the perspective that he has acquired on a certain subject, but I do not really take cognizance of his communication as knowledge. I do not take it seriously as a contribution to the information about this subject, but rather I listen for what drives the other to say what he says, for an unconscious motive. . . . Since it is the idea of the other, it is for me an "ideology." My main task in my intercourse with my fellow-man becomes more and more . . . to see through and unmask him. . . . With this changed basic attitude . . . the mistrust between man and man has become existential.[29]

Dag Hammarskjöld, like Pope John, believed in mutual trust as the necessary moral basis for disarmament and was not shy in suggesting such an approach, as when he broke into a dead-locked Security Council debate on disarmament to say firmly, "I hope that each one of the governments around this table will wish to try out the line of trust." [30]

Hammarskjöld considered it his personal task to strengthen these bonds of trust between nations. He therefore deliberately trusted the men with whom he was negotiating—men whose opponents always said they were unworthy of trust and incapable of it themselves—to the point of making himself extremely

vulnerable on a personal level. To read the story of Hammarskjöld's diplomatic successes, and the story of the U.N.'s growing
habit of passing "Leave it to Dag" resolutions on seemingly insoluble conflicts, is to confront the power of a man emptying
himself in order to permit the more powerful workings of Truth
and Love in international affairs. Hammarskjöld's power of reconciliation was the expression, in his encounters with the world's
men of power, of the deepening surrender to God's will traced
in *Markings*.

Some of Dag Hammarskjöld's friends have expressed their bewilderment at *Markings* for its testimony to a level of life they
never knew existed in the man (because he was not a churchgoer
or user of pious phrases). But *Markings* does not transcend Hammarskjöld's involvement in world affairs by a private mysticism.
The final and largest section of the diary records a seeking of
God's will precisely in and through its author's U.N. diplomacy.
A correlation of *Markings*' entries with the pattern of Hammarskjöld's work reveals a power of transcendence not apart from
but *within* the conflicts to whose resolution he was committed.
The transcendent Truth in which he rooted his life was *a transcendence made immanent* in Hammarskjöld's power to reconcile
men preparing for war.

One example of Hammarskjöld's power through voluntary
powerlessness can be found in the Secretary-General's first major diplomatic mission for the United Nations, his negotiations
with Communist China for the release of eleven American airmen held by the Chinese after the conclusion of the Korean War.
In December 1954 China announced that the Americans had
been tried and sentenced as spies. With pressures increasing on
Washington for retaliatory action, the United States and its
Korean War allies introduced a resolution in the General Assembly, "not knowing what else to do," requesting the Secretary-
General to undertake "continuing and unremitting efforts" to
secure the release of the fliers "by the means most appropriate
in his judgment."

Hammarskjöld made use of this resolution by first of all stripping himself of its power. Rather than forwarding it to Peking through diplomatic channels as expected, he cabled Chinese Premier Chou En-lai requesting a personal conference regarding the American prisoners. He did not make this request on the basis of the U.N. resolution which gave him an unlimited power in the matter because he knew the Chinese would resent and probably reject a formal resolution, having been excluded from the world body themselves. Instead he sought a way out of the conflict by making himself personally accessible to the Chinese.

His entry in his diary during this time quotes from Psalm 62: "God spake once, and twice I have also heard the same: that power belongeth unto God; and that thou, Lord, art merciful: for thou rewardest every man according to his work." [31]

And two weeks later, as he made last-minute preparations for the trip which the Chinese had agreed to: "To have faith—not to hesitate!" [32]

Chou En-lai received Hammarskjöld in Peking with great courtesy and the two men conferred for several days. When Hammarskjöld returned to New York, his terse comment to reporters concerning the Chinese-American conflict was that "everybody is afraid of everybody." For the next six months China did nothing with the fliers, and observers began to believe the mission had been a failure; but three times the Chinese Embassy in Stockholm asked the date of Hammarskjöld's birthday and what he might appreciate as a remembrance. The reply given was, "The release of the airmen." On July 29, 1955, while the Secretary-General was celebrating his fiftieth birthday, he received a cable from the Foreign Minister of Communist China announcing that the United States airmen were being released.

Under the date of July 29, 1955, Hammarskjöld notes in his diary: "God sometimes allows us to take the credit—for his work." [33] Three days later he refers again to Psalm 62, then accuses himself: "A troubled spirit? Isn't the cause obvious? As soon as, furtively, you sought honor for yourself, you could no longer transform your weakness into strength." [34]

Dag Hammarskjöld practiced a politics of reconciliation which was equally a politics of resistance to global injustice. His commitment against war was one with his understanding of the revolutionary development necessary in the poorer nations. In fact he conceived of the United Nations as existing first of all for these smaller nations. When on October 3, 1960, he was confronted by his gravest challenge to his U.N. leadership, Nikita Khrushchev's "*troika*" proposal and demand for Hammarskjöld's resignation, the Secretary-General resisted the Soviet Premier by appealing successfully over his head to the global community of smaller powers:

It is not the Soviet Union or, indeed, any other big powers who need the United Nations for their protection; it is all the others. In a sense the Organization is first of all *their* Organization, and I deeply believe in the wisdom with which they will be able to use it and guide it.

I shall remain at my post during the term of my office as a servant of the Organization in the interests of all those other nations, as long as *they* wish me to do so.[35]

Dag Hammarskjöld's death was in the service of the powerless of the earth, in the continent where he had felt most deeply the need for change, Africa, and in a final effort to achieve the peace necessary for change by rendering himself powerless to his opponents. His decision to accede to the Katanga rebel leader Moise Tshombe's demand that the Secretary-General meet him on the hostile ground of Ndola, Rhodesia, dismayed U.N. subordinates, who felt he was flying into a trap. Hammarskjöld was aware of the risks. But he thought that Tshombe needed a sense of victory over him through such a concession in order to be prepared to negotiate peace.

The only book Hammarskjöld had taken with him on his last trip to the Congo, found after his death on the table next to the bed in Leopoldville where he spent his last night, was *The Imitation of Christ*. Thomas a Kempis', and the Gospel's, theme of the disciple's openness to crucifixion is repeated constantly through the last half of *Markings*. The same theme is used by Gandhi to define the essence of non-violent power present in the Satyagrahi:

It is only when the Satyagrahi feels quite helpless, is apparently on his last legs and finds utter darkness all around him, that God comes to the rescue. God helps when one feels oneself humbler than the very dust under one's feet. Only to the weak and helpless is divine succour vouchsafed.[36]

Dag Hammarskjöld experienced this darkness of solitude and dust of humiliation both literally and figuratively as he crawled from his crashed plane nine miles from Ndola, and in his last hours of agony, alone and exposed to the night, clutched at the grass found later in his fist. A scene strangely like it was described by him in a poem written ten months before his death:

> The moon was caught in the branches:
> Bound by its vow,
> My heart was heavy.
>
> Naked against the night
> The trees slept. "Nevertheless,
> Not as I will. . . ."
>
> The burden remained mine:
> They could not hear my call,
> And all was silence.
>
> Soon, now, the torches, the kiss:
> Soon the grey of dawn
> In the Judgment Hall.
>
> What will their love help there?
> There, the question is only
> If I love them.[37]

Hammarskjöld loved them and suffered their killing into peace. The cease-fire which he was seeking on his final trip took place two days after his death. The various parties to the conflict came together almost immediately after the shock of his death and under the suspicion, never laid to rest, that it had been caused by one of them. The deeper truth was expressed by a woman member of the Secretariat, in reply to the question of who killed Hammarskjöld: "Everybody killed him."

Is there a politics without violence? Gandhi and Hammarskjöld died to violence, the violence of us all, so perhaps there is not.

But if the meaning of the question is, Can men practice politics without doing violence? the answer is an imperative: They must if humanity is to live. The fact that some men can do so is evident enough in the struggles of a Hindu ascetic and a Swedish diplomat to lay the basis for the hope that a politics of revolution and peace is within the grasp of many more. To face the cost of such a politics, in the cross, is to affirm simultaneously the resurrection of humanity that is its outcome.

NOTES

1. Walter James, *The Christian in Politics* (Oxford University Press: 1962), p. 193.
2. Daniel's article first appeared in the French weekly *L'Express,* then in *The New Republic,* and was reported in *Newsweek,* December 23, 1963.
3. Elie Abel, *The Missile Crisis* (Bantam: 1966), p. 169.
4. Kennedy made the comment at a luncheon with twenty-two Maryland and Delaware newspaper executives on March 14, 1963 (AP story, March 16, 1963).
5. Abel, *The Missile Crisis,* p. 134.
6. Max Weber, *Politics as a Vocation* (Fortress Press: 1965), p. 1.
7. *Ibid.,* p. 2.
8. *Ibid.,* p. 52.
9. Robert C. Good, "Reinhold Niebuhr: The Political Philosopher of Christian Realism," *Cross Currents* (Summer 1961), p. 267.
10. M. K. Gandhi, *An Autobiography or The Story of My Experiments with Truth* (Navajivan Publishing House: 1927), p. 318.
11. M. K. Gandhi, *Satyagraha in South Africa* (Navajivan Publishing House: 1928), p. 318.
12. George F. Kennan, "Foreign Policy and Christian Conscience," *The Moral Dilemma of Nuclear Weapons* (The Church Peace Union: 1961), p. 69. Kennan's address appeared originally in *The Atlantic Monthly,* May 1959.
13. Howard Zinn, *SNCC: The New Abolitionists* (Beacon Press: 1965), p. 220.
14. Quoted by Gopinath Dhawan in *The Political Philosophy of Mahatma Gandhi* (Navajivan Publishing House: 1946), p. 292.
15. *Ibid.,* p. 297.
16. *Ibid.,* p. 331.
17. *Ibid.,* p. 336.

18. *Ibid.*, p. 64.
19. *In Place of War* (Grossman Publishers: 1967), p. 89. Although it skirts the relation between the moral quality of a body politic and its capacity for a non-violent defense of its society, this pamphlet offers an excellent analysis of the strategy of non-violent national defense.
20. Adlai E. Stevenson, "From Containment to Cease-Fire and Peaceful Change," *The Quest for Peace* (The Dag Hammarskjöld Memorial Lecture Series), eds. Andrew W. Cordier and Wilder Foote, p. 57.
21. *Ibid.*, p. 61.
22. From a speech by U Thant in Montreal, June 1, 1967, to the council of the International Civil Aviation Organization, a U.N. special agency (Canadian Press story, June 3, 1967).
23. A proposal for the internationalization of the Peace Corps was made in 1967 to the U.S. Senate Committee on Foreign Relations by Seth Tillman, a consultant to the committee. The proposal appears in a "Latin American Diary" describing Tillman's trip to Latin America in December 1966 to study "something of the philosophy, purpose, and self-assessment of the Peace Corps and its volunteers." A portion of the diary was published in *worldview* (July-August 1967), pp. 4–7.
24. Stevenson, "From Containment to Cease-Fire and Peaceful Change," p. 65.
25. Quoted by Henry P. Van Dusen, *Dag Hammarskjöld: The Statesman and His Faith* (Harper & Row: 1967), p. 108. For the details of Dag Hammarskjöld's life I have drawn freely from Van Dusen's book and from Emery Kelen, *Hammarskjöld* (G. P. Putnam's Sons: 1966).
26. Kelen, *Hammarskjöld*, p. 42.
27. Dag Hammarskjöld, *Markings* (London, Faber paper edition: 1964), p. 101.
28. Gandhi, *Satyagraha in South Africa*, p. 159.
29. Quoted by Sven Stolpe, *Dag Hammarskjöld: A Spiritual Portrait* (Charles Scribner's Sons: 1966), p. 45.
30. Kelen, *Hammarskjöld*, p. 98.
31. Hammarskjöld, *Markings*, p. 94.
32. *Ibid.*
33. *Ibid.*, p. 98.
34. *Ibid.*, p. 99.
35. Quoted by Kelen, *Hammarskjöld*, p. 211.
36. Gandhi, *Satyagraha in South Africa*, p. xiv.
37. Hammarskjöld, *Markings*, p. 165.

11

The Crux of History

THE WAY OF TRUTH in a world of injustice is revolution. There is a sense in which every Christian must follow Ivan Karamazov in his revolt against a world in which children suffer. As Jean Daniélou has observed, "Because of the scandal of the suffering of the innocent the world stands convicted, and revolt is justified." [1] Such a world cries out for transformation, and any man of faith who keeps his gaze heavenward while his suffering neighbors appeal for a new earth will, we are told (Matthew 25), depart ultimately with the curse of the Son into the eternal fire. In the contemporary world of affluence and poverty, where man's major crime is murder by privilege, revolution against the established order is the criterion of a living faith. Pope Paul has put it in the form of a program: "The new name of peace is development" (*Populorum Progressio*). Jesus stated its alternative: "Truly, I say to you, as you did it not to one of the least of these, you did it not to me" (Matthew 25:45). The murder of Christ continues. Great societies build on dying men.

But Ivan's revolt against injustice needs Alyosha's love and acceptance of responsibility in order to become the grain of wheat which—as Dostoevsky quotes from John's Gospel in his epigraph —by dying will bear much fruit. Ivan's revolt turns against the Creator, blaming Him for the sins of men, and becomes a sterile gesture toward his own autonomy. The revolt against injustice becomes a revolt against dependence. Alyosha, on the other hand, hears the counsel of Father Zossima, who by an acceptance of man's responsibility for man points toward the Revolution of Peace:

There is only one means of salvation, then take yourself and make yourself responsible for all men's sins, that is the truth, you know, friends, for as soon as you sincerely make yourself responsible for everything and for all men, you will see at once that it is really so, and that you are to blame for every one and for all things.[2]

The innocents of the world suffer, just as the Son suffered, because every living man makes them suffer. It is man's responsibility, in and through the cross of the Son, to see that the innocents stop suffering. Man either gives life by himself taking on their suffering in that community of Christ working toward a new earth or he murders by turning from the God in man to the idolatry of a distant deity. There is only one God, and he has become man. Man can possess no life in God apart from God's life in the Suffering Servant.

The Servant's suffering love is the power to redeem evil. Evil is not absolute. Its existence in the world is profound, yet dependent on the prior existence of Good. Evil is relative to the Good and can be redeemed by the Love on which even it is dependent. When evil is thought to be absolute, as in the thought of Jean-Paul Sartre, the only way remaining for the man who in conscience knows the world's suffering is to respond to the executioners with absolute violence. Thus the anguished cry for a return violence by Frantz Fanon. But violence cannot liberate the wretched of the earth. To press this way upon them, as Che Guevara and other men hungering for justice have sought to do, is to confuse revolution with the evil it must overcome. History knows no liberation through the sword. Arnold Toynbee has made the point well:

An instrument that has once been used to destroy life cannot then be used to preserve life at the user's convenience. The function of weapons is to kill; and a ruler who has not scrupled to "wade through slaughter to a throne" will find—if he tries to maintain his power thereafter without further recourse to the grim arts which have gained it— that sooner or later he will be confronted with a choice between letting the power slip through his fingers or else renewing his lease of it by means of another bout of bloodshed. The man of violence cannot both genuinely repent of his violence and permanently profit by it.[3]

To use a term of Martin Buber, whose thought offers a supreme affirmation of the possibilities of redemption, the way of redeeming evil lies along a "narrow ridge" between the false positions of reducing evil to illusion or objective error on the one hand and of absolutizing its existence on the other.[4] Such a dialectical attitude toward evil, acknowledging evil's profound presence at the same time as its possibilities of redemption, draws one into the cross at the world's center, as Buber shows in *I and Thou*:

Love is responsibility of an *I* for a *Thou*. In this lies the likeness— impossible in any feeling whatsoever—of all who love, from the smallest to the greatest and from the blessedly protected man, whose life is rounded in that of a loved being, to him who is all his life nailed to the cross of the world, and who ventures to bring himself to the dreadful point—to love *all men*.[5]

This is not to enlist Martin Buber in Christianity but to point to that common Judeo-Christian witness of the *ebed Yahweh* which Buber himself identified so closely with Jesus. "The life-history of Jesus cannot be understood, in my opinion," he wrote, "if one does not recognize that he . . . stood in the shadow of the Deutero-Isaianic servant of the Lord." [6] Neither Christians nor Jews have yet begun to come to terms with Martin Buber's statement of the place of Jesus in the Jewish community:

I firmly believe that the Jewish community, in the course of its renaissance, will recognize Jesus; and not merely as a great figure in its religious history, but also in the organic context of a Messianic development extending over millennia, whose final goal is the Redemption of Israel and of the world. But I believe equally firmly that we will never recognize Jesus as the Messiah Come, for this would contradict the deepest meaning of our Messianic passion. . . . There are no knots in the mighty cable of our Messianic belief, which, fastened to a rock on Sinai, stretches to a still invisible peg anchored in the foundations of the world. In our view, redemption occurs forever, and none has yet occurred. Standing, bound and shackled, in the pillory of mankind, we demonstrate with the bloody body of our people the unredeemedness of the world. For us there is no cause of Jesus; only the cause of God exists for us.[7]

Perhaps it is only within the community of a revitalized *ebed Yahweh* commitment to the world, extending equally across both Israel and the Church, that the Judeo-Christian faith can reach its height—in a Jerusalem where the cause of God and the cause of Jesus will become one cause of Love. The point where Christians can begin to walk toward that Holy City is by confessing that at the heart of Jesus' self-understanding is the *ebed Yahweh* of Judaism. Jesus' demand in the world today is not that the Jew recognize him as Christ but that the Christian recognize him as Jew.

It is Christians' living denial of Jesus' humanity which is the incarnational heresy characteristic of the modern Church. Only through an existential reaffirmation, in the lives of Christians, of Jesus' suffering, loving humanity can his messianic character begin to become generally manifest again. St. Paul told the Colossians that he had to suffer in order to complete Christ's sufferings in the Church (Col. 1:24). Even though mankind is already justified by Christ's suffering, this redemptive act has to be made present in the world through its embodiment in the life of the Church.

In his book *The Grave of God*, Father Robert Adolfs calls for the re-creation of such a "kenotic Church," a Church which will empty herself of wealth and power and become poor again in the deepest evangelical sense so as to rule only by love; a servant Church reflecting the Son who emptied himself of all claims to wealth and power for the sake of man. A group of Protestant Christians in East Germany which has sought out of necessity to live such a vision put it more sharply: "It is not the church we try to preserve now, but the Gospel." [8] Perhaps it was Peter Maurin, though, who possessed the deepest sense of the revolution rising in the Church for the sake of the world:

It is about time
to blow the lid off
so the Catholic Church
may again become
the dominant social dynamic force.[9]

But even as the Church still hesitates before blowing the lid off her crucified Power, Christ's presence in the world today is manifest in scattered communities of men of all faiths whose lives are centered on the redemptive reality of suffering love, as it works to transform them and their societies. Danilo Dolci and his development teams in Sicily, Cesar Chavez and the Mexican farm workers, Vinoba Bhave and his walking revolution, U Thant and his co-workers for global peace—in such communities circling the earth and in their common commitment to the redemptive reality the face of Christ appears, just as it appeared in the lives of Gandhi, King, Hammarskjöld, and Pope John. "Our ultimate end," said Martin King, "must be the creation of the beloved community." Christ becomes present now as he became present in such men, in the constant crucifixion of self and resurrection of man which is the liberating basis for the Revolution of Peace. The humanity of God is men suffering and loving. His divinity becomes manifest in the community of grace their suffering love reveals.

The baptism into Christ which men are undergoing today, both within and without the Church, is not of water but of blood—their suffering for the community of man, a suffering accepted out of love and the hope for a new earth. This baptism of suffering draws men into the heart of the redemptive event, crucifixion, and through their response of faith and hope in mankind raises them in Christ to the community of love which is God's life in man. Christ's love and power, given through the sacrament of suffering, is the Holy Spirit. The power of the Holy Spirit is re-making the earth. Beside it nuclear weapons are impotent.

But we remain distant from an understanding of the reality of power. Those men who have understood the power of the Spirit, and in whom we sense its radiating life, remain enigmas in their efforts to tell us what it is. For an age in which a breakaway technology has determined the meaning of "power," the power of the Spirit is always a sign of contradiction. Never has man's self-defined power been so enormous and so impotent.

A remarkable statement by Gandhi, the most powerful man of our time, indicates the amount of reconstruction necessary if we are ever to understand the meaning of true power. On one occasion during a period of evening prayer a member of Gandhi's Ashram asked him: "Bapuji, what would be your first act if at this moment you would have power to shape the destinies of mankind?" After the suspense of silence, with all eyes pinned on Gandhi, he replied: "I would pray for the courage instantly to renounce that power." [10]

Paul defined his power with a smiliar paradox in his second letter to the Corinthians: "I will all the more gladly boast of my weaknesses, that the power of Christ may rest upon me. For the sake of Christ, then, I am content with weaknesses, insults, hardships, persecutions, and calamities; for when I am weak, then I am strong" (12:9–10).

When man knows his weakness and accepts full responsibility for the evil in himself and in the world, he becomes strong in love and in the Spirit. By taking on the cross man is raised. By embracing the earth in love and responsibility as Alyosha did, man is prepared by God to build the City of Man into the City of God.

With enormous power and authority man's evil stands resistant to him at the center of history. In apparent surrender man in God lies on the cross and accepts the full impact of evil's hammerblows, and evil falls back finally in exhaustion as the cross is raised against the sky. With its destructive energy spent, the evil in man waits expectantly as the Son cries out in agony to the Father. But the cry only affirms that God is truly man, that heaven and earth have met in the cross, and that man's evil is therefore overcome. For as the suffering and the cry affirm God's humanity, the death and the open tomb initiate man's divinity. As the man of the cross dies, the centurion who nailed

him there is raised to life: "Truly this was the Son of God."
Evil's violence accepted in love is evil overcome, for evil is man's
effort to create himself, and cannot withstand his power in God
to be re-created in love. Within history, which is from one standpoint the history of his sin, evil is one side of man. When man
accepts that side of himself on the cross, he is reconciled to
himself through suffering love. Evil demands suffering love as its
cost of reconciliation. It is only when man reverses the cross and
seeks to destroy his evil with a sword that he becomes impotent
and self-destructive in facing his darker self. The Revolution of
Peace is man taking responsibility for his evil in the cross and
thereby becoming himself in God.

The world's beauty and mystery is the cross at its center extending outward through history and divinizing man through the
power of Love. The non-violent cross is not unique to the prophets
of peace mentioned here. The cross of suffering love is God's continuing presence in each man on this earth. The Son lives today
as he redeemed, in the community of peace being constantly created through the sacrifice of love. A man cannot live without
loving someone, however much his life as a whole may be con-
sumed by hatred or deadened by indifference. For that someone
he will suffer gladly and thus realize his humanity. To love is
to suffer in joy, for the perfect union sought by love can be
approached only through sacrifice. Love's price of suffering extended across the world is the price of redeeming man's violence.
The violence within man is what prevents him from realizing a
perfect union of love, and can be overcome progressively only
through the fire of voluntary suffering. Suffering itself is evil,
the result of sin. Love seeks union and community, not suffering.
But in a world in which man has first crucified his brother, love's
only way to union is through the reversal of violence in suffering.
And the way has been divinized. By becoming man God has
sacramentalized man's suffering so that man might become God
through the cost of love. Love is the Power, but a Power incarnate
on the cross.

Humanity is therefore defined by its attention to the cross at its center. The tension in every man between humanity and in-humanity is identical with his movement between the overcoming love of the crucified and the impotent Cain instinct of the execu-tioner. Dehumanization is de-Christification. Love is by nature Christocentric.

In the age of Hiroshima and Vietnam, it cannot be denied that history still awaits the fullness of redemption. Any Christian in-sistence on the finality of Christ's redemptive act is in effect false if it is not joined with an admission of the continuing failure of Christianity to embody the Spirit of redemption. The world con-tinues to groan for the fullness of Christ in its midst.

Some men of conscience have even insisted that with the oc-currence of our inconceivable crimes the God of History has died finally and irrevocably, that after Auschwitz man can no longer comfort himself with the illusion that God lives or acts in history. But the truth is not that God has died but that man has relied on his presence in the wrong way. Man has been forced by his-tory to surrender his belief in a God whose omnipotence signified for man a haven from his own evil. The God who protected man from his own history is dead. The God who suffers in man through that history and thereby raises him to life is the only God of the living. Auschwitz has not destroyed belief. It has only purged it of mythology. The God incarnate in the *ebed Yahweh* still lives and gives life. The children of Israel who suffered at Ausch-witz live on in the God who suffered with them. Neither God nor history ended with Auschwitz. The humanity of God cried out at Auschwitz with the enormity of the suffering filling his body, but the end of history will confirm the truth that with that cry men were reborn. With Ernie Levy the miracle of resurrection deepens. After Auschwitz history has passed into that phase in which mankind must feel more and more profoundly the power of its children's tears.

The cross is resurrection, and at the heart of the world is the dance of its children who have died. They dance in the shadows of the living's struggle for a new earth, and the realized joy of the children of Auschwitz and Hiroshima can be sensed by men of faith even as they confront the tears of the living. The children of the resurrection dance from their love of the world whose final truth has been given them in new life, while the world of continuing history spins toward this same consummation on the strength of its life-giving cross. The children's dance of life is the world community which men suffer for now and realize in anticipation where two or three become one in love.

History still awaits the fullness of the Spirit because man has only begun to realize that the Truth up ahead, and the Love incarnate in man's suffering after Truth, are the same God. The Truth is man's end. But the Truth is also the way, and the way is Love. That the God of Truth and the God of Suffering Love are one is the meaning of the cross, and the way of man's transfiguration into God.

NOTES

1. Jean Daniélou, *The Scandal of Truth* (Helicon Press: 1962), p. 42.
2. Fyodor Dostoevsky, *The Brothers Karamazov*, translated by Constance Garnett (Modern Library Paperback: 1950), p. 384.
3. Arnold J. Toynbee, *War and Civilization*, selected by Albert V. Fowler from *A Study of History* (Oxford University Press: 1950), p. 144.
4. See Maurice S. Friedman, "The Problem of Evil," *Martin Buber: The Life of Dialogue* (Harper Torchbooks: 1960), pp. 11–15.
5. Martin Buber, *I and Thou* (second edition) (Charles Scribner's Sons: 1958), p. 15.
6. Quoted by Friedman, *Martin Buber*, p. 275.
7. Quoted by Ernst Simon, "Martin Buber: His Way between Thought and Deed", *Jewish Frontier*, XV (February 1948), 26.
8. *Pro-Existence: Christian Voices in East Germany*, papers edited by Elisabeth Adler (London: SCM Press, 1964), p. 13.
9. Peter Maurin, "Blowing the Dynamite," *The Green Revolution: Easy Essays on Catholic Radicalism* (Academy Guild Press: 1961), p. 3.
10. Recounted by Karel Hujer, "Gandhi's Non-Violence: A Way of Life," *Reconciliation Quarterly* (Fourth Quarter, 1966), p. 723.

Index

ABC warfare, 103, 104
Abel, Elie, 259
Acts of the Apostles, 63, 131, 183, 269
Adolfs, Robert, 287
Adzhubei, Alexei, 93, 258
Affluence, 7–8, 12, 13, 14, 16, 18, 22, 270, 284; and violence, 228
Africa, 6, 230, 280
Again, the Justice of Deterrence, 168
Aggression: and the individual, 242–43; nature of, 218–20; non-violent, 221; and sin, 226–27; value of, 219–20; and war, 224, 239
Alfrink, Cardinal, 109, 156
Algeria, 6
Allport, Gordon, 242
American Friends Service Committee, 270
American University, 22
Amery, Carl, 50, 51, 52
Anti-Semitism, 139–40, 141–43, 149; Church's role in, 149–50, 151
Apocalypse, and the state, 196–98
Apostles, and Zealotism, 183–85
Aquinas, Thomas, 139–40, 157
Arab-Israeli War, 272

Ardrey, Robert, 219
Arms race: morality of, 110–26; and total war, 113–14
Asia, 6
Atheism, 36, 103; and truth, 37–38
Atheist with Gandhi, An, 36
Augustine, St., 140, 157, 208, 261; and the just-war doctrine, 200–201
Auschwitz, xiii, 3, 5, 149, 152, 291
Austria, 174
Autobiography of Malcolm X, The, 228

Barth, Karl, 49
Batchelder, Robert, 165
Bay of Pigs, 40, 259
Beck, Archbishop George A., 104
Belief, politics of, 260–62, 275
Belzec, 149
Benedict XV, 212
Bergen-Belsen, 149
Berkhof, H., 192–93
Beyond the Pleasure Principle, 224
Bhave, Vinoba, 15–17, 18, 19, 23, 24, 269, 288
Bhoodan-Gramdan movement, 15–17, 269

Bonhoeffer, Dietrich, 29, 31–33, 37–38, 56
Brown, Rap, 218
Brown, Robert McAfee, 101
Buber, Martin, xiv, 277, 286
Buchenwald, 5, 149
Butler, Bishop Christopher, 110, 111–17, 120–22, 124, 130

Cain instinct, 218, 221–22, 231, 239, 291; and aggression, 226; and the cross, 226; and sin, 225, 253; and violence, 227, 247–48; and war, 242
Cambridge University, 277
Camus, Albert, 3
Capovilla, Monsignor Loris, 97
Castro, Fidel, 258, 259
Central America, 6
Central Intelligence Agency (CIA), 258
Chakravarty, Dr. Amiya, 73–75
Chavez, Cesar, 288
Chelmno, 149
Children of Sanchez, The, 227–28
Chou En-lai, Premier, 279
Christ, 17–18, 58, 100, 109, 119, 126–29, 130, 140, 142–43, 146–48, 158, 166, 171–73, 177, 193, 195, 197–98, 200, 202–203, 206, 220–21, 225–26, 228, 261–63, 272, 284, 289, 291; and crucifixion, 32, 33, 66, 72–73, 92, 97, 109, 150–51, 178, 185; and the ebed Yahweh, 62–66, 72, 286–87; humanity of, 59–61, 65–66, 72, 75, 83, 221, 287; as living truth, 48–50; and the modern Church, 52–53, 211; and natural law, 210; and non-violence, 191–92; presence of, 52–54, 211; relationship to John the Baptist, 60–61; relationship to the Zealots, 182–87; as revolutionary, 32, 182–83, 186–89, 269; and the state, 182–83, 185, 188–92, 196, 206–208, 260; and suffering love, 53–54, 55, 64–65, 71, 211, 226; transforming power of, 204; and war, 106, 248–49, 252–53
Christ and Culture, 202–204
Christ and the Caesars, 189

Christian Church, 198, 201–203
Christian in Politics, The, 257
Christian theology, and the state, 190
Christianity, 17–18, 29–30, 93, 127, 130, 200–201, 211, 286; and anti-Semitism, 142, 150–51; institutional, 261; and militarism, 201–202; non-violent, 199; political theory of, 260–61; and revolution, 54–55, 188; the sect in, 202–203, 204; and truth, 37–38, 48–50; growth in understanding, 252–54; victory of, 204; and war, 112; see also Gandhi; Revolution
Christianity and Crisis, 81
Christological problem, 57–66
Christology: existential, 60, 65–66; non-violent, 48; ontic, 60; Servant, 66
Church and State, 182, 200
Church in the Modern World, The, 109, 127, 155
Churchill, Winston, 83
City of God, 289
Civil-rights movement, 266
Civil War (American), 52
Communism, 17, 43, 188, 191, 201, 235, 257, 258, 260, 261, 269
Communist China, 278–79
Congo, 271, 273, 280
Conscience, 130, 137, 161–62, 164, 168, 170–71, 173; barriers to, 108; Christian, 128, 156–57, 191; and the Church, 138; revolution of, 128, 130, 191–92; and the revolutionary, 8, 11
Conscientious objection, 106, 108, 121, 138, 166–69, 171–72, 175–77
Conscription, 242–43
Constantine, 50, 109, 178, 203, 252–53, 261; and the Christian Church, 199–200, 202, 205, 208–209, 217, 260
Contraception, 155
Council of Chalcedon, 59, 60
Council on Religion and International Affairs, 159
Cox, Harvey, 26–27, 30–32
Creative tension, 221

Cross: and aggression, 221; living, 66; meaning of, 109, 261–62, 292; non-violent, 109, 156, 290; rejection of, 225–26; and resurrection, 204, 261, 291; revolution of, 33, 55; as suffering love, 254; universal, 212; victory of, 197, 199–200; and war, 240

Crucifixion: logic of, 71; power of, 18, 288; as redemptive process, 92; and resurrection, 75; and war, 128; world as, 3–4, 15, 18–19, 23–24, 26, 253

Crusades, 201

Cuba, 257–60

Cullmann, Oscar, 62, 63, 64, 182, 183–84, 186

Daniel, Jean, 258

Daniélou, Jean, 284

De Ecclesia, 151–52

Dearden, Archbishop John F., 52

Death, redemptive, 151

Death instinct, 223–25

Declaration on the Relation of the Church to Non-Christian Religions, 148–49

Defense: immoral, 115, 116; military, 109, 127; non-violent, 109, 269–70

Deicide, 143, 150

Democracy, 266–68

Deterrence, 127, 155, 171; morality of, 161–66, 169–70, 173

Detroit, 232; archdiocese of, 51–52

Dewart, Leslie, 30, 36–37

Dharasana salt works, 66, 70

Dhawan, Gopinath, 268

Dionysius the Areopagite, 30

Disarmament, 212, 277; unilateral, 124, 171, 172

Dissent, politics of, 270

Doctor Zhivago, 9–10, 233

Doctrines, racist, 229

Dogma, cultural, 58

Dolci, Danilo, 20–21, 23, 24, 126, 288

Dollard, John, 227

Donne, John, 245

Dora, 149

Dostoevsky, Feodor, 11, 284

Dresden, xiii, 5, 165; bombing of, 169–70

Dunne, Father John, 59, 60–61

East Germany, 287

Ebed Yahweh, xiv, 61, 62, 291; see also Christ

Ecclesiology, Christocentric, 51

Egypt, 271–73

Eichmann, Adolf, 50, 55

Einstein, Albert, 87, 224

Elijah Muhammad, 229, 230, 231

Ellul, Jacques, 29

Ends, relationship to means, 43–44; see also Means

England, see Great Britain

Eros instinct, 224

Ethic: Christian, 158, 208; Christocentric, 210, 211; of responsibility, 262–63; of ultimate ends, 262, 264–65, 275

Europe, 205

Fanon, Frantz, 270, 285

Fascism, 139

Fear, law of, 87, 94

Fischer, Louis, 70

Flahiff, Archbishop George, 105

Florida, 218

For Whom the Bell Tolls, 243–45

Fostering of Peace and the Promotion of a Community of Nations, The, 101

France, 15, 258

Francis of Assisi, St., 100, 188

Frank, Anne, 236–37

Freud, Sigmund, 223–25, 227

Fuchs, Father Josef, 210–11

Future of Belief, The, 30, 36–37

Gamaliel, 183

Gandhi, Manilal, 67

Gandhi, Mohandas, xiv, xv, 18, 20, 23, 24, 33–39, 44, 67–69, 83, 85, 91, 92, 94, 95, 97, 98, 100, 126, 130, 230, 232, 261, 263–64, 271, 275–77, 280–81, 288–89; and atheism, 36; on Christ, 55–56, 64–65; relationship to Christ, 46, 48, 54, 55, 57, 75, 76; on Christian-

Gandhi, Mohandas (*continued*)
ity, 55–56, 57; on communism, 268–69; on the cross, 57, 71, 72, 75–76; fast of, 73–75; non-violent tactics of, 70, 84, 86, 88, 95; political ethics of, 265–69; on Sermon on the Mount, 56, 57, 69, 70; and truth, 34–39, 41, 42, 45, 46, 48, 76, 88–90

Garrone, Archbishop, 107

Genocide, 143, 160–64, 166, 169, 170, 172, 266; Church's role in, 137–38

German Catholics and Hitler's Wars, 158

Germany, 53, 91, 139–41, 236, 240

Gestapo, 169

God: and history, 291; humanity of, 288; as love, 38, 292; and man, 23–24, 26–29, 33, 38, 53, 90, 94, 288; and politics, 31–35; power of, 91, 207; presence of, 30–31, 37, 38, 143–45; and secularization, 30, 31–32, 33, 35, 38; suffering, 32–33; as truth, 34–39, 44, 46, 89, 91; wrath of, 195, 206, 207

Golgotha, 71, 221, 226, 276

Good, Robert C., 263

Gospel According to Matthew, The (movie), 188

Grant, Bishop Charles, 105, 110, 117

Grave of God, The, 287

Gray, J. Glenn, 250

Great Britain, 23, 53, 70, 73, 91, 110, 170

Guernica, xiii

Guevara, Che, 285

Guilt: Christian, 150; moral, 173; transformation of, 226

Hales, E. E. Y., 83

Hammarskjöld, Dag, xiv, xv, 22–24, 261, 271, 273, 275–82, 288

Hannan, Archbishop Philip M., 103, 107, 127

Hemingway, Ernest, 243

Herberg, Will, 82

Heresies, incarnational, 54, 55, 60, 66

Hersey, John, 233

High Noon, 260

Hiroshima, xiii, 4–5, 41, 159, 160, 165, 170, 240, 291

Hitler, Adolf, 91, 139, 174, 177

Holy Roman Empire, 205

Holy Spirit, 49, 54, 210, 288

Homo habilis, 217–18

Hungary, 6, 10, 258

Hunger, 6–8, 12, 20

I and Thou, 286–87

Imitation of Christ, The, 280

Imperative: moral, 168; natural-law, 211; non-violent, 193, 197, 208, 211, 212, 236; of reason, 211

In Place of War, 270

Incarnation, 225, 226; belief in, 55; doctrine of, 49, 54; mystery of, 66; redeeming truth of, 76

Incarnational heresy, 50

India, 7, 15–17, 23, 66, 67, 70, 90, 259, 264–66, 269

Injustice, revolt against, 8–10, 20–21, 23, 42, 55, 90, 187, 232, 234, 275, 284–85

Irving, David, 165, 169

Isaac, Jules, 148

Isaiah, xiv, xv, 61–63, 195

Israel, 147, 150–52, 183, 186, 195, 219, 233, 237, 238, 271, 286–87, 291

Italy, 20, 53, 85

Jagerstatter, Franz, 174, 177

James, William, 253

Janow, 149

Japan, 219; *see also* Hiroshima; Nagasaki

Jeremiah, 195

Jerusalem, 201, 235, 287

Jewish Fighter Organization, 235

Joan of Arc, 253

John of the Cross, St., 30

John the Baptist, 60–61, 185

John XXIII, xiv, 22–23, 24, 33, 81–98, 126–27, 147–48, 156, 277, 288; on disarmament, 86–88; and nationalism, 85; and non-violence, 211; on peace, 94, 100, 101; on role of Catholic Church, 97; and suffering love, 96–97; on war, 84–85, 97; on world peace, 81–98

Johnson, Lyndon B., 112, 115, 120, 222, 264–65

Journal of a Soul, 84, 85, 96, 97

Judaism, 286–87; and *ebed Yahweh,* 61, 62

Judas Iscariot, 184

Just Man, 145–48

Justice, 140, 206, 232; divine, 195; rule of, 88; and violence, 88, 285

Just-war doctrine, 101–102, 103–105, 106, 125–28, 130–31, 141, 155–78 *passim,* 182, 200–202, 217, 239

Kahn, Herman, 13, 41, 160

Katanga, 280

Kennan, George F., 240, 264

Kennedy, John F., 20, 22, 40, 257–60, 274

Khrushchev, Nikita, 93, 257–60, 275, 280

King, Martin Luther, xiv, 23, 126, 221, 231, 288

Kingdom of God, 27–28, 44, 45, 184, 185; and revolution, 28

King-Hall, Commander Stephen, 13

Klackenburg, Henrik, 276

Knowles, John, 87

Korea, 14

Korean War, 278

Lamed Vav, xiv

Land redistribution, 15–16

Last of the Just, The, xiv, 137–53 *passim*

Latin America, 7

Law of Moses, 209

Lawler, Justus George, 156

Lercaro, Cardinal, 156

Levy, Rabbi Solomon, 140–41

Levy, Rabbi Yom Tom, 139

Lewis, Oscar, 227–28

Life: affirmation of, 233–34, 236, 239; Christocentric, 202; power of, 10–11; reverence for, 129, 258, 276; and revolution, 9–10; as suffering, 14

Limits of Nuclear War, The, 160–61

Lorenz, Konrad, 218–19

Louis of France, St., 139–41, 253

Love, 150, 196, 231, 287; Christian, 129; Christic, 83–84; commandment of, 194; community of, 131, 288; confrontation of, 93; law of, 87; and natural law, 210; nonviolent, 28, 92, 98, 106, 147, 194–96, 201, 206, 211, 234, 261; and peace, 94, 101; and politics, 278; power of, 18–19, 21, 23–24, 88, 96, 98, 285, 290; redemptive, 205, 212, 285; resistance of, 192; and resurrection, 145; and the revolutionary, 8; rule of, 287; spiritual, 109, 149; transcendent, 53; and truth, 234–35; universal, 94; and violence, 249–50; *see also* Suffering love

Luther, Martin, 206, 249

McKenzie, Father John, 63, 190, 209, 211

Mafia, 20, 70

Maidanek, 149

Malcolm X, xiv, 228–32

Man: aggression in, 221; common good of, 102; community of, 81; conscience of, 8–9, 94, 108, 228; crucifixion of, 11, 23–24, 28, 64–66, 72–73, 226–27, 234, 288–90; dehumanization of, 18–19, 171, 245–47, 261, 291; dignity of, 86, 88, 93, 127, 232–34; divinity of, 289–90; enslavement of, 193; liberation of, 193; morality of, 219, 263; nature of, 21–22, 86, 90–92, 94, 211, 219, 221, 234–36, 238, 253; and nuclear war, 103–104; political, 42; rejection of Christ by, 226; responsibility of man to, 129; resurrection of, 288; revolutionary power of, 11–12; self-destruction of, 5–6, 101, 172–73, 174, 271; self-discovery of, 26; and suffering, 145–47; transformation of, 156, 220–21, 224; *see also* Just Man

Mankind: family of, 84–85, 94, 101, 212, 225, 230, 231, 274; violence in, 217–18

Maritain, Jacques, 44

Markings, 276, 280

Marx, Karl, 17, 18, 32, 269

Marxism, 10, 17–18, 93, 127, 268–69

Maurin, Peter, 287

Mauthausen, 149

Maximos, Patriarch of Antioch, 104

Means, 167; autonomy of, 43, 45; civilization of, 39, 42–43; end-creating, 43–44; moral, 117, 262, 264; non-violent, 265

Mexico, 227, 288

Milieu-Catholicism, 50–54

Milieu-Christianity, 55–56, 58–59, 66

Military power, futility of, 6–7, 9–15, 89, 93–94, 175

Miller, Webb, 66–69

Mind, technical, 41–42

Mitzvah, 44–45

Moral corruption, 14

Moral law, 118

Morality: Christian, 209, 262; public, 161; and violence, 220

Murder, 5, 6–7, 8–9, 22, 24, 41, 43, 102, 105–106, 110, 117, 126, 128, 176, 217–18, 226, 231, 234, 247, 251–52, 284; and Gospel of Peace, 128; *see also* Genocide

Murray, Father John Courtney, 81–83, 102

Muslim faith, 229–30

Nagasaki, 5, 41, 159, 240

Naidu, Mrs. Sarojini, 66

Nasser, Gamal Abdel, 272–73

National Broadcasting Company, 258

Nationalism, 85, 93, 121, 128, 188–89, 198, 236–37, 257, 261, 274–75; and violence, 270

Nation-state, obsolescence of, 21–22

Natural law, 121, 208–13; and sin, 211–12; trinitarian perspective of, 210–11; and violence, 211–12

Nazis, 51, 91, 139–41, 143–46, 158, 177, 235–39; and Judaism, 232–34

Neuengamme, 149

New Testament, 64, 183, 189, 198, 201, 203–205, 209

New York *Pacem in Terris* Convocation, 81–82

Newman, John Henry, 267, 269

Niebuhr, H. Richard, 202–205, 208

Niebuhr, Reinhold, 81–83, 208, 260–61, 263

Non-violence, 17–18, 28, 94, 109, 147, 157, 176–77, 198, 207, 211, 221, 230–31, 234, 252, 265–68, 270–71, 273; and the Cain instinct, 222–25; and Christ, 191–92; and Christianity, 201; effectiveness of, 92; essence of, 130; faith of, 86, 87; imperative of, 174–75, 176; as love, 95; as natural law, 86, 90, 212; power of, 94, 126, 131, 232; purpose of, 71, 72; rule of, 267; techniques of, 95; victory of, 88–89; and war, 108–109; *see also* Satyagrahi

North Atlantic Treaty Organization (NATO), 259

Nuclear Age, 5–6, 8–9, 16, 22–24, 81, 128, 155–56, 160–62, 170–72, 176, 261; peace in, 100; violence in, 84

Nuclear deterrence, morality of, 106, 110–26

Nuclear war, 138, 240–41, 257, 260; morality of, 101–30, 159–78

Nuclear weapons, 4–6, 8, 9, 11, 22, 102–106, 110, 112, 114–16, 117–19, 123–25, 127, 156, 159, 160–63, 166, 171, 192, 240–41, 247, 257–59, 266, 269, 288

On Aggression, 218

Original sin, 225–26

Osborne, William, 51, 52

Pacem in Terris, 23, 101, 126–27, 155, 211; criticism of, 81–82, 93; and Gandhi's non-violent techniques, 95; perspective of, 82; power of, 94; and treatment of power, 82–83; on truth, 88, 90–91; on violence, 83, 84–85, 86

Pakistan, 73

Palestine, 183, 189

Panitz, Rabbi David, 151
Pasolini, Pier, 188
Pasternak, Boris, 9–10, 31, 233
Pastoral Constitution on the Church in the Modern World, 101, 107, 117, 129
Paul, St., 49, 183, 211, 229, 287, 289; and revolution of conscience, 192; and natural law, 209, 210; on the state, 193–96, 206–208, 209
Paul VI, 100, 128, 284
Peace, 41, 63, 66, 72, 105, 108, 111, 130, 137, 147, 166, 172, 174, 184, 185, 201, 274; and the arms race, 119–20, 123–24; community of, 271–72; doctrine of, 177; global, 251, 288; Gospel of, 55, 125–26, 138, 140–41, 155–56, 173, 175, 177, 178, 203, 207, 209–10, 262–63; and John XXIII, 100; and love, 101; and militarism, 127; revolution of, 11–12, 15–17, 20, 24, 26, 28, 55, 76, 198, 253, 275, 285, 288, 290; struggle for, 277; truth of, 94; universal, 96; Vatican II on, 101
Peace Corps, 20, 93, 274
Pfaff, William, 14
Pius XII, 103–105, 107
Politics: non-violent, 269, 270; of peace, 275; of protest, 266–67, 274–75; of reconciliation, 279; of rule, 266–67; and salvation, 263
Ponary, 149
Pontius Pilate, 18, 92, 183, 185–86
Poverty, 12, 15, 23, 284; and violence, 227–28, 231, 239
Power, 7, 51, 83, 127, 161, 192–93, 196, 198, 207, 231, 268; Christic, 51, 289; of the cross, 130, 187, 196, 198–99, 288–89; cultural, 51; of God, 24, 207; government, 167; imperial, 205; of life, 10–11; of love, 15, 18–19, 23–24, 290; national, 212; nature of, 6, 19, 289; non-violent, 22, 57, 83, 91, 96, 126, 131, 231, 280; political, 51, 175, 265–66, 273; reality of, 288; of redemption, 226; of the Spirit, 288–89; of

the state, 196, 266; of suffering, 12–13, 14–15, 146–47, 177; of transcendence, 278; of transformation, 21–23; of truth, 19, 21, 23–24; understanding of, 94; of violence, 147; of war, 240; against the weak, 14–15; *see also* Military power; Suffering; Truth
Princeton Theological Seminary, 264
Prophetism, 100–101
Protestantism, 157, 203
Pustkow, 149

Racism, and violence, 228–32, 239
Rahner, Karl, 49, 59, 204–205
Ramsey, Paul, 101–102, 103, 111, 157–76, 202
Reality, political, 159
Reason, morality of, 209, 211
Redemption, and crucifixion, 72, 73, 91, 291
Reform, non-violent, 266
Resistance: non-violent, 191–92, 195, 197, 212, 232, 238; redemptive, 236; suffering, 176–77, 234–35
Responsibility, moral, 173, 208
Resurrection, of humanity, 282
Revolution: Christian, 49, 187, 192, 199; of conscience, 191–92; and ideology, 10–11; morality of, 7–9, 21–22, 254, 261, 267–68; non-violent, 183, 191, 220, 267, 285; spiritual, 102; and suffering, 13, 14; theological, 101; and transformation, 21–22; and truth, 234, 284; *see also* Peace
Rights, moral, 167
Ritter, Cardinal Joseph, 52, 117–19, 121–23, 130
Roman Catholic Church, 20, 23, 38, 48–53, 56, 58–59, 64–65, 83, 98, 100, 104, 119, 126, 128, 138, 141, 145, 147, 177, 191, 197, 209, 260, 269; in America, 50–52, 54, 100, 127–28; and Christian-Jewish relations, 148–53; and the cross, 205–206; as diaspora, 204–205, 207; in Germany, 50, 54; and natural law, 209–10; and persecution of Jews, 142; and

Roman Catholic Church (*continued*)
racism, 51–52, 54; and revolution, 287–88; and the state, 212;
theology on war of, 105, 107,
109–10; and universalism, 205;
and violence, 217; and war, 128–
30, 155, 177–78

Roman Empire, 182–88, 190, 195–
99, 206, 207, 208, 248

Rome, 32, 100, 150, 158

Roncalli, *see* John XXIII

Rusk, Dean, 260

*Russia and the West under Lenin
and Stalin*, 240

Russian Revolution, 9, 240, 269

Salvation, 91, 130, 147, 171, 262

Sartre, Jean-Paul, 285

Satyagraha, 88, 92, 94, 95, 264,
276–77, 280–81; *see also* Non-
violence

Schoonenberg, Father Piet, 225

Schroffer, Bishop, 107

Schwarz-Bart, André, xiv, 137–53

Schwarzschild, Steven, 44

Schweitzer, Albert, 276

Secular City, The, 26–27

Secularization, 26–28, 29; *see also*
under God

Segregated Covenant, The, 51

Selective Service Act, 167

Separate Peace, A, 87

Sicily, 7, 12, 20

Skarzysko, 149

Sobibor, 149

Social ethics, Christian, 204

*Social Teachings of the Christian
Churches, The*, 202

Society: morality of, 263; and transformation, 204

South Africa, 91, 219, 264, 266

South America, 6

Southeast Asia, 14

Soviet Union, 173, 258–59

Spain, 53

Spanish Civil War, 243

Spirit: of man, 91, 92; power of,
88, 98; resurrection of, 98; victory of, 198

State: conduct of, 182–213 *passim*;
nature of, 262; non-violent, 267–
68

State in the New Testament, The,
182

Stauffer, Ethelbert, 189

Stein, Walter, 124, 156, 162

Stevenson, Adlai, 271–72, 275

*Story of My Experiments with
Truth, The*, 35

Strategic Air Command, 93, 159

Study of History, A, 240

Suenens, Cardinal, 97

Suffering, 116, 130, 166, 174, 177,
188; baptism of, 288; and the
innocent, 284–85; and the Jews,
137, 140, 145, 152, 205; power
of, 12–13, 14–15, 18, 19, 21, 23,
54, 70–71, 147, 177, 285; redemptive, 46, 231; and violence, 19,
284–85, 290; and war, 247–48

Suffering love, 22–24, 33, 36–37,
49, 55, 64–66, 70–73, 75, 95,
142, 197, 198, 211, 212, 234–35,
254, 260, 265, 267, 288, 290;
redemption of, 177, 248–50, 251,
252, 288; victory of, 198; and
war, 248–52

Suicide, global, 101

Sweden, 105

Taylor, Bishop John, 105–106

Technology: dangers of, 5–7, 11, 28,
34, 39–40, 42–43, 93, 102, 128,
162, 165, 171, 245–46, 265; military, 162; and modern warfare,
40–41

Teilhard de Chardin, Pierre, 94,
101, 248

Territorial Imperative, The, 219

Theresienstadt, 149

Third Reich, 141; *see also* Nazis

Third World, 12, 14–15, 270, 280

Thomas a Kempis, 280

Tillich, Paul, 81–82, 83, 190, 249

To Feed the Hungry, 20

Torah, 237

Totalitarianism, 243

Toynbee, Arnold, 232, 240, 285–86

Toynbee, Philip, 173–74

Transformation: of guilt, 226; and
society, 204; spiritual, 267

Treblinka, 149, 237

Troeltsch, Ernst, 202–205, 208

Trust, and politics, 276–77

Truth, 28–29, 35–39, 42, 45–46, 48–49, 88–91, 93–95, 112, 127, 156, 162, 234–35, 251, 278, 284, 292; experiments in, 44–46, 48, 54, 76, 83, 96, 126, 261; incarnation of, 48–50; and Malcolm X, 229–31; and politics, 42, 45, 278; power of, 17–20, 21, 23–24, 42, 88–89, 90–93, 94

Tshombe, Moise, 280
Tucker, Robert, 111, 119–20
Turkey, 259

Uganda, 219
United Nations, xv, 22, 128, 275, 277–80; and non-violent politics, 270–74; peace force of, 272–74
United Nations Food and Agriculture Organization, 6
United Press, 6
Universal Church, 23
U Thant, 22, 24, 272–73, 288

Vatican II, xiv, 100–31 *passim*, 147, 156; on Jewish-Christian relations, 137–53 *passim*
Viet Cong, 89
Vietnam, 3, 6, 7, 10, 13–14, 15, 18, 30, 40, 43, 91, 93, 100, 128, 167, 171, 175, 219, 246, 264–65, 271, 274, 291
Vilna, 149
Violence, 14, 17–18, 106, 108, 140, 142, 168, 174–75, 183, 185, 191, 201, 217, 227, 261, 290; and aggression, 219–20; and Christianity, 200; definition of, 18; and exploitation, 269–70; and the Jews, 232–34; and justice, 176–77; and man, 290; in the Nuclear Age, 261; and politics, 257–82 *passim;* power of, 147; rule of, 86; tradition of, 141; and truth, 89; of war, 239, 249, 271

Wall, The, 233–34, 235–39
War: and aggression, 239; and Christianity, 141, 239; Gospel and, 109–10, 128; and the individual, 241–47, 249; and justice, 127, 174–76; limited, 161, 171–72; modern, 102, 104–105, 107, 109, 120, 123, 126, 130, 156, 157, 172, 174, 176, 224, 239, 242, 245; morality of, 112, 158; and natural law, 212; object of, 13–14; as a political instrument, 241; and saints, 252–54; suffering resistance to, 174; total, 102–108, 109–10, 111, 113–23, 126–27, 130, 161, 166, 171–73; as organized violence, 220, 239, 242, 246, 253; *see also* Just-war doctrine; Nuclear war
War and the Christian Conscience, 157, 159, 160, 166–69, 172–73
Warfare: discriminate, 168; holy, 201
War-peace polarity, 87
Warriors, The, 250
Warsaw Ghetto, 232–33, 235–39
Washington, D.C., 103, 104, 258, 278
Weber, Max, 262–63, 266, 267
Weil, Simone, 18
Wheeler, Bishop Gordon, 105, 110, 117
Wilde, Oscar, 221
World: powers of, 207; transformation of, 207, 284
World Medical Association, 103, 107
World War I, 97, 240, 248
World War II, 165, 240

Zahn, Gordon, 158
Zealotism, 191
Zealots, 182–89
Zionism, 235